Sociology of Education Series
Aaron M. Pallas, Series Editor

Advisory Board: Sanford Dornbusch, Adam Gamoran, Annette Lareau, Mary Metz, Gary Natriello

---

Still Separate and Unequal:
Segregation and the Future of Urban School Reform
Barry A. Gold

I Compagni:
Understanding Children's Transition from Preschool to Elementary School
William A. Corsaro and Luisa Molinari

Different by Design:
The Context and Character of Three Magnet Schools,
Reissued with a New Introduction
Mary Haywood Metz

Contradictions in Women's Education:
Traditionalism, Careerism, and Community at a Single-Sex College
Barbara J. Bank with Harriet M. Yelon

Transforming Teaching in Math and Science:
How Schools and Districts Can Support Change
Adam Gamoran, Charles W. Anderson, Pamela Anne Quiroz,
Walter G. Secada, Tona Williams, and Scott Ashmann

Where Charter School Policy Fails: The Problems of Accountability and Equity
Edited by Amy Stuart Wells

Comprehensive Reform for Urban High Schools:
A Talent Development Approach
Nettie E. Legters, Robert Balfanz,
Will J. Jordan, and James M. McPartland

School Kids/Street Kids: Identity Development in Latino Students
Nilda Flores-González

Manufacturing Hope and Despair:
The School and Kin Support Networks of U.S.-Mexican Youth
Ricardo D. Stanton-Salazar

Restructuring High Schools for Equity and Excellence: What Works
Valerie Lee with Julia Smith

Finding One's Place:
Teaching Styles and Peer Relations in Diverse Classrooms
Stephen Plank

PreMed: Who Makes It and Why
Mary Ann Maguire

Tracking Inequality: Stratification and Mobility in American High Schools
Samuel Roundfield Lucas

Working for Equity in Heterogeneous Classrooms:
Sociological Theory in Practice
Edited by Elizabeth G. Cohen and Rachel A. Lotan

Culture, Instituti ... ce
Edited by Bruce Fu ... rfield

From the Series Editor

ONE OF SOCIOLOGY'S unique contributions to the study of education policy is a concern for how the targets of education policy experience the array of mandates, rewards and sanctions, and resources that are intended to change their behavior. All too often, policymakers' expectations about the impact of a new policy are off the mark, and sociologists can help explain why this is so. Writing in this tradition, Barry Gold provides a window into the thinking of teachers and administrators forced to confront conflicting mandates.

Like many states, New Jersey has struggled to address widespread inequalities associated with geographic differences in wealth and property tax revenues. Over a period of seven years, policymakers shifted from a focus on money alone to a combination of resources and mandates about how schools should be organized—first, whole school reform and, later, standards-driven classroom reform. The latter period coincided with the initial implementation of No Child Left Behind, the most influential federal education legislation in our nation's history.

Gold's case studies of how New Jersey schools engaged with these policy reforms connect the inner lives of schools with the broader political and social context. He provides vivid descriptions of how schools and teachers were buffeted about by powerful external forces that demanded one set of goals in one year and dramatically different goals the next. Staff and resources came and went; standardized tests were introduced, then discarded in favor of other assessments. The one constant was that teachers set aside a broad spectrum of goals for students' academic and social development in favor of a narrow focus on test preparation. Gold's account makes clear that test scores went up but raises the troubling question of whether real learning occurred.

Barry Gold persuasively argues that the impact of federal and state education policy can only be understood in the context of time and place. But place has a special meaning in settings that are scarred by racial and social class segregation. An ecology of segregated schools leads teachers and administrators to distinguish the kinds of students a particular school serves from the students enrolled in neighboring schools. If they perceive a reform as legitimate for their students, they may well embrace the reform with enthusiasm. Conversely, if teachers and administrators judge a reform as inappropriate for their students, they will resist it. This perception of legitimacy is the key to understanding why some schools resist coercive policies so strenuously.

Still Separate and Unequal: Segregation and the Future of Urban School Reform provides a fresh perspective on the relationship between urban schools and their external environments. Barry Gold has clarified the dynamics of organizational responses to school reform initiatives, explaining why resistance to change can be so fierce. The sobering message is that tinkering with incentives does not come close to addressing the structural roots of the problem, which lie in segregation itself.

—Aaron M. Pallas

Still Separate *and* Unequal

Segregation and the Future of Urban School Reform

BARRY A. GOLD

Teachers College
Columbia University
New York and London

Published by Teachers College Press, 1234 Amsterdam Avenue, New York, NY 10027

Copyright © 2007 by Teachers College, Columbia University

All rights reserved. No part of this publication may be reproduced or transmitted in any form or by any means, electronic or mechanical, including photocopy, or any information storage and retrieval system, without permission from the publisher.

Library of Congress Cataloging-in-Publication Data

Gold, Barry A.
Still separate and unequal : segregation and the future of urban school reform / Barry A. Gold.
p. cm. — (Sociology of education series)
Includes bibliographical references and index.
ISBN-13: 978-0-8077-4756-8 (pbk : alk. paper)
ISBN-13: 978-0-8077-4757-5 (cloth : alk. paper)
1. Segregation in education—United States. 2. Urban schools—United States. 3. Educational change—United States. I. Title.

LC212.52.G65 2007
370.9173'2—dc22 2006028931

ISBN-13: 978-0-8077-4756-8 (paper)
ISBN-13: 978-0-8077-4757-5 (cloth)

Printed on acid-free paper
Manufactured in the United States of America

14 13 12 11 10 09 08 07 8 7 6 5 4 3 2 1

For Lauren and Ian

Contents

Acknowledgments xi

Introduction 1

Separate and Equal 1

Still Separate and Unequal 1

The Urban Education Revolution 2

Different Explanations for Separate and Unequal 2

Objectives of the Book 3

Organization of the Book 4

PART I: The Urban Education Revolution

1 *Abbott v. Burke V*: New Jersey's Revolution in Urban Education Reform 7

Unequal Education 7

The *Abbott V* Decision 8

The Socioeconomic Context of *Abbott v. Burke* 11

Abbott v. Burke: A Brief History 14

Abbott in Perspective 20

2 No Child Left Behind: The Federal Solution to *Brown* 21

A Revolution in Education 21

A High-Quality Education for All Children 22

Enforcing NCLB 26

The Critics and Supporters of NCLB 26

A Long Revolution: *Abbott V* and NCLB in Urban Schools 29

3	**The Urban Education Revolution in Perspective: A Theory of Educational Change**	30
	Explaining *Abbott V* and NCLB	30
	Theories of Educational Change	30
	Abbott V and NCLB in Theoretical Perspective	37

PART II: Implementing the Revolution

4	**The Bridge Street School: Unanticipated Incremental Change**	41
	The Social Context of Education: Newark	41
	The Newark School District	44
	The State Takeover of Newark's Schools	46
	The Bridge Street School Community	47
	The Bridge Street Elementary School	47
	Bridge Street Before *Abbott V*	48
	Bridge Street and *Abbott V*, Year 1—2000–2001	48
	Bridge Street and *Abbott V*, Year 2—2001–2002	64
	Bridge Street and *Abbott V*, Year 3/NCLB, Year 1—2002–2003	69
	Bridge Street and *Abbott V*, Year 4/NCLB, Year 2—2003–2004	72
	Bridge Street and *Abbott V*, Year 5/NCLB, Year 3—2004–2005	75
	Analysis of the Bridge Street School	77
	Conclusions	80
5	**The College Avenue School: The Normal Appearance of Change**	81
	The Social Context of Education: Elizabeth	81
	The Elizabeth School District	83
	The College Avenue School Community	83
	The College Avenue Elementary School	84
	College Avenue Before *Abbott V*	85
	College Avenue and *Abbott V*, Year 1—1998–1999	85
	College Avenue and *Abbott V*, Year 2—1999–2000	90
	College Avenue and *Abbott V*, Year 3—2000–2001	94
	College Avenue and *Abbott V*, Year 4—2001–2002	96
	College Avenue and *Abbott V*, Year 5/NCLB, Year 1—2002–2003	97

College Avenue and *Abbott V*, Year 6/NCLB, Year 2—2003–2004 98
College Avenue and *Abbott V*, Year 7/NCLB, Year 3—2004–2005 100
Analysis of the College Avenue School 101
Conclusions 103
The Change Cycle: Ending and Beginning 104

6 The Church Street School: Immediate Sustained Rigid Change 105
The Church Street School Community 105
The Church Street School 106
Church Street Before *Abbott V* 106
The Church Street Student Population 106
Church Street and *Abbott V*, Year 1—1998–1999 107
Church Street and *Abbott V*, Year 2—1999–2000 111
Church Street and *Abbott V*, Year 3—2000–2001 113
Church Street and *Abbott V*, Year 4—2001–2002 115
Church Street and *Abbott V*, Year 5/NCLB, Year 1—2002–2003 116
Church Street and *Abbott V*, Year 6/NCLB, Year 2—2003–2004 118
Church Street and *Abbott V*, Year 7/NCLB, Year 3—2004–2005 119
Analysis of the Church Street School 119
Conclusions 121
The Change Cycle: Ending and Beginning 122

7 The Park Avenue School: Chronic Resistance to Change 123
The Park Avenue School Community 123
The Park Avenue School 124
Park Avenue Before *Abbott V* 124
Park Avenue and *Abbott V*, Year 1—1998–1999 125
Park Avenue and *Abbott V*, Year 2—1999–2000 129
Park Avenue and *Abbott V*, Year 3—2000–2001 130
Park Avenue and *Abbott V*, Year 4—2001–2002 133
Park Avenue and *Abbott V*, Year 5/NCLB, Year 1—2002–2003 134
Park Avenue and *Abbott V*, Year 6/NCLB, Year 2—2003–2004 136
Park Avenue and *Abbott V*, Year 7/NCLB, Year 3—2004–2005 138
Analysis of the Park Avenue School 139
Conclusions 141
The Change Cycle: Ending and Beginning 141

PART III. Explaining the Revolution

8 What Changed? Why Separate Cannot Be Equal 147
The NCLB Revolution 147
The Key Questions 147
Major Common Findings 148
Explaining the Changes 154
Abbott V, NCLB, and the Structure of Urban Education 154
Why Separate Cannot Be Equal 155

9 Segregation and the Future of Urban School Reform: Planning for a Post-Abbott and Post-NCLB Era 157
The Legacy of *Abbott V* and NCLB 157
What Next? 159
The Findings in Perspective 160
A Revised Model of Urban Education and Change 161
Segregation and the Future of Urban School Reform 163
Alternative Strategies 168
Expanding Education Policy 170

APPENDIX A. Education Equity in New Jersey: A Summary of Cases and Continuing Litigation 175

APPENDIX B. Research Methods 181
The Research Design: Comparative and Longitudinal 181
The Research Sites 182
The Role of Theory: Explaining Change 184
Data Collection Methods: Ethnography 185
Data Analysis: Continuous and Interactive 185

Notes 186

References 193

Index 204

About the Author 212

Acknowledgments

OVER THE 7 YEARS of research for this book, I acquired many debts of gratitude. Even before entering the field to collect data, I owed a key debt to the late Matt Miles, who gave me my first opportunity to study education innovation and indelibly influenced my approach to understanding how schools change.

I thank Michael Ryan, who, by discussing his experiences in an urban school district in New Jersey at a dinner party, unknowingly initiated this research. Patricia Brock provided valuable data and interesting discussions on events in the College Avenue School during my first 2 years of fieldwork. At various times, Diana Ward, Vasanthakumar Bhat, and Peter Gotlieb provided a critical audience for the arguments presented in this book. Michael Lundy read a draft of the manuscript and encouraged me with his supportive remarks. Alan Sadovnik provided detailed and important suggestions for improving the book, as did two anonymous reviewers selected by Teachers College Press.

I am particularly appreciative to Frank Cullen, whom I have known from our earliest days as graduate students, for his thoughtful comments on a preliminary draft. I also thank Herb Green of the Public Education Institute of Rutgers University for organizing stimulating conferences on a variety of topics on education reform.

Susan Liddicoat of Teachers College Press supported this book from its beginnings as a proposal until her retirement, a short time before I finished the project. Marie Ellen Larcada then became my editor and was helpful and patient during the final stages of writing. Lynne Frost's editorial skills greatly improved the book.

Several papers that I have presented at annual meetings of the American Educational Research Association have been incorporated into this book. I have benefited from comments of Association members.

I also thank the Spencer Foundation for supporting this project. During the complexities of extended fieldwork and the demands of writing, it was comforting to know that someone else thought that the time and effort were worthwhile. Of course, the Spencer Foundation is not responsible for the data, analysis, arguments, or conclusions present herein. These are my responsibilities, as are any shortcomings.

I owe my greatest debt to the teachers, administrators, government officials, and most of all the students, who are the main characters in this book. Teachers and students welcomed an outsider into their classrooms who sat quietly for hours, took notes on a yellow legal pad, asked a few questions, and left, only to repeat this strange behavior a few weeks later.

I hope that the questions were the right ones, that the observations were accurate, and that this research, although critical in many ways of the reform efforts it reports, proves to be constructive for the future improvement of urban education.

My wife, Bonnie, a fourth-grade teacher in an affluent suburban school in New Jersey during the time of this study, not only experienced some of what is reported in this book—her students always scored among the highest in the state on standardized tests—but also patiently listened to preliminary interpretations of the data and asked for important clarifications. Even when she disagreed with my conclusions, the discussions refined my views and improved the basic arguments of the book.

Finally, my parents contributed to this book because, for better or worse—mainly better, I think—I was born and raised in New Jersey.

Introduction

Separate and Equal

In 1954, in *Brown v. Board of Education,* the United States Supreme Court ruled that separate but equal education was unconstitutional. In a series of decisions over the next five decades, the Supreme Court, federal and state courts, and state and federal legislation retreated from *Brown* (Orfield & Eaton, 1996). By the beginning of the 21st century, the discredited doctrine of separate but equal was again the education policy of the United States (Clotfelter, 2004; Reed, 2001).

The two landmark education reforms that are the subjects of this book attempted to create separate and equal urban education. In 1998, when the New Jersey Supreme Court ruled in *Abbott v. Burke V,* it provided extensive reforms—including per-pupil funding equal or superior to the state's wealthiest school districts—designed to improve educational opportunities for poor minority students trapped in segregated, isolated, inadequately funded, underperforming urban schools. But it did not mandate school integration as part of the solution for improving urban education.

In 2002, with the signing by President George W. Bush of the No Child Left Behind (NCLB) legislation, the federal government enacted an unprecedented program of urban education reform that featured accountability. But NCLB did not include integration as a step toward improving underperforming urban schools.[1]

The central question this book will answer is, Can separate education be equal?

Still Separate and Unequal

In June 2005, after 7 years of implementation of the *Abbott V* mandated remedies—universal preschool, class size reduction, site-based management, the use of a Whole School Reform model in elementary classrooms, and secondary school reform—and 3 years of NCLB reforms, three of the four racially and economically segregated elementary schools profiled in this book remained unequal, as measured by standardized tests. The fourth school had achieved Adequate Yearly Progress for 3 consecutive years. Unlike the other schools, instead of attempting to implement *Abbott V*, since 1999 this school has focused on test preparation.[2]

In addition, for 2004–2005, according to NCLB criteria, Newark and Elizabeth, the districts that included the schools, were "in need of improvement" for 2 consecutive years. According to the New Jersey Department of Education, the sanctions imposed by NCLB could involve the loss of federal funds, replacement of administrators and teachers, removal of schools from the district, parents being offered the choice of sending their children to schools in other districts, and restructuring or abolition of the district.

The Urban Education Revolution

Although *Abbott V* and NCLB did not close the achievement gap, they revolutionized the schools described in this book by creating a new type of urban education. The reforms narrowed the curriculum and transformed classrooms into preparation centers for standardized tests. These changes only served to *increase* the differences between urban and suburban schools.

A second part of the revolution is that *Abbott V* and NCLB legitimated the notion that separate and equal education is possible. Over the 7 years of implementation, instead of recognizing that the inability to improve urban education is a consequence of accumulated inequalities resulting from intergenerational segregation, politicians and educators simply declared that, despite its persistence, the achievement gap could be closed within the existing social structure.

The purported reasons for failure focused on selection of ineffective programs by administrators and teachers, inept implementation of the reforms, absence of dynamic educational leadership, and inefficiency in urban school districts, including administrative and political corruption. Additional arguments were that it was too soon to expect results—although test scores in a few schools indicated dramatic improvement—and that minority populations lack the appropriate values and behaviors required for high academic achievement.

Different Explanations for Separate and Unequal

The schools described in this book remained separate and unequal in part because of difficulties in managing change, but primarily as the result of the influence of racial and economic segregation on the decision making and behavior of administrators and teachers. The segregated social structure of New Jersey created and, even under intense pressure to change, reproduced a specific type of urban education for poor minority students. Ironically, *Abbott V* and NCLB reinforced the view that urban children require a different education than suburban students. As a result, in addition to increasing the differences in the type of education between suburbs and cities, the reforms reinforced them.

The ethnographies of elementary school change presented herein reaffirm the *Brown* decision that separate schools cannot be equal. The successful reform of urban education, even if narrowly defined as closing the achievement gap, requires the integration of poor, minority urban students into mainstream American education and society.

Objectives of the Book

To explore the issue of whether separate schools can be equal, the question that guided the research over 7 years is, How did *Abbott V* and NCLB affect the learning and classroom behavior of low-income students in isolated, racially segregated urban elementary schools? The research used a broad measure of learning that included test scores and informal learning that occurs in classrooms.

To answer this question requires first identifying the social and political conditions that affected the selection of the types of reforms and, consequently, learning. Thus, the book describes three decades of litigation in New Jersey aimed at equalizing funding and programs intended to improve urban education. In addition, the features of NCLB that formed its strategy for improving education are discussed.

Another purpose of the study was to propose effective reforms aimed at improving urban education. The most promising approach is to reconfigure the social and economic environment of education by desegregating city schools. However, because the short-term prospects for integration appear remote—in fact, schools in many cities are resegregating (Kozol, 2005)—this book examines a range of options for refocusing the debate over state reforms, NCLB, vouchers, and charter schools.

The final objective is to understand the impact of two revolutions in American social policy and to identify a third revolution. The first revolution was the retreat from *Brown*. The Supreme Court recognized unequivocally in *Brown* that integration is essential for improving the educational opportunities of low-income minority students. The second revolution was the accomplishment, through court orders and legislation, of the postdesegregation policy of separate but equal education that culminated in *Abbott V* and NCLB.

The third revolution, the product of separate and equal, occurred with the changes in schools and classrooms that *Abbott V* initiated and NCLB exacerbated by focusing on accountability. Instead of equalizing educational opportunity for poor minority students in urban schools, this third revolution has transformed urban schools by narrowing the curriculum and limiting instructional methods.

Organization of the Book

This book is divided into three sections. Part I, The Urban Education Revolution, traces the development through the judicial and legislative processes of the revolutionary reforms that the schools were required to implement.

Chapter 1 is a portrait of New Jersey, including discussion of its current social and economic structure and a history of *Abbott v. Burke*. Chapter 2 is a description of NCLB, its remedies for underperforming schools, and the major criticisms of the law. Chapter 3 places *Abbott V* and NCLB in the theoretical framework of the punctuated legitimacy theory of education change.

Part II, Implementing the Revolution, documents implementation of *Abbott V* and NCLB in four elementary schools in Newark and Elizabeth, New Jersey. The primary focus is on how the reforms generated through the legal system and legislative processes affected classrooms and student learning.

Chapters 4 through 7 present the data—primarily from 7 years of classroom observations and interviews with teachers—that generated the findings that support the conclusions of the book. In addition to providing a history of Newark and its school district, Chapter 4 describes the Bridge Street School[3] and shows how the school transformed the reforms from rapid major change into minor incremental change. Chapter 5 focuses on the Elizabeth school district and examines how the College Avenue School responded to reforms that created the symbolic appearance of change yet nevertheless radically altered education in the school. Chapters 6 and 7 focus on the Church Street and Park Avenue schools, which are in neighborhoods of Elizabeth that differ significantly from the neighborhood of the College Avenue School. Church Street underwent sustained rigid change, and Park Avenue responded to *Abbott V* and NCLB with strenuous resistance.

Part III, Explaining the Revolution, is an analysis of why the reforms could not close the achievement gap. Through examination of the reforms and their implementation, recommendations are developed for reformulating policies to increase the future success of urban education reforms.

Chapter 8 is a comparative analysis of what changed in the districts, schools, and classrooms, and argues that separate education cannot be equal. Chapter 9 explores the possible effects of segregation on *Abbott V* and NCLB if they are changed significantly, as well as the effects of segregation on reforms such as voucher plans and particularly on the future of urban education change in a post-Abbott and post-NCLB era. The discussion argues that integration is the only strategy for improving equality of educational opportunity.

Appendix A is a chronology of key decisions in the Abbott cases that, in addition to the history of *Abbott* in Chapter 1, provides a context for understanding the changes in approaches and results. Appendix B discusses research issues, such as how representative the schools in the book are of urban schools in New Jersey and the United States.

PART I

The Urban Education Revolution

CHAPTER 1

Abbott v. Burke V

New Jersey's Revolution in Urban Education Reform

Unequal Education

In *Savage Inequalities* (1991), Jonathan Kozol documented the extreme inequality in the funding of suburban and urban schools in New Jersey and demonstrated how the state testing program, which was intended to improve achievement, distorted the education process in schools in Camden, Jersey City, and Paterson. The unequal conditions for learning were evident in Kozol's (1991) quote of an urban educator:

> "If they first had given Head Start to our children *and* pre-kindergarten, *and* materials *and* classes of 15 or 18 children in the elementary grades, *and* computers *and* attractive buildings *and* enough books and supplies *and* teacher salaries sufficient to compete with the suburban schools, and then come in a few years later with their tests and test-demands, it might have been fair play. Instead, they leave us as we are, separate and unequal, underfunded, with large classes, and with virtually no Head Start, and they think that they can test our children into a mechanical proficiency." (p. 143)

Commenting on the *Abbott v. Burke* litigation, which at the time of his study was extremely contentious, Kozol (1991) observed that

> Whatever the next step that may be taken in New Jersey, no one believes that people in Princeton, Millburn, Cherry Hill and Summit are prepared to sacrifice the extra edge their children now enjoy. *The notion that every child in New Jersey might someday be given what the kids in Princeton now enjoy is not even entertained as a legitimate scenario* [emphasis added]. In the recent litigation [*Abbott v. Burke*] the defendants went so far as to deride attempts to judge one district by the other's standards. Comparing what was offered in the poorest districts to the academic offerings in Princeton was unfair, they charged, because, they said, the programs offered in the schools of Princeton were "extraordinary." (p. 171)

Six years later, Kozol's conclusion that prospects for altering the extreme inequality of education in New Jersey were nonexistent would have to undergo dramatic revision because of the New Jersey Supreme Court's *Abbott V* ruling.

The *Abbott V* Decision

Forty-four years after the U.S. Supreme Court's landmark *Brown v. Board of Education of Topeka* decision, a 28-year court battle to improve urban education in New Jersey's cities resulted in the New Jersey Supreme Court's *Abbott v. Burke V* decision.[1] *Abbott v. Burke V* mandated that the state assist the 30 lowest income and lowest achievement urban school districts in New Jersey to improve student academic performance.[2] A February 9, 2002, *New York Times* editorial commented that the 1998 *Abbott V* decision "may be the most significant education case since the Supreme Court's desegregation ruling nearly 50 years ago" ("A Truce," 2002, section A, p. 18).

The Education Experts

The New Jersey Supreme Court's view was that equal funding for education was only one element required for a program to increase educational opportunity and achievement for inner-city students. However, in developing a comprehensive reform plan the Court did not accept as the best education practices for the Abbott districts what wealthy suburban districts did to organize schools and instruct children. The Court also rejected the proposal of the Education Law Center that each Abbott district and school perform a needs assessment to create a school-specific reform plan.

Instead, the Court solicited advice from nationally recognized education experts in the areas of school finance, curriculum, school facilities, and a variety of other disciplines. The experts testified that city schools required a new type of governance, modernization of facilities, early childhood education, and most importantly, effective classroom instruction techniques based on scientific research. As a result, the education reform the court developed in *Abbott V* was intended to meet the specific needs of urban students.

The Abbott Mandates

The court's remedy, Whole School Reform in New Jersey, was based on the experts' recommendations and developed by the New Jersey Department of Education as a systematic and comprehensive reform. In addition to equalizing and even surpassing the education funding between suburban and urban school districts, the *Abbott V* mandates included

- preschool funded by the state
- building repair and construction

The reforms targeted toward elementary schools, the focus of this study, were

- zero-based budgeting for each school
- a School Management Team (SMT) for each school
- use of technology in all classrooms
- reduction in class size to 23 students in elementary schools
- implementation of a Whole School Reform (WSR) model, to be adopted in a school by a majority vote of the faculty

In addition to these mandates, Abbott districts—along with all districts in the state—would use the previously implemented New Jersey Core Curriculum Content Standards (CCCS) and standardized—"high stakes"—testing for 4th, 8th, and 11th grades.

The 1998 *Abbott V* reforms focused on preschool and elementary grades, but the Court also intended to reform secondary education. However, it was not until 2004 that the New Jersey Department of Education initiated a secondary school reform to create small learning communities in middle and high schools. Four pilot districts initiated the program in September 2005.

Plessy v. Ferguson Revisited

The *Abbott V* reforms targeted low-income, mainly minority students in racially and economically segregated communities. Of the 264,070 students under the Abbott mandates—21% of the school enrollment in New Jersey—most were either African American or Latino. According to the 1996–1997 population data used by the Court, the breakdown by race of the Abbott population was 119,066 African Americans (45%), 98,098 Latinos (37%), 39,355 Whites (15%), and 7,551 Native Americans and Asian/Pacific Islanders (3%). (See Table 1.1 for a population breakdown for New Jersey as a whole, as of the 2000 Census.)

The Education Law Center, the initiator of the Abbott litigation, preferred to desegregate public education in New Jersey. But, among the last of the Northern states to end segregation officially, with an amendment to the state constitution in 1947, New Jersey had de jure segregation in 43 districts until 1948—one of every 13 districts in the state. "By 1951," according to Charles Clotfelter, "forty of those districts had integrated their schools and the remaining three had pledged to do so" (2004, p. 18).

More important than a heritage of de jure segregation, de facto segregation developed in most of New Jersey because of residential patterns. In 1972, to

TABLE 1.1. Racial and Ethnic Distribution of the New Jersey Population, 2000 Census

	New Jersey number	New Jersey %	U.S. %
White	6,104,705	72.6	75.1
Black or African American	1,141,821	13.6	12.3
American Indian and Alaska Native	19,492	0.2	0.9
Asian	480,276	5.7	3.6
Native Hawaiian and Other Pacific Islander	3,329	0.0	0.1
Some other race	450,972	5.4	5.5
Two or more races	213,755	2.5	2.4
Hispanic or Latino (of any race)	1,117,191	13.3	12.5

New Jersey ranks 10th in the nation in population, with a 2000 population of 8,414,350.
Source: United States 2000 Census.

comply with a New Jersey Supreme Court order to desegregate, suburban Morris Township and urban Morristown integrated their schools across municipal lines. In 1973, the State Commissioner of Education was fired and integration attempts ended.

At the time of the *Abbott V* decision, with the exception of a continuing battle over desegregation in Englewood, which had encountered a variety of implementation problems, there were no large-scale attempts to integrate suburban and urban schools in New Jersey. In 2004, however, in a case involving the possible withdrawal of the North Haledon School District from the Passaic County Manchester Regional High School District, the New Jersey Supreme Court reaffirmed the state's prohibition of segregation, ruling that "racial imbalance resulting from de facto segregation . . . is inimical" to the constitutional guarantee of a thorough and efficient education (New Jersey Supreme Court, 2004, Section III A).

Because of the historic difficulty in achieving desegregation in New Jersey, legal advocates for minority students shifted to a strategy of seeking equal funding. Paul Tractenberg, a founder of the Education Law Center and a pivotal figure in the history of *Abbott v. Burke,* observed that

> We were almost compelled to give up on the possibility of any serious movement towards statewide desegregation. In a sense, we ended up saying, if they [schools] are going to be separate, let's at least make them truly equal. (quoted in Schwaneberg, 2004, p. 17)

In *Abbott V* the New Jersey Supreme Court retreated from the 1954 *Brown v. Board of Education* doctrine that separate schools cannot be equal to a position that resembled the 1896 *Plessy v. Ferguson* separate but equal ruling. The goals of *Abbott V* were not desegregation but financial equity and education improvement by using planned organization change in racially and economically segregated school districts.

The Socioeconomic Context of *Abbott v. Burke*

An understanding of the social and economic structure of New Jersey is essential before one can appreciate the conditions that resulted in *Abbott V* rather than interdistrict, county-based, or statewide integration. The social arrangement of New Jersey also provides the context for understanding the responses of school districts, administrators, and teachers to *Abbott V* and NCLB.

Cities and Suburbs

New Jersey's cities were once among the nation's most powerful industrial centers but eventually became—and remain—symbols of urban decay. Trenton, Camden, Elizabeth, Newark, and Paterson experienced severe declines in their industrial base after World War II that only accelerated with the relocation of knowledge-intensive work to the suburbs. Although it began decades before the war, the migration of African Americans to New Jersey's cities increased after the war, overburdening urban resources and accelerating the relocation of Whites to nearby suburbs. In the 1970s, the construction of highways to formerly remote parts of the state, coupled with the rapid expansion of the knowledge sector of the economy, continued to erode the economic foundation of the cities (Wilson, 1996).

The result of these long-term social processes was that New Jersey was bifurcated geographically along racial and economic lines (Anyon, 1997; Massey & Denton, 1993), and today it is one of the most residentially segregated states in the country (Logan et al., 2001). The Harvard Civil Rights Project reported that in 2000–2001 New Jersey's schools were the eighth most segregated in the nation for African American students and seventh for Latino students (Braun, 2005; Frankenberg, Lee, & Orfield, 2003).

The Dollars and Cents of Residence

A feature of the sociogeography of New Jersey that contributes to social class and race relations is that some of the wealthiest towns in the country are only a short distance from many of the most economically depressed, racially segregated inner-city neighborhoods in the United States. This spatial arrangement—which is common to most metropolitan areas in the country—evolved over decades because of social preferences and government economic policies.

Eventually, however, as Massey and Denton (1993, p. 17) noted, "The residential segregation of Blacks and Whites has been with us so long that it seems a natural part of the social order, a normal and unremarkable feature of America's urban landscape."

Significant economic inequalities underlie and contribute to what, on the surface, appears to be a natural division by race. For example, the 1999 median family income for Essex County was $54,818 and the per capita income was $24,943.[3] However, illustrating the wide range of income in Essex County, Millburn, a predominantly White town with a 2000 population of 19,765, had a 1999 median family income of $158,888 and a per capita income of $76,796. Millburn's school system, as Kozol (1991) noted, is one of the best in the state. Ten minutes away by car, Irvington, with a population of 60,615 that is predominantly African American, with a large subcommunity of Haitian immigrants, had a $41,098 median family income and a per capita income of $16,874 in 1999.

Irvington, an Abbott district, was a White ethnic working- and middle-class suburb of Newark until the mid-1960s. It deteriorated rapidly as the result of an influx of immigrants that overburdened social welfare agencies, an increase in poverty, White flight, and periodic political corruption. Crime has increased over the past decades, and a record was set with 30 homicides in 2003, most the result of rivalry between the Crips and the Bloods.

In Union County, Westfield, which is predominantly White, had a 1999 median family income of $112,145 and a per capita income of $47,187. Plainfield, which is a 10-minute drive away, is a predominantly African American Abbott district, and had a 1999 median family income of $50,774 and a per capita income of $19,052. Union County overall had a median family income of $65,234 and a per capita income of $26,992.[4]

Other Dimensions of Residence

The visual contrasts between houses in Millburn and Irvington (Essex County) or in Westfield and Plainfield (Union County), or in other radically different communities within the same county are striking. The type, variety, and quality of retail stores also differ: suburban malls feature stores such as Macy's, Nordstom's, Neiman Marcus, and expensive boutiques, whereas urban areas have almost no shopping.

To some extent, residential location is self-restricted, even for African American families with enough income to live in White suburbs. In an analysis of residential patterns in northern New Jersey, the *Star-Ledger* ("The Voice of New Jersey," based in Newark) reported that African American families with incomes in 2000 of $114,000 or more—the top fifth of New Jersey's income scale—clustered in predominantly African American communities near minority-dominated urban centers (Gebeloff, 2005). Clement Price, a history professor at Rutgers University, Newark, explained this phenomenon by observing that

"We're still in the throes of the suburban cultural shift that has to do with race, the residuals of that discrimination. There is a very strong sensibility in New Jersey that suburban meant White and urban meant non-White. That is passed down" (quoted by Gebeloff, 2005, p. 1).

Thus, the social and cultural landscape created—and then maintained—geographic, economic, and racial segregation. However, the widespread perception is that the correlation of social class and race in New Jersey is the product of naturally occurring social forces rather than a result of the social practices of the dominant groups or a consequence of government policies (Anyon, 1997, 2005; Gans, 1995).

Regardless of how it developed, segregation remains a critical feature of race relations in New Jersey and in the United States. Massey and Denton (1993, p. 9) wrote that

> Our fundamental argument is that racial segregation—and its characteristic institutional form, the Black ghetto—are key structural factors responsible for the perpetuation of Black poverty in the United States. Residential segregation is the principal organizational feature of American society that is responsible for the creation of the urban underclass.

Mount Laurel: Ordering Residential Patterns

The 1975 New Jersey Supreme Court Mount Laurel ruling—the fair housing equivalent of *Roe v. Wade* or *Brown v. Board of Education*—attempts to redress the effects of race on population distribution. It also directly affects education reform, because *Abbott V* targeted segregated communities.

A 2001 *New York Times* article, "Mount Laurel: A Battle That Won't Go Away" (Capuzzo, 2001, Section 14, p. 1), summarized the ongoing conflict over housing as follows:

> Despite rulings that challenged each New Jersey municipality with the "moral obligation" to provide "an appropriate variety and choice of housing for all categories of people who may desire to live there," a tour through any part of the state reveals something else: vast suburbs that are largely White and affluent, interrupted by cities, mostly full of the state's poor and minority populations.

To avoid building affordable housing in middle- and upper-income communities, a practice developed that permitted affluent towns to transfer their Mount Laurel housing allotment—usually with a multimillion dollar payment—to working-class communities, thereby fulfilling their moral obligation. The working-class communities then built the housing but, in most cases, restricted occupancy to low-income Whites. The result of this practice, as noted in the *Star-Ledger,* was that "Three decades after the court's ruling, the state's record on building affordable housing is decidedly mixed. But when it comes to the court's secondary goal of integrating the suburbs, Mount Laurel has been a flop" (Chambers, 2005, Section 10, p. 1).

Despite the New Jersey Supreme Court's efforts to remedy residential segregation through the Mount Laurel decision and its rulings in other desegregation cases, the *Abbott V* decision actually reinforces segregation as part of the social architecture of New Jersey. In fact, the social and economic conditions that shaped the geopolitical dynamics of New Jersey were the very reasons that systemic reform of urban education became necessary. These conditions set the stage for the 28-year legal battle that resulted in the *Abbott V* reforms and for continuing court battles over the implementation of *Abbott V.*

Abbott v. Burke: A Brief History

To understand the implementation of *Abbott V* in the elementary schools described in Chapters 4 through 7, it will be helpful to place the history of the Abbott litigation in the context of the social structure of New Jersey outlined above. (See Appendix A for a chronology of the Abbott decisions.)

The Origin of *Abbott V*

An 1875 amendment to the New Jersey constitution of 1844, which replaced the original state constitution of 1776, introduced the idea of a "thorough and efficient" education (Williams, 1990). The New Jersey State Constitution of 1947, in Article VIII, Taxation and Finance, Section IV, Paragraph 1, states that

> The Legislature shall provide for the maintenance and support of a thorough and efficient system of free public schools for the instruction of all children in the state between the ages of five and eighteen years.

The phrase "thorough and efficient" became the centerpiece of litigation that began in 1970 when *Robinson v. Cahill* charged that New Jersey's funding for schools discriminated against poor districts and created disparities in education. Three years later, the New Jersey Supreme Court ruled that heavy reliance on property taxes—which suburban communities had more ability to collect—discriminated against poor districts.

School funding cases faced a setback at the federal level in 1973, when in *San Antonio Independent School District v. Rodriguez,* the U.S. Supreme Court ruled that education funding was not a "fundamental interest" under the federal constitution. In effect, the *Rodriguez* decision shifted the focus of litigation throughout the country to the education clauses in state constitutions, the focus of *Cahill v. Robinson.*

Starting in 1981, the Abbott cases focused on attempts by the state to meet the New Jersey constitution's "thorough and efficient" clause. At almost every step in the process, politicians voiced reservations about the Abbott cases. As late as 1996, in her State of the State Address, Governor Christine Todd Whitman said, "Money alone does not equal learning. On the other side of the equation, we can point to districts that produce solid academic results while spending below the sate average." She used the example of a middle-class suburb that had below average per pupil expenditures and just above average SAT scores (Gold, 1999).

Abbott IV and *V*

In 1997, the *Abbott IV* ruling ordered funding parity for poor urban schools with the wealthiest school districts in the state.[5] In May 1998, *Abbott V* specified the educational programs to be implemented in the 30 Abbott districts. These programs, outlined earlier in this chapter and discussed in detail in Chapters 4–7, when combined with the equalization of per pupil expenditures, were unprecedented in United States history.

However, reflecting the ongoing contentiousness surrounding the 1998 ruling, there have been five additional Abbott rulings—ending with *Abbott X* in June 2003—that reaffirmed *Abbott IV* and *V.* In addition to these rulings, political and administrative actions from 1998 until 2006 have created actions and a context affecting implementation of the *Abbott V* mandates.

The McGreevey Era

A February 9, 2002, *New York Times* editorial titled "A Truce in New Jersey's School War" captured the different approaches to Abbott taken by Governor James McGreevey and his predecessor, Christine Whitman.

> James McGreevey took office as New Jersey's governor less than a month ago, but he has already made history by moving to settle one of the most bitterly fought education lawsuits in America. After 20 years of foot-dragging and obfuscation by governors and legislators of both parties, Mr. McGreevey has told the state's Supreme Court that he will abide by the court's rulings in *Abbott v. Burke.*
>
> . . . Mr. McGreevey's decision to institute the ruling should clear the air on this racially charged issue and set New Jersey on the road to full educational opportunity in 30 underprivileged districts.
>
> . . . The McGreevey administration has appointed former Democratic state senator, Gordon MacInnes, to oversee the reconstruction of the 30 so-called Abbott Districts around the state. Mr. MacInnes recently said that the state had attempted to create the appearance of compliance without doing much to help the impoverished children on whose behalf the suit had been brought. Building new schools and strengthening the curriculum will be expensive, but well worth the cost in terms of the lives that will be salvaged. (Section A, p. 18)

A June 6, 2002, *Star-Ledger* editorial noted that:

> The Newark school system spends $16,000 a year on each child. Nearly half of the city's students drop out before graduating from high school. It is obvious that money is no longer the root problem.
>
> Gordon MacInnes, the new state czar for urban education, admitted that the state has no idea whether the reforms ordered by the court for funding urban districts are working. It was a moment that exposed the bankruptcy of Christie Whitman's approach. She presented herself as a fiscal conservative but did little to ensure that the huge infusions of money ordered by the court were spent effectively. ("Measuring School Reforms, 2002, p. 20)

McGreevey's Approach to *Abbott V*

When Governor McGreevey took office, New Jersey faced a projected $7 billion deficit. The cause was a combination of Whitman administration fiscal policies that relied heavily on borrowing, declines in tax revenue as a result of the September 11 terrorist attacks, and the dot-com bust. McGreevey had difficulty funding many state programs, including education. For the Abbott districts, his solution was to freeze funding at the 2001 level.

Abbott V Phase II

Early in McGreevey's term the state reduced its emphasis on implementing court-ordered Whole School Reform models to focus on "standards-driven classroom reform" that emphasized the state's Core Curriculum Content Standards. Abbott Phase II announced three changes in focus for the 2002–2003 school year:

- The Core Curriculum Content Standards were revised and progress indicators were added for kindergarten and second grade;
- The State launched an Early Literacy effort, which required stronger pedagogical and logistical connections between Abbott pre-K and K–3; and,
- Sweeping new federal legislation—No Child Left Behind—took effect, with immediate but uncertain implications for schools and districts failing to make Adequate Yearly Progress.

In addition to the budget freeze and adjustments in the implementation of the Abbott ruling, McGreevey took other actions not favorable to the Abbott districts. The Education Law Center accepted many of these as necessary under the budget constraints, including a "hiatus" in Abbott implementation. However, in the view of the Education Law Center, it eventually became clear that McGreevey was not fulfilling his commitment to implement the Abbott mandates. The result was more litigation.

New School Construction

After years of delay by Whitman, the McGreevey administration began the repair of old schools and the construction of new schools mandated by *Abbott V*, funded with $6 billion of state revenues. The view of the director of the School Construction Corporation was that "I believe if you give these children facilities they have not had for years, that it has to make a difference in the way they are educated and their ability, down the road, to compete for the better jobs" (quoted in Chambers, 2004, p. 16).

Property Tax Reform: A Constitutional Convention?

In late August 2004, Governor McGreevey appointed a property tax convention task force to explore ways to amend the state constitution to reduce local property taxes, the major source of revenue for funding local education. In addition to the usual political aspects of property tax levels—New Jersey had the highest in the country—property taxes became an even more sensitive issue because *Abbott IV* had decoupled property taxes from the Abbott districts.

To solve the property tax problem, an influential state leader proposed an amendment to the constitution to provide a "thorough and efficient" education for Abbott districts by equaling the state average per pupil expenditure instead of the parity with the wealthiest districts that *Abbott V* mandated. This proposal intended to reduce property taxes in New Jersey and to lower per pupil funding for the Abbott districts.

David Sciarra, the director of the Education Law Center, wrote in the *Star-Ledger* on September 29, 2004, that

> The constitutional convention is a blatant attempt to turn back the clock to the not-too-distant past, when the quality of a child's education in New Jersey was determined by where you lived, your family's income, and the color of your skin. (p. 17)

The Governor Resigns

On August 12, 2004, Governor James McGreevey announced his resignation because of a scandal. He resisted efforts to force him from office immediately, and instead set a departure date of November 15, 2004, in order to avoid a special election to replace him. Along with many citizens, Jon Corzine, the senior United States senator, who wanted to replace McGreevey, declared that there was a "crisis of confidence" in New Jersey (Orr, 2004, p. 1).

The Acting Governor's Budget

Richard Codey, who succeeded McGreevey, submitted the state budget for 2006. Again, the message was that New Jersey had to reduce its expenditures. The budget kept school funding at the same level as for the 3 previous years except for a $49 million increase for the Abbott districts. Reflecting the division between suburban and urban districts, the business administrator of South Brunswick, a middle-class district, said, "I try not to pit ourselves against the Abbotts, but when you see our spending less than the state average and theirs above even the wealthiest districts, it becomes difficult sometimes not to feel that way" (quoted in Mooney, 2005a, p. 11).

A Shift in Attitude

In the summer of 2004, an important shift occurred toward collaboration between the state and the Abbott districts. John Mooney, the *Star-Ledger* education reporter, observed that "Meetings like this [between the state and local education officials] are part of the state's more collegial approach with its Abbott districts over the past few months, a balm after the previous three years under Gov. James E. McGreevey's administration. The two sides had been constantly at odds—and in court—over how the Abbott mandates are carried out" (Mooney, 2004b, p. 23).

The School Construction Program—Again

In the fall of 2004, reports began to appear in local newspapers that the school construction program was running out of money. As a result, many planned new schools and renovations in urban districts were unlikely to go forward. Early in 2005, the cost of the building program and its management became an issue of concern. By March 2005, investigations into the school building program were under way and, after review of the old contacts, the state Inspector General suspended new contracts (McNichol, 2005, p. 1).

On July 27, 2005, the New Jersey Schools Construction Corporation prioritized 59 projects that it could complete and stopped work on 200 new schools. Senator Jon Corzine, who soon became governor-elect, called the school construction program a "disgrace" and said, "It's the worst kind of theft to overpromise, underdeliver and undercut New Jersey's basic obligation to our kids" (quoted in Chen, 2005, p. B7). Revised estimates of the cost of completion of the new schools were $20 billion (McNichol & Chambers, 2005, p. 1).

Revising and Sustaining *Abbott V*

On May 18, 2005, the *Star-Ledger* front page headline read, "State Looks to Shrink Needy Schools List" (Mooney, 2005b, p. 1). Under the Abbott statutes, the state was required to review the list of qualifying districts every 5 years.

Education Commissioner William L. Librera submitted a proposal to the legislature that "would tighten rules ensuring schools that benefit from the landmark mandates are the most in need" (Mooney, 2005b, p. 1) and proposed to reduce the 31 districts by half.[6]

The response to this proposed revision was a threat of legal action. "Abbott is not just about school funding," said David Sciarra of the Education Law Center, "It's really about education quality which the commissioner ignores" (quoted in Mooney, 2005b, p. 10). A May 29, 2005, *Star-Ledger* editorial cautioned that adjusting the Abbott districts should proceed carefully: "With property owners clamoring for relief, it's tempting to slash Abbott districts. But taking a meat-cleaver approach to these districts would be a mistake" ("The Abbott Districts," 2005, Section 10, p. 2).

Another Lawsuit

In June 2005, the Education Law Center filed a lawsuit in Superior Court claiming that the New Jersey Department of Education had not formulated a plan for managing the Abbott program, as required by law, for 2004–2005 through 2006–2007. In October 2005, the Department of Education submitted a management plan for the Abbott districts, required in a Superior Court ruling. (Chapter 9 discusses the plan.) The Education Law Center characterized the plan as demonstrating "major shortcomings" in the Department's management of the Abbott districts and not offering solutions for the management deficiencies.

Evaluating Abbott

In March 2005, the State Department of Education solicited bids for the first evaluation of the *Abbott V* programs, to begin in the 2005–2006 school year. In July 2005, the Department announced that it had indefinitely suspended the bidding process for the evaluation.

Changing of the Guard

Education Commissioner Librera resigned in September 2005, and in November 2005, Jon Corzine became the governor-elect. In the past, the governor had exerted significant influence on the direction and implementation of Abbott. Corzine would eventually gain more control over the future of Abbott than his predecessors, because during his term two New Jersey Supreme Court justices would retire and three others would face reappointment.

New Initiatives

In September 2005, departing Acting Governor Codey signed legislation that would withdraw the state from administering the three school districts—

Paterson, Jersey City, and Newark—that it had taken over and operated without demonstrated improvement. The intent of the legislation was that the state and the districts would work cooperatively to assist the return to local control.

Also in September, the state began implementing the Abbott Secondary Initiative in four Abbott districts. This reform focused on breaking large middle and high schools into smaller schools to create "learning communities."

Governor Corzine's Lawsuit

In April 2006, a few months after taking office, Governor Corzine filed a lawsuit with the New Jersey Supreme Court to freeze financial aid to Abbott districts and requested fiscal audits of selected districts.

In May, responding to the Governor's case that the state was in dire financial condition and that Abbott districts had not demonstrated significant progress on standardized tests, the Court ruled that Abbott funding would be frozen and audits would be conducted. However, districts could appeal their budgets, leaving open the possibility of funding increases.

Abbott in Perspective

The social and economic segregation that developed in New Jersey's urban regions was highly correlated with race. Apartheid conditions created the need for the Abbott rulings and influenced the response of politicians, educators, and citizens to the funding and type of urban education reform. The class- and race-based social structure of New Jersey exerted significant influence on the entire legal and political process.

Despite the long-term conflict over equity funding in New Jersey and the problems encountered under *Abbott V*, compared with Kozol's pessimistic 1991 assessment of the prospects for change, *Abbott V* provided an opportunity for a revolution in the reform of urban education in New Jersey. In addition to equalizing funding and mandating specific programs, it provided a framework for comparing the performance of schools in such disparate districts as Princeton and Camden. These comparisons, then, could form the basis for further legal action to improve educational opportunity for poor minority students.

THE NEXT CHAPTER will present the history and features of the No Child Left Behind Act of 2001 and will show how its provisions for accountability and corrective action for low-performing schools contributed to the revolution in New Jersey education.

CHAPTER 2

No Child Left Behind

The Federal Solution to Brown

A Revolution in Education

On January 8, 2002, President George W. Bush signed a reauthorization of the federal Elementary and Secondary Education Act (ESEA). Implementation of the No Child Left Behind Act of 2001—the most sweeping reform of ESEA since its enactment in 1965—began in schools in fall 2002, four years after implementation of *Abbott V.*

Senator Edward M. Kennedy proclaimed No Child Left Behind (NCLB), which had broad bipartisan support in Congress, to be "An entirely new concept, a new initiative, a new endeavor" comparable to the enactment of Social Security and the race to the moon (quoted in Schemo, 2004, p. B9). After 2 years of implementation, Rod Paige, the U.S. Secretary of Education, agreed with Kennedy: "What the President is asking is revolutionary: accountability for results while preserving local control and flexibility; expanded options for parents; using what works in the classroom" (quoted in Mooney, 2004a, p. 1).

James Liebman and Charles Sabel (2003b) understood the implications of NCLB to be even more dramatic. In their view, over the past 30 years, various education reforms have converged, including state reforms and NCLB, reflecting

> a new form of collaboration among courts, legislatures, and administrative agencies on the one side and between these organs of government and new forms of public action on the other. It thus redefines the separation of powers and recasts the administrative state more generally, while opening the way to new forms of citizen participation in the orientation and operation of key public institutions. At the limit, school reform raises the prospect of a broader redefinition of our very democracy. (p. 184)

Less exuberant, but nonetheless positive about its prospects, the *Wall Street Journal* editorialized that the passage of NCLB

> will now force the debate to come to grips with a stark reality, namely that public schools, no matter how high-flown their intended purpose, are at bottom public *bureaucracies,* which by now have shown themselves to be the American institution least amenable to reforms of the sort that have already occurred throughout the private sector. ("Mr. Bush's ABC's," 2001, p. A18)

Because NCLB overlapped with the *Abbott V* ruling, this book examines how the two programs combined to affect the learning of children in high-poverty, low-achievement urban elementary school classrooms.

A High-Quality Education for All Children

Title I of No Child Left Behind, "Improving the Academic Achievement of the Disadvantaged," will be quoted at length because its goals and the means for achieving them are expressed in remarkably clear language.[1]

Statement of Purpose and Plan

As described in Title I, the purpose of NCLB is to

> ensure that all children have a fair, equal, and significant opportunity to obtain a high-quality education and reach, at a minimum, proficiency on challenging state academic achievement standards and State academic assessments. This purpose can be accomplished by—
>
> (1) ensuring that high-quality academic assessments, accountability systems, teacher preparation and training, curriculum, and instructional materials are aligned with challenging State academic standards so that students, teachers, parents, and administrators can measure progress against common expectations for student academic achievement;
>
> (2) meeting the educational needs of low-achieving children in our Nation's highest-poverty schools, limited English proficient children, migratory children, children with disabilities, Indian children, neglected or delinquent children, and young children in need of reading assistance;
>
> (3) closing the achievement gap between high- and low-performing children, especially the achievement gaps between minority and nonminority students, and between disadvantaged children and their more advantaged peers;
>
> (4) holding schools, local educational agencies, and States accountable for improving the academic achievement of all students, and identifying and turning around low-performing schools that have failed to provide a high-quality education to their students, while providing alternatives to students in such schools to enable the students to receive a high-quality education;

(5) distributing and targeting resources sufficiently to make a difference to local educational agencies and schools where needs are greatest;

(6) improving and strengthening accountability, teaching, and learning by using State assessment systems designed to ensure that students are meeting challenging State academic achievement and content standards and increasing achievement overall, but especially for the disadvantaged;

(7) providing greater decision making authority and flexibility to schools and teachers in exchange for greater responsibility for student performance;

(8) providing children an enriched and accelerated educational program, including the use of schoolwide programs or additional services that increase the amount and quality of instructional time;

(9) promoting schoolwide reform and ensuring the access of children to effective, scientifically based instructional strategies and challenging academic content;

(10) significantly elevating the quality of instruction by providing staff in participating schools with substantial opportunities for professional development;

(11) coordinating services under all parts of this title with each other, with other educational services, and, to the extent feasible, with other agencies providing services to youth, children, and families; and

(12) affording parents substantial and meaningful opportunities to participate in the education of their children. (NCLB Act, Section 1001)

Key Features of NCLB

An important element of NCLB is a mandate that educational practices should reflect scientific research. An example, which is relevant to this study because it reflects the use of the Whole School Models mandated by *Abbott V*, is the NCLB Act's stipulation that local education agencies should "take into account the experiences of model programs for the educationally disadvantaged, and the findings of relevant scientifically based research" (NCLB Act, Section 1112(c)(1)(F)). Another provision of NCLB requires that districts certify that teachers possess the proper teaching credentials for the subjects they teach. In addition, NCLB focuses on the school as an organization and seeks to "replace old ways of thinking about parental involvement with new ways of organizing more-equitable and effective programs of school, family, and community partnerships" (Epstein, 2005, p. 179).

Implementation of NCLB

NCLB required each state to formulate and submit a plan to the Secretary of Education that demonstrated that it had adopted challenging academic content standards and student academic achievement standards for all schools and children in the state. These standards applied to math and reading or language arts; science standards were to take effect beginning in 2005–2006.

Based on annual standardized tests that should "involve multiple up-to-date measures of student academic achievement, including measures that assess higher-order thinking skills and understanding" (NCLB Act, Section 1111(b)(3)(C)(vi)), states are required to determine if schools achieve Adequate Yearly Progress (AYP). The state defines AYP and must demonstrate that it applies to all schools in the state and results in continuous and substantial academic improvement for all students. The tests—which eventually will cover grades 3 through 12—should disaggregate the achievement of economically disadvantaged students, students from major racial and ethnic groups, students with disabilities, and students with limited English proficiency.

Each state was required to establish a starting point for the measurement of achievement and a timeline for AYP. "The timeline shall ensure that not later than 12 years after the end of the 2001–2002 school year, all students in each group . . . will meet or exceed the State's proficient level of academic achievement on the State assessments . . ." (NCLB Act, Section 1111(b)(2)(F)). In addition, states must participate in the biennial academic assessment of fourth- and eighth-grade reading and mathematics using the National Assessment of Educational Progress (NAEP) test. This requirement measures how challenging the state tests are; a wide difference in performance on the state test and the NAEP would indicate problems in the education system.

The state is required to publish annual report cards that present the results of the annual test for each district and school. One intention of the report cards is to provide information that permits comparisons from year to year and among the various groups. Another intention is to inform parents of the quality of the schools their children attend.

States also must report annually to the Secretary of Education on their progress in developing and implementing the annual tests, along with results of the tests. The report also must include data on the number of "highly qualified" teachers in the state, local educational agency, and school.

Corrective Actions

Although the AYP requirements apply to all schools, the NCLB Act specified corrective actions applying only to Title I schools that fail to achieve AYP. According to NCLB, "a local educational agency shall identify for school improvement any elementary or secondary school . . . that fails, for 2 consecutive years, to make adequate yearly progress" (NCLB Act, Section 1116(b)(1)(A)). Any school identified as needing improvement must provide all students enrolled in the school with the option of transfering to another public school in the district—including a public charter school—that has not been identified for improvement.

Schools needing improvement are required to develop an improvement plan "in consultation with parents, school staff, the local educational agency serving the school, and outside experts" (NCLB Act, Section 1116(b)(3)(A)). The school must also use 10% of its Title I funds for professional development and institute a teacher mentoring program.

After 3 years of a school failing to achieve AYP, parents continue to have the option of transferring to another school and can use Title I funds to purchase supplemental educational services from outside vendors. After 4 years of not achieving AYP, a school district is required to take "corrective action":

> (I) Replace the school staff who are relevant to the failure to make adequate yearly progress.
>
> (II) Institute and fully implement a new curriculum, including providing appropriate professional development for all relevant staff, that is based on scientifically based research and offers substantial promise of improving educational achievement for low-achieving students and enabling the school to make adequate yearly progress.
>
> (III) Significantly decrease management authority at the school level.
>
> (IV) Appoint an outside expert to advise the school on its progress toward making adequate yearly progress, based on its school plan.
>
> (V) Extend the school year or school day for the school.
>
> (VI) Restructure the internal organizational structure of the school. (NCLB Act, Section 1116(b)(7)(C)(iv))

The school district is responsible for disseminating information to the public and parents regarding the corrective actions undertaken at this stage.

If a school does not achieve AYP after having operated under corrective action status for 1 year, NCLB requires the district to undertake, in addition to the actions listed above, one of the following remedies, which, in effect, will reconstitute the school:

> (i) Reopening the school as a public charter school.
>
> (ii) Replacing all or most of the school staff (which may include the principal) who are relevant to the failure to make adequate yearly progress.
>
> (iii) Entering into a contract with an entity, such as a private management company, with a demonstrated record of effectiveness, to operate the public school.
>
> (iv) Turning the operation of the school over to the state educational agency. . . .
>
> (v) Any other major restructuring of the school's governance arrangement that makes fundamental reforms, such as significant changes in the school's staffing and governance, to improve student academic achievement in the school and that has substantial promise of enabling the school to make adequate yearly progress. . . . (NCLB Act, Section 1116(b)(8)(B))

The state has responsibility for providing technical assistance to schools undergoing corrective action and for determining if the school district failed to carry out its responsibility for improving the school. After 2 consecutive years of achieving AYP, a school will be relieved of the requirements of corrective action.

For school districts that fail to achieve AYP, NCLB provides further corrective action administered by a state. Among the allowed actions are the following:

> (v) Appointing . . . a receiver or trustee to administer the affairs of the local educational agency in place of the superintendent and school board.
>
> (vi) Abolishing or restructuring the local educational agency.
>
> (vii) Authorizing students to transfer from a school operated by the local educational agency to a higher-performing public school operated by another local educational agency. (NCLB Act, Section 1116(c)(10)(C))

Enforcing NCLB

The NCLB legislation did not provide the federal government with significant enforcement tools. It relied on voluntary compliance, except for the possible withdrawal of federal education funds from a district (approximately 7% of the expenditures of most school districts) and the imposition of the progressive corrective sanctions for schools and districts.

For example, early in the implementation of NCLB, the Secretary of Education's office threatened to withdraw Title I funds from communities that selected educational programs that did not meet its standards. A widely publicized case was the selection of a reading program in New York City that the Secretary's office considered not sufficiently based on scientific research. The threat to withdraw federal funds resulted in New York changing the program to one endorsed by the Secretary's office. Other cities and states, however, have challenged various parts of the law, and some resist compliance or implement NCLB symbolically.

The Critics and Supporters of NCLB

There are many criticisms of NCLB from a wide variety of sources (Meier & Wood, 2004). Governors, teachers, teachers' unions, parents, and taxpayers have expressed concerns about NCLB ranging from claims that the Bush administration failed to fund it to objections over the federal government interfering in local education.

Another view is that NCLB is an expedient attempt to deal with the long-term problems of race relations in the United States, because the interests of Whites temporarily converged with the needs of Blacks (Bell, 2004). At the beginning of the 21st century, the interest convergence of NCLB appears to be the increasing threat to American corporations from global business competition, requiring production of more highly skilled workers in the USA.

Unanticipated Outcomes

Like most social policies and interventions, it is probable that NCLB will produce short- and long-term unanticipated consequences (Merton, 1936) and reverse outcomes (Sieber, 1981). For example, studies of the effect of standardized tests on classrooms have found that creative teaching declined because standardized tests pressured teachers to narrow the curriculum and use rote instructional methods (McNeil, 2000; Johnson & Johnson, 2002).

Another potential reverse outcome is that NCLB "creates incentives to increase segregation by class and race and to push low-performing students out of school entirely" (Ryan, 2004, p. 934). Also, because of the new demands placed on teachers to have students pass tests, NCLB may deter talented people from entering the teaching profession.

A possible long-term reverse consequence of NCLB is that states could reject federal intervention in education, reinforcing states' rights. Several lawsuits have already contested the right of the federal government to require certain provisions of NCLB without providing funding for them.

Standardized Tests

One implication of these arguments is that the quality and interpretation of standardized tests, and how they are used, is essential for NCLB's success or failure (Popham, 2004). Problems with tests include the possibility that they could measure student performance inaccurately and misidentify students and schools that make significant progress on their own terms as "in need of improvement." Finally, because NCLB lets states devise their own instructional content and standardized tests, there may be extensive variation in curriculum and its measurement. This variation will create differences in the usefulness of the tests as part of a comparative framework for judging student performance.

The Privatization of Education

Another criticism of NCLB is that its real objective is to advance the conservative political agenda of undermining the public education system. By demonstrating that public schools are not able to achieve AYP, NCLB could lead some to the conclusion that the only solution is for private education to replace public schools. For example, in New Jersey the teachers' union viewed

NCLB as a Trojan horse poised to destroy public education. Adding credibility to this viewpoint, NCLB provides for the use of private for-profit tutoring companies and for the takeover of a failing school by a private education company.

The New Accountability

Another, more positive, view of NCLB is that although it increases the federal government's role in states, it preserves local control and forges new relationships among the levels and branches of government (Liebman & Sabel, 2003a). NCLB reaffirmed the right of American citizens to have an education. It also defined high-quality education and provided a means of determining the adequacy of the education that was offered. Through the diagnostic use of standardized tests, NCLB provided a roadmap that could lead to continuous improvement.

But critics of NCLB have argued that instead of continuous improvement based on a "race to the top" in which states would compete to achieve higher test scores, NCLB could produce a "race to the bottom" (Ryan, 2004, p. 949). This possible perverse outcome of NCLB questioned why states would establish ambitious goals and risk large numbers of students and schools not performing well. Instead, a more likely strategy was that state education officials would devise easier tests to make students, schools, and communities look good (Ryan, 2004, p. 949).

Pressures for states to race to the bottom include employer preferences for locating in communities with high-quality schools from which to select a work force. Another factor is that the quality of neighborhood schools influences property values. Rigorous tests that many students fail could impair the ability of a state to compete with other states in attracting new businesses and could possibly reduce home prices and property tax revenues (Ryan, 2004).

A Comparative Framework for Improvement

Regardless of how states, school districts, and schools would eventually respond, NCLB created a national framework for comparing the performance of schools. Among schools of similar demographics, comparative studies of schools with high achievement levels and their low-performing peers could identify practices that schools "in need of improvement" should implement. As a result, NCLB created a potential strategy for a new civil rights movement: demonstration (through litigation, if necessary) that a remedy for the inability of a particular subpopulation to achieve adequately is implementing successful educational programs (Liebman & Sabel, 2003a).

A Long Revolution: *Abbott V* and NCLB in Urban Schools

Similar to *Abbott V* in New Jersey, NCLB was the federal culmination of the evolution of *Brown v. Board of Education*. In response to the rulings that modified the intent of *Brown* to desegregate schools to achieve equal educational opportunity, NCLB articulated the historically unprecedented goal "to ensure that all children have a fair, equal, and significant opportunity to obtain a high-quality education" (NCLB Act, Section 1001). Like *Abbott V*, NCLB accepted the doctrine of separate but equal education.

The differences between *Abbott V* and NCLB are significant, however. By mandating a comprehensive reform program, *Abbott V* intended to change major elements of the organization of urban schools in New Jersey quickly and fundamentally. NCLB set specific goals within a time frame for all states but did not specify programs for school improvement. More important, NCLB shifted responsibility for educational achievement from the individual and subgroup to the organizational properties and instructional programs of schools, and provided a framework for implementing the change.

THE NEXT CHAPTER will present a theory of educational change to explain the historic *Abbott V* and NCLB reforms. Then subsequent chapters will describe and analyze implementation of these reforms in four elementary schools.

CHAPTER 3

The Urban Education Revolution in Perspective

A Theory of Educational Change

Explaining *Abbott V* and NCLB

The punctuated legitimacy theory views change as alternations between long periods of equilibrium and short periods of rapid revolutionary change (Gersick, 1991; Gould, 2002; Parsons & Fidler, 2005). The theory focuses on the interaction of organizations with environmental forces and the resulting dynamics within organizations that contribute to the erosion, loss, reconstruction, and maintenance of legitimacy as the cause of organization change (Gold, 1999).

The punctuated legitimacy theory explains developments during the 7 years of *Abbott V* and 3 years of NCLB implementation for each of the schools described in Chapters 4 through 7.[1] It also informs the comparative analysis in Chapter 8 and the discussion of policies and practices for improving urban education in Chapter 9.

Theories of Educational Change

Incremental Change Theory

With few exceptions, most studies of education change are atheoretical (e.g., Barnes, 2002; Duke, 1995; Fink, 2000; Levine, 2002; Silin & Lippman, 2003). Even when not stated explicitly, however, a theory of incremental organizational change underlies most studies of education reform (though there are rare exceptions, such as when a charismatic leader creates a sharp break with the past and then sustains that change; see, e.g., Bensman, 2000). The three stages of incremental change are

1. *Adoption*—the process that leads up to and includes a decision to adopt or proceed with a change;

2. *Implementation of initial use*—the first experiences of attempting to put an idea or reform into practice; and
3. *Institutionalization*—whether the change gets built in as an ongoing part of the system or disappears because of a decision to discard or through attrition. (Fullan, 1991, pp. 47–48)

According to this theory, planned, controlled, incremental reform results in the emergence of significant change between Phases 2 and 3, in approximately 3 years. A central concern is resistance or barriers to change, which can occur at any stage of the change process and can arise from internal or external sources. Depending on its management, resistance ends the change, distorts its intentions, or creates unanticipated consequences. The primary explanation for change failure is individual or group resistance to new ideas and practices (Fink, 2000). One consequence of implementation failure—which often occurs shortly after the initiation of change—is the creation of barriers to further innovation (Fullan, 1991, p. 74; Louis & Miles, 1990, p. 186).

The Punctuated Equilibrium Theory

The punctuated equilibrium theory is more comprehensive than the incremental theory. As a framework for studying organizational change over an extended period, this theory can place *Abbott V* and NCLB in a historical perspective to help explain their successes and shortcomings.

The basic argument of punctuated equilibrium is that organizations experience "relatively long periods of stability (equilibrium), punctuated by compact periods of qualitative, metamorphic change (revolution)" (Gersick, 1991, p. 12). The organizational deep structure consists of variables that change, and these changes demarcate equilibrium and revolutionary periods.[2] The components of deep structure are

1. core beliefs and values regarding the organization, its employees, and its environment;
2. products, markets, technology, and competitive timing;
3. the distribution of power;
4. the organization's structure; and
5. the nature, type, and pervasiveness of control systems. (Tushman & Romanelli, 1985, p. 176)

Institutional and ecological theories indicate that the deep structure of specific types of organizations (e.g., financial institutions) have common elements because the environment they operate in exerts similar influences (DiMaggio & Powell, 1983; Hannan & Freeman, 1989; Meyer & Rowan, 1977; Scott, 1995). This perspective applies to the deep structure of schools (Tye, 2000) and urban education (Tyack, 1974), as well.

During equilibrium periods, organizational activity remains relatively stable and carries out the deep structure choices, engaging in incremental adjustments that leave the deep structure intact. Contributing to the maintenance of equilibrium are cognitive frameworks, motivational barriers to change, inertial constraints of system stakeholders, and the benefits that systems derive from persistence.

Revolutionary periods occur when the dismantling of the deep structure leaves the system temporarily disorganized. One reason for deep structure dismantling is organizational failure, which "may be extremely important in setting the stage for revolutionary change" (Gersick, 1991, p. 22). Failure precipitates an organizational crisis that increases performance pressures on internal participants by various stakeholders and attracts new leadership whose "explicit task [is] to break the old deep structure and establish a new one" (Gersick, 1991, p. 23). Typically, "a subset of the system's old pieces, along with some new pieces, can be put back together into a new configuration, which operates according to a new set of rules" (Gersick, 1991, p. 19), creating significant, even revolutionary, change (Weick & Quinn, 1999). In some cases, instead of change occurring, a new organization replaces the old one.

Determining the extent of change in districts, schools, and classrooms requires identification of the key elements of the change process. These include change triggers, creation of punctuations, measurement of the stability or change in organizational deep structure (i.e., incremental versus revolutionary change), and assessment of innovation failure or success.

Change triggers are either external or internal actions that create punctuations and produce movement between periods. Revolutionary change occurs when at least three deep structure elements change within 2 years, resulting in disassembly and reconfiguration of the deep structure (Romanelli & Tushman, 1994, p. 1154). The success or failure of innovation is judged by participants and other stakeholders, based on their evaluation of the extent of implementation of the intended changes and whether or not they produced the desired results.

The Punctuated Legitimacy Theory

The punctuated equilibrium theory does not adequately explain the transition from equilibrium to revolutionary periods. For example, research testing the theory found that a crisis occurs at the midpoint of an organizational time frame that produces new leadership and results in revolutionary change (Gersick, 1994). Although a crisis at a specific time in an organization's life cycle can precipitate a revolutionary period, another possibility is externally initiated forced change. Furthermore, changes that organizations experience within equilibrium and revolutionary periods are often more complex than a single crisis (Gold, 1999). Over time, actions accumulate to create a variety of organizational scenarios. One of these is a long, slow decline that participants do not view as a crisis, eventually adjust to, and finally accept; yet, in the process, they have legitimated suboptimal performance.

Whether as the result of a single crisis or long decline, a primary cause of change is the delegitimation of an organization. The loss of legitimacy, which different stakeholders contribute to and could view as a crisis, sets in motion attempts to reconstruct and then sustain organizational legitimacy.

The Moral Basis of Legitimacy

Legitimacy is a multidimensional concept that explains individual, group, organization, and societal actions (Zelditch, 2001). Kelman (2001) emphasized that "at its core" legitimacy

> refers to the *moral basis* of social interaction. [Legitimacy is] an issue that arises in an interaction or relationship between two individuals, or between one or more individuals and a group, organization, or larger social system, in which one party makes a certain *claim,* which the other may accept or reject. Acceptance or rejection depends on whether the claim is seen as just or rightful. Legitimacy can be evaluated at least on two levels. One level concerns the legitimacy of the claim itself, or of the action, policy, demand, or request that reflects that claim. The other concerns the legitimacy of the claimant—of the person, group, organization, or larger social system that makes the claim or provides the backing for it. (p. 55)

For actions within organizations, the moral dimension of legitimacy is a stream of judgments that produce, reproduce—and occasionally challenge—the legitimacy of the practices of the organization. These judgments involve issues such as assessment of the legitimacy of the authority structure (Weber, 1947) and, more fundamentally but usually only on specific occasions, the arrangement of organizational components, including the values represented by deep structure assumptions.

As Kelman (2001) notes, in addition to its moral component—but also an element of it—legitimacy involves the use of power and authority. The ability of an individual or group to enforce a claim to legitimacy is central to organization change, particularly when external forces, such as *Abbott V* and NCLB, initiate the change.

Socially constructed agreements—laws, contracts, policies, procedures, and rules—have claims to legitimacy. For example, *Abbott V,* a state Supreme Court order, and NCLB, a federal law, are the products of institutions central to American democracy that have high legitimacy claims. However, through a variety of mechanisms, court orders and laws often encounter delegitimating efforts that can eventually result in their revision, existence as unenforced symbols of social ideals, or termination (Rosenberg, 1991). For example, some commentators viewed NCLB as legitimate and revolutionary in its potential to improve equality of educational opportunity in America (Liebman & Sabel,

2003b), whereas others concluded that it was a defective law that should be replaced (Meier & Wood, 2004; Noddings, 2005).

The multiple complex issues involved in large-scale planned educational change raise questions with moral implications that affect its claim to legitimacy. The basic question concerning legitimacy for *Abbott V* and NCLB is, Do the planned changes provide more benefits for students than the education they currently receive?

Planned Change and Legitimacy

Planned change—particularly when it is externally initiated—challenges the legitimacy of the taken-for-granted nature of the social world of an organization by proposing new arrangements (Schutz, 1967). The anticipation of a new type of organization creates uncertainty that can generate various forms of resistance, including legitimating existing behavior and delegitimating the future organization.

Further, if planned change intends to reconfigure elements of the deep structure of an organization, the issue of legitimacy affects the entire change process. Because it challenges fundamental values and ideas concerning the correctness of social arrangements, legitimacy is at the core of organizational change. Consequently, in a shift from granting legitimacy without the inspection of organizational processes or outputs (Meyer & Rowan, 1977), periods of externally initiated change challenge the legitimacy of education institutions (Gold, 1999; Coburn, 2004). The result is interactions between schools and their environments based on strategies to change or protect the core behaviors and structures and, in the process, challenge, maintain, or reconstruct the moral and institutional legitimacy of education.

However, although the rational creation of meaning by organization members to justify practice is an essential component of legitimacy, it does not necessarily result in rational decisions that successfully maintain or reconstruct legitimacy (Gold, 1999). To understand the processes that construct legitimacy requires an evolutionary model of organizations and an examination of ways in which cognitive frameworks mediate the complex interactions between the organization and its environment.

Evolutionary Processes

The evolutionary processes of variation, selection, retention, and diffusion within an ongoing struggle for resources (Aldrich, 1999) contribute to the alternation of equilibrium and revolutionary periods. This process is similar to the three-stage theory of change, but connects the organization directly to its environment because historically determined opportunities and constraints influence the type of change, for example, by creating particular variations.

Variation is intentional "when people actively attempt to generate alternatives and seek solutions to problems" (Aldrich, 1999, p. 22) and blind when it "occurs independently of environmental or selection pressures" (Aldrich, 1999, p. 22). A key feature of planned change is intentional variation, yet it occurs within a specific context.

Selection involves the "differential elimination of certain types of variations" (Aldrich, 1999, p. 22). One type of selection is external, in which forces outside an organization affect its routines and competencies. The second type occurs when internal forces alter the behavior and structure of the organization (Aldrich, 1999, p. 22). Following selection, retention and diffusion occur when "selected variations are preserved, duplicated, or otherwise reproduced" (Aldrich, 1999, p. 22).

These processes take place within a struggle for scarce resources that are valued and sought after by similar types of organizations. A feature of planned change is that the environment assigns values to limited resources by indicating the preferred features of organizations, over which a struggle ensues.

Externally initiated and mandated change appears to make the evolutionary processes irrelevant because it forces change. However, the same evolutionary processes shaped the mandated changes. In addition, unless the use of force ensures fidelity to the planned change, evolutionary processes contribute to its management and implementation through selection, retention, and diffusion.

Legitimacy and Cognitive Frameworks

Legitimacy issues affect every stage of the evolutionary process of planned change. Even under forced compliance, rather than accepting the purposes, plans, and strategies endorsed by the environment—the creation of variation—the organization, through a dominant cognitive framework, interprets and shapes the processes of selection, retention, and diffusion.

The cognitive framework, a central element of the deep structure that contributes to equilibrium or change, shapes the organization's core beliefs. During the course of planned organization change, a variety of individuals and groups make numerous decisions at different levels in the system. Cognitive frameworks are basically decision-making and sense-making mechanisms, and, as with all decisions, psychological, social, and institutional constraints affect the rationality of policy formulation and implementation (Boudon, 2003; Ingram & Clay, 2000; Shafir & LeBoeuf, 2002).

In *Abbott V* and NCLB, the number of organizations and individuals involved was extensive. Decision makers ranged from the President of the United States to classroom teachers and ordinary citizens. Multiple cognitive frameworks influenced this array of actors and the interactions of schools with their environments. Of course, the type of legitimacy represented and the ability to exert and enforce authority varied among the actors and organizations.

The Eco-Cognitive Framework

Although multiple cognitive frameworks exist and compete in a diverse group, as predicted by the punctuated legitimacy theory, legitimacy emerged immediately as a key variable. On the first day of fieldwork, a Latina principal talked voluntarily about her experiences with race and class in Elizabeth and their potential effects on *Abbott V.* In fact, she questioned the legitimacy of *Abbott V* as appropriate for the needs of the Latino children in her school and the African American students in nearby schools. In addition, she articulated the view that poor inner city Latino and African American students require a different pedagogy than is practiced in the suburbs. These views reoriented the research from a narrow focus on technical aspects of educational change to exploring ways in which the social context of urban schools would affect *Abbott V.*

The cognitive framework of the principal and of most other urban educators created legitimacy based on the distribution of social class and race in New Jersey, which correlated highly with the concentration of poor minorities in cities and wealthy Whites in suburbs. This geographic distribution provided empirical data for administrators and teachers that reinforced assumptions that inevitable social forces, combined with voluntary choices, produced what became the taken-for-granted residential segregation by race and class. The forces of history or government social and economic policies accompanied by the expansion of the global economy (Anyon, 1997; Massey & Denton, 1993; Sassen, 1991) were not regarded as determinative of the situation in New Jersey.

The ecological-cognitive decision-making framework (the eco-cognitive framework) was the central evolutionary mechanism that influenced the implementation of *Abbott V* and NCLB. It affected whether administrators and teachers implemented the court-ordered Whole School Reform model and to what extent. It also influenced fundamental issues such as the selection of textbooks and the use of phonics drill or constructivist pedagogy for reading instruction. It also shaped the response to NCLB, including how to prepare students for tests and how much time to devote for test preparation. In other words, by interpreting the local social structure in a particular way, the eco-cognitive framework connected the legitimacy of the externally initiated coercive changes to the local environment. Macro education policies underwent organizational mediation that affected the deep structure of the schools and classrooms.

Finally, the eco-cognitive framework, in addition to being a product of the evolutionary processes that produced a particular geographic social distribution, incorporated the moral dimension of legitimacy. It mediated, and in a variety of ways altered, the reform process through professional judgments based on whether the selection and retention of variations created by *Abbott V* and NCLB were appropriate for inner city students.

Legitimacy, The Eco-Cognitive Framework, and the Deep Structure of Classrooms

To understand changes in learning it is essential to examine changes in the deep structure of classrooms. Variables that effect learning, the ultimate objective of both reforms, are

1. The ways in which students are grouped for instruction,
2. The materials and activities through which the curriculum is taught,
3. The evaluation system that teachers use to assess student learning,
4. The motivational system that teachers use to engage student learning,
5. The responsibility that students have in directing and evaluating their learning,
6. The climate of relationships within the class, with parents, and with the school. (Weinstein, 2002, p. 103)

These variables, in addition to structuring the conditions of learning, affect the development of social skills transmitted through socialization into classroom processes and organization. For example, as a result of classroom social arrangements students learn about authority, acquire different levels of motivation to learn, and develop personal and group identity.

This view of learning includes more than standardized test scores, which are one approach to measuring learning. Among other shortcomings, tests have problems ranging from psychometric defects to culture bias and misalignment with curricula (Popham, 2004), and they do not capture the richness of what children learn in schools.

The decisions of policy makers, administrators, teachers, and others involved in school reform have the potential to affect the deep structure of classrooms, which in turn affects cognitive achievement and informal learning in ways that "may expand or constrain learning and performance opportunities for all children" (Weinstein, 2002, p. 103).

Abbott V and NCLB in Theoretical Perspective

After an extended period of decline in the quality of urban education, *Abbott V* and NCLB initiated external change that replaced the leadership and programs of urban schools with court mandates and federal legislation. Both tried to change the key components of the deep structure of urban education in a short time.

Abbott V and NCLB complemented each other. *Abbott V* focused on organizational inputs (particularly per pupil funding), throughputs (in the form of a Whole School Reform model, class size reduction, and new management processes), and outputs (measured by tests). NCLB focused on the outputs

by specifying criteria for success or failure and accountability, providing corrective actions which, if necessary, could restructure all elements of an educational system.

However, *Abbott V* and NCLB did not directly change the *environment* of urban education, leaving the community structure, culture, and economy unchanged. This is important because research has identified the effects of the socioeconomic status of families and neighborhoods as the most important predictor of academic achievement (Coleman et al., 1966; Rothstein, 2004; Sirin, 2005).

From the perspective of evolutionary theory, *Abbott V* and NCLB selected specific organizational solutions for the problems of urban education defined as "closing the achievement gap" between the affluent White majority and the low-income minority population. From an array of possible solutions—for example, student health, economic conditions, and the effect on learning of the population diversity of a school—the judicial and legislative judgment was that these factors were either unimportant, not able to change, or politically and socially unpalatable.

Both reforms were the product of specific cognitive frameworks, and they created new cognitive frameworks or reinforced old ones that limited the reforms to the organizational properties of schools. As products of the legal, legislative, and sociopolitical environment of New Jersey and the United States, *Abbott V* and NCLB reflected a series of choices American society has made over the past 50 years concerning education reform.

Within these constraints, both reforms broke with past education reforms because of the comprehensive solutions they proposed. Even though the reforms fashioned their remedies from existing solutions, separately and particularly together, they created a revolutionary period in the history of educational change.

Putting the experiences of four schools into theoretical perspective, and previewing the argument of the book, *Abbott V* dismantled the deep structure of the schools and tried to change it, but met with resistance based on the eco-cognitive framework. Instead of promoting enduring change, the dismantled deep structure set the stage for NCLB, primarily the focus on standardized tests. Instead of restructuring the organization of urban schools and classroom instruction to create a more enriched urban education—as *Abbott V* intended—the reforms narrowed the options for behavior in schools and classrooms and resulted in a revolution in the meaning and practice of urban education.

THE NEXT FOUR CHAPTERS look inside two school districts, four schools, and a variety of types of classrooms to see what changed because of *Abbott V* and NCLB.

PART II

Implementing the Revolution

CHAPTER 4

The Bridge Street School

Unanticipated Incremental Change

The Social Context of Education: Newark

The cultural, economic, social, and physical characteristics of the neighborhood, city, and region of each school created a context that influenced administrators' and teachers' responses to the *Abbott V* elementary school mandates and NCLB reforms (Arum, 2000; Coleman et al., 1966; Rothstein, 2004). To establish the context, this chapter begins with a brief history of Newark, as well as portraits of the school district, the neighborhood, and the school. Next, an ethnographic account of the changes over 7 years in the Bridge Street School focuses on the responses to the reforms from first- and fourth-grade teachers, the entire faculty, and administrators. The chapter concludes with an analysis of the changes in the school.

One of the oldest settlements in the United States, Newark in the late 19th century and into the 20th century was a thriving industrial center. Beginning in the 1930s, however, banks refused loans to many Newark neighborhoods, and government policies spurred the development of highways that facilitated suburban growth. These and other economic activities beyond local control, particularly intensification of the global economy, had negative consequences for Newark's long-term development (Sassen, 1991).

In the 1940s and 1950s, Italians and other ethnic groups who had lived in urban villages throughout the city gradually moved to nearby suburbs (Gans, 1962). The Jewish population, with aspirations for upward mobility enabled by increasing wealth, moved out more rapidly than the other groups (Helmreich, 1999).

In the 1950s and 1960s, migration of African Americans from the south to Newark accelerated. The African American population did not create the social and economic problems in Newark but, rather, arrived well after the beginning of Newark's economic deterioration (Anyon, 1997). Even jobs that unskilled urban workers could perform were no longer available because the local labor market had disappeared (Wilson, 1996). This left members of poor minority groups, many of whom could not afford cars, in the inner city, increasing racial and economic segregation (Rae, 2001). To find work, many Newark residents had to travel by bus to the suburbs for minimum wage jobs in retail stores and fast-food outlets.

Over the course of the 20th century, the impact of the automobile on the spatial organization of Newark in relationship to its metropolitan region was profound. The automobile facilitated the exodus of the White population, and the resulting shift of white-collar work to suburban office parks and creation of high-tech industries outside the city only exacerbated Newark's deindustrialization. This process accelerated in the 1970s, when the western counties of the state became accessible by highways that enabled Whites to live and work even further from the city.

Civil Disorder

A dramatic outcome of the segregation and abject poverty created by this migratory pattern was a race riot in 1967 that, in addition to destroying several neighborhoods, became an enduring economic, social, and psychological turning point for Newark. Current and former residents vividly remember the riot and, after almost four decades, it still often serves as a benchmark for measuring Newark's progress.

Community and Stability

Despite the impoverished conditions of much of Newark, several neighborhoods thrived because close-knit ethnic groups gave them cohesion and a distinctive character. For example, a Portuguese community, which was separated by railroad tracks from the rest of the city, had a positive reputation throughout the region because of its hard-working residents and its distinctive restaurants—and it had several of Newark's highest scoring schools on standardized tests. In addition, several working- and middle-class African American and Italian neighborhoods retained a sense of community and, in some cases, maintained clear boundaries separating them from other ethnic and racial groups.

There were other sources of stability, and periodically coordinated attempts were made to revitalize Newark. Institutions of higher education clustered near the central business district, and the headquarters of Prudential Insurance dominated the main business street. Recent development has included the New Jersey Performing Arts Center, a minor league baseball park, and the replacement of several low-income high-rise housing projects with affordable townhouses.

Newark Today

Despite the improvements, in the early 21st century Newark still has one of the highest poverty rates in the United States. It has struggled with a high infant morality rate, one of the highest incidences of AIDS in the country, a significant homeless population, organized youth gangs that are becoming increasingly violent, high unemployment, and inadequate housing.

In fact, for at least four decades, many Newark neighborhoods have been extremely distressed. Most have few retail stores, rubble-strewn vacant lots, and neglected and abandoned houses. In addition to the visual reminders of Newark's plight, the *Star-Ledger*—the regional newspaper of northern New Jersey—regularly reports a stream of violent crimes. For many people, the urban ills of Newark continue to define it far more strongly than its prospects for revitalization.

Indeed, many suburban residents view Newark as a place to avoid and a financial burden for county taxpayers. One reason is that political corruption has periodically erupted in Newark and undermined suburbanites' confidence in the management of the city. Another reason is the perception that the high welfare rate, the overburdened criminal justice system, and persistent social problems contribute to disproportionately high suburban property taxes. To indicate their displeasure with Newark, in 2004 and 2005 several wealthy suburban towns threatened to secede from the county.

Newark's Population

In the 1990 census—the source of the data the New Jersey Supreme Court used to designate Abbott districts—Newark's population was 275,221. There were 161,000 African Americans, who composed 58.5% of the population. The 69,000 Latinos made up 25% of the population, and 78,600 Whites formed 28% of the population.[1] In 1990, the median family income was $25,800.

In 2000, the population of Newark had decreased to 273,500, distributed as follows: African Americans, 146,250 (53.5%); Latinos, 80,600 (29.5%); and Whites, 72,500 (26.6%). The median family income was $30,700. In 2000, almost 16,000 families in Newark—74,000 individuals—were below the poverty level. The unemployment rate in the city was 9.2%, compared with 7.7% for all Abbott districts and 4.2% for the state as a whole.

An important population characteristic that changed between 1990 and 2000 in Newark was that children were more likely to live in a segregated neighborhood. Newark was one of the most racially segregated cities in the country and one of the most segregated for African American and Latino children (Logan et al., 2001). Despite an increase in the ethnic population of the

United States, "The average White person continues to live in a neighborhood that looks very different from those neighborhoods where the average Black, Hispanic, and Asian lives. This conclusion holds even more strongly among children" (Logan et al., 2001, p. 1).

In 2000, Essex County, the county where Newark is located, had a population that was 44.5% White, 41.2% African American, 15.4% Latino, and 3.7% Asian. New Jersey's population was 72.6% White, 13.6% African American, 13.3% Latino, and 5.7% Asian. The median family income for the county was $45,000 in 2000, and the median income in New Jersey was $55,000, the highest in the United States.

The Newark School District

In 2000, the Newark school district had a total enrollment of 42,000 students. White students totaled 3,600, African Americans 25,200, and Latinos 13,000. Eighty-one percent of the students were eligible for free or reduced-price lunch, compared with 73% for all Abbott districts and 28% for the state. The high school graduation rate was 50%; the rate was 67% for the state, and most suburbs in the county had 100% graduation rates, with almost all students bound for college.

The district had 4,200 full-time teachers in 2001–2002, with an average experience of 16 years, compared with 14 years experience for all Abbott districts and the state. The average teacher salary in Newark was $60,500, compared with $52,500 for Abbott districts and $53,700 for the state. The 2005 starting teacher salary in Newark was $44,500, one of the highest in the county. The Newark school district had 79 school buildings, with an average age of 85 years, compared with 61 years for buildings in Abbott districts.

Per pupil funding for Abbott districts was the lowest in the state in 1989–1990. By 1997–1998, however, Abbott districts on average had parity with, and several exceeded, the highest spending school districts in the state. For example, in 2001–2002 the average for all Abbott districts was $11,741, and the wealthiest districts spent an average of $9,344. While all Abbott districts on average had per pupil funding higher than the wealthiest districts, differences among Abbott districts were significant: Asbury Park spent the most at $15,315 and Perth Amboy the least at $9,897 per pupil.

Figure 4.1 illustrates the changes in Abbott district budgets compared with other poor non-Abbott districts, middle-income districts, and the I and J districts, which are the wealthiest.[2]

As presented in Table 4.1, during the 7 years of *Abbott V* documented in this book, the average annual per pupil expenditure for Newark was $12,792, compared with $9,495 for the state. That is, Newark spent 34.7% more than the state average.

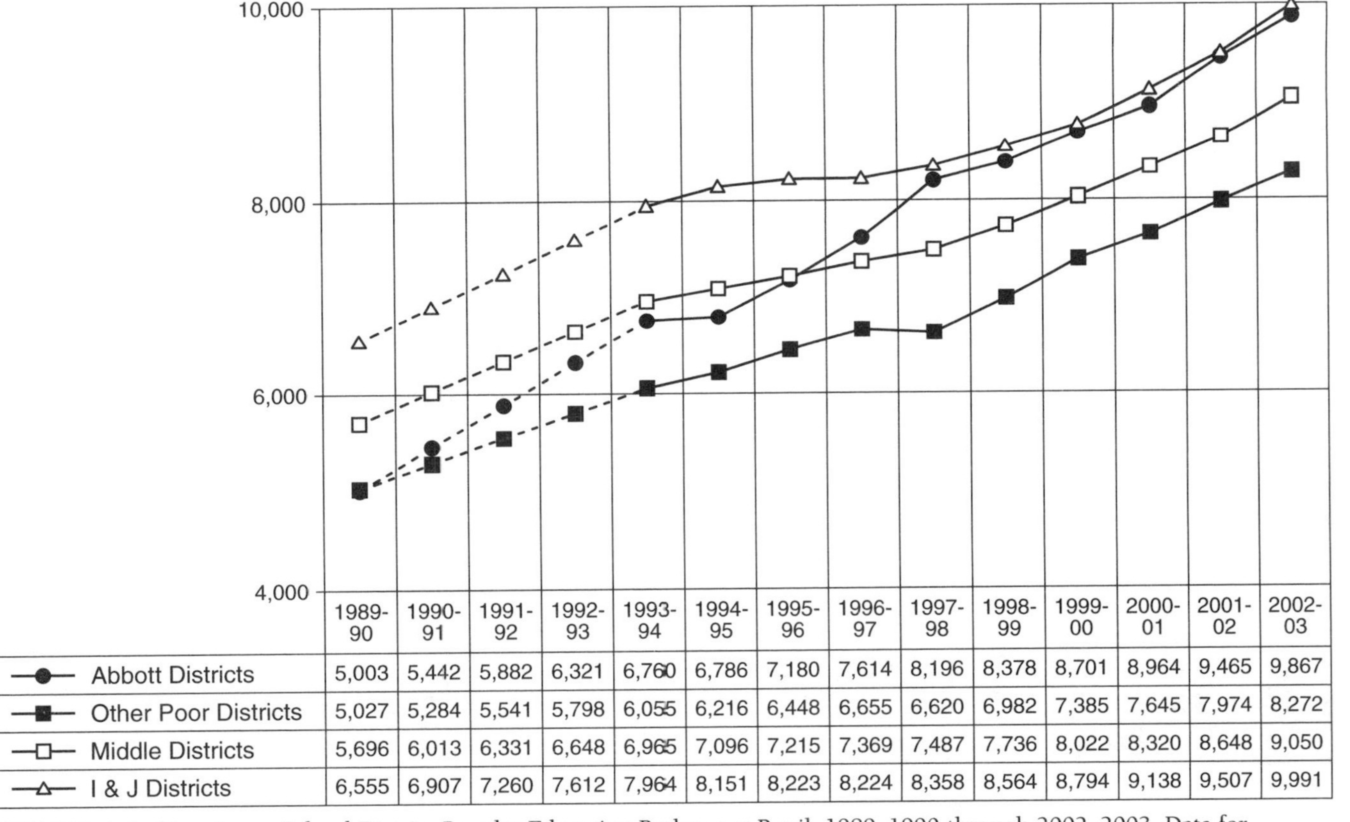

	1989-90	1990-91	1991-92	1992-93	1993-94	1994-95	1995-96	1996-97	1997-98	1998-99	1999-00	2000-01	2001-02	2002-03
Abbott Districts	5,003	5,442	5,882	6,321	6,760	6,786	7,180	7,614	8,196	8,378	8,701	8,964	9,465	9,867
Other Poor Districts	5,027	5,284	5,541	5,798	6,055	6,216	6,448	6,655	6,620	6,982	7,385	7,645	7,974	8,272
Middle Districts	5,696	6,013	6,331	6,648	6,965	7,096	7,215	7,369	7,487	7,736	8,022	8,320	8,648	9,050
I & J Districts	6,555	6,907	7,260	7,612	7,964	8,151	8,223	8,224	8,358	8,564	8,794	9,138	9,507	9,991

FIGURE 4.1. New Jersey School District Regular Education Budget per Pupil, 1989–1990 through 2002–2003. Data for 1990–1991 through 1992–1993 are interpolated. *Source:* Adapted from Ernest C. Reock, Jr. (2004).

TABLE 4.1. Newark Per Pupil Expenditures Compared With State Average Expenditures, 1997–1998 Through 2004–2005

	Newark	State Average
1997–1998	$ 9,939	$ 7,958
1998–1999	10,027	8,194
1999–2000	10,328	8,692
2000–2001	13,841	9,236
2001–2002	13,546	9,688
2002–2003	13,546	10,273
2003–2004	15,312	10,709
2004–2005	15,796	11,215
Average	$12,792	$ 9,495

Source: New Jersey Department of Education.

The State Takeover of Newark's Schools

For several decades, parents, employers, and politicians recognized that the education systems of several major cities in New Jersey had failed. Using a 1987 statute, the New Jersey Department of Education took control of Jersey City's schools in 1989, and it took control of the Paterson school district in 1991.

In 1995, three years before the *Abbott V* ruling, the state took over the Newark school district. The takeover increased the managerial apparatus of the district by adding a regulatory and administrative level, in an attempt to rationalize the management of what had become a patronage-riddled, bureaucratically inept system (Wong & Shen, 2001). To signify change, the first state-appointed superintendent came from outside New Jersey.

Despite the changes in management, after more than a decade of state control, a study of the three districts found that little, if any, improvement had occurred. In fact, the report concluded that the state should return the districts to local control as soon as possible, because "rather than enhancing local capacity, state takeover seems to diminish it" (Tractenberg et al., 2002, p. 8). The state commissioner of education agreed with this conclusion and, after several years of discussion coupled with intentional delay, in October 2005 the state devised an exit strategy. According to the current Newark superintendent, "The state takeover got lost after Abbott. Most of my tenure has been trying to enact regulations related to Abbott, and now, of course, No Child Left Behind has rolled into that" (quoted in Addison & Mooney, 2005, p. 13).

The Bridge Street School Community

The Bridge Street Elementary School is in the neighborhood where the 1967 riot occurred. A recently built movie theatre (which closes periodically because of a lack of patrons), a supermarket operated by a regional chain, and a home improvement store—all the first in Newark since the riot—along with privately financed low-income housing, started a minor and sporadic revitalization of the neighborhood.

In 2003, indicating changes in the community, several teachers were surprised that, for the first time in memory, a few students were required to pay for lunch. But, a few blocks from the school there were still abandoned houses, vacant lots, and padlocked retail stores. According to the 2000 census, several census tracts[3] near the school had average family incomes of $11,200–19,200, a few had incomes of $20,038–26,520, and several had incomes of $27,165–35,929. Regardless of the precise income levels, from a middle-class perspective, the neighborhood was unmistakably an inner city ghetto.

In 2004, a neighborhood that overlaps the Bridge Street School catchment area had 114 shootings with 22 fatalities. This prompted the intervention of criminologists at Rutgers University, who designed and implemented "Operation CeaseFire," an antiviolence plan. The violence in Newark has increasingly originated from drug-related gang wars among the Latin Kings, Bloods, and Crips (Schuppe, 2005).

The Bridge Street Elementary School

The Bridge Street School, built in 1968, had 600 students in preschool to sixth grade and was housed in a large building with an unattractive brick exterior.[4] However, the interior was well maintained, with large classrooms and clean hallways that displayed students' work in thoughtful arrangements.

In 2000, at the beginning of the Abbott elementary reforms, the Bridge Street principal was an African American woman who had formerly been a teacher of the handicapped in Newark. On the school Web site she stated her educational philosophy: "It is my belief that all children can achieve if given the appropriate tools. The most essential tool is expectation." The two vice principals were a White Italian female and a White Jewish male.

The faculty of 60 teachers was almost half African American, with the other half split between Italians and Jews. Most of the faculty was female. All of the teachers had earned a Bachelor's degree, and 25% had Master's degrees. The faculty turnover rate for 2003–2004 was 7.9%, compared with 6.3% for the state.

In 2004–2005, 84% of the students were African American and 16% were Latino. Ninety percent of the students spoke English as their first language, and the remaining 10% lived in households where Spanish was the primary language. Eighty-three percent received free or reduced-price lunch, and the student mobility rate was 35%.

Bridge Street's students were usually well behaved in classrooms and when passing through the halls. In part, this was attributable to most teachers' continuous emphasis on appropriate behavior and their willingness to scold students—on occasion, harshly. However, even with the threat and application of strict discipline, a few teachers had difficulty controlling their classes.

Although the school was in a neighborhood that had experienced systematic destruction during the riots followed by almost 40 years of neglect and persistent poverty, Bridge Street did not fit the stereotypical image of a ghetto school that is falling apart physically, socially, and academically.

Bridge Street Before *Abbott V*

Prior to the *Abbott V* funding and elementary curriculum reforms, the Bridge Street School had undergone a series of minor adjustments in its educational program until the 1995 state takeover of the Newark school district. An important period was 1987 through 1993, with the appointment of a dynamic principal who, it was hoped, would correct a variety of instructional, student, and faculty problems at Bridge Street. With adroit political skills, he recruited high-quality teachers and acquired extra resources for instruction. His efforts improved the school significantly.

The dynamic principal retired, then his successor left after only 1 year, and student discipline and teacher morale suffered. The current principal was appointed at the beginning of state control, and the next year she restored and maintained productive working conditions, and standardized test scores improved. However, there were no significant innovations and, in the view of many teachers, under state control the district and school deteriorated because conflicting goals prevented needed changes.

Bridge Street and *Abbott V*, Year 1—2000–2001

Learning About *Abbott V*

Many teachers were either unaware of or had little knowledge of the *Abbott v. Burke* litigation. They were familiar with the controversy over the "thorough and efficient" clause in the New Jersey Constitution but had not followed the lengthy and complex series of court decisions. One teacher said, "*Who* and *what* is this '*Abbott*'?" When they did find out about *Abbott V*, it surprised most teachers to discover the responsibility the court placed on them to implement it.[5] A vice principal summarized the feelings of the faculty: "The state forced Whole School Reform down our throats."

Some teachers thought that *Abbott V* was another in a series of reforms that would quickly fail. Others concluded that because it was a court order, enforcement would be strict. The prospect of coerced change toward the end of their career prompted several teachers to consider early retirement.

Selecting a Whole School Reform Model

Initially, the only court-approved research-based Whole School Reform (WSR) model was Success for All/Roots and Wings, developed by Robert Slavin of Johns Hopkins University. After objections to only one model, the court added Community for Learning/Adaptive Learning Environments Model, the Accelerated Schools Project, the Comer School Development Program, the Modern Red School House, and Co-Nect Schools.

In March 2000, a small group of Bridge Street administrators and teachers visited several schools in other districts that had started to implement a WSR model. One of the schools they visited, and that impressed them favorably, was the Church Street School in Elizabeth (described in Chapter 6), which had implemented the Community for Learning/Adaptive Learning Environments Model (CFL/ALEM) in November 1998.

As required by the New Jersey Supreme Court *Abbott V* mandates, the Bridge Street faculty voted in October 1999 for a WSR model, despite uncertainty and confusion. They selected CFL/ALEM, though for many the decision was less than enthusiastic. Most teachers felt pressured to vote for CFL/ALEM because the principal preferred it. Also favoring the selection of CFL/ALEM was the fact that the majority of teachers reacted negatively to Success for All. Based on the experiences of colleagues in other schools, many at Bridge Street believed that Success for All would severely limit the professional judgment of teachers because it used scripted lessons.[6] Finally, most teachers felt rushed and complained that the only information they had on which to base a decision was descriptions of the WSR models provided by New Jersey Department of Education (Datnow, 1999; Erlichson, Goertz, & Turnbull, 1999; Shafir & LeBoeuf, 2002).[7] Figures 4.2, 4.3, and 4.4 show the state Department of Education's descriptions of Success for All, CFL/ALEM, and The Comer School Development Program, respectively.

The Community for Learning/Adaptive Learning Environments Model (CFL/ALEM)

CFL/ALEM is a school reform and instruction program developed at Temple University's Center for Research in Human Development and Education (CRHDE). It is not a curriculum or teaching style but rather a management technique for organizing and improving the classroom learning environment. Built on a foundation of learning centers that students rotate among for 20-minute instructional periods, CFL/ALEM requires individualization of instruction, peer and cooperative learning instead of whole class instruction, and student self-selection and self-scheduling of time at the learning centers throughout the week. The following description comes from the Community for Learning Web site (http://www.temple.edu/LSS/cfl.htm):

A Typical CFL Classroom

A visitor to a well-run elementary Community for Learning classroom will witness a beehive of activity. Teachers and students are all busy, with many

New Jersey State Department of Education

Description of Success for All/Roots & Wings (SFA)

Success for All is clearly the whole school reform program that shows the most promise of enabling students in the Abbott districts to achieve the Core Curriculum Content Standards (CCCS). This elementary school program is based on years of research of effective practices in beginning reading and cooperative learning. SFA is an approach to school improvement that involves changes to every aspect of elementary school organization, instruction, and curriculum. The program focuses on preventing school failure by relentless concentration on having every child read successfully by the end of third grade. During the 1999–2000 school year, over 800,000 students will be enrolled in SFA classes in 1,700 schools in 46 states, Canada, and Great Britain. Essential program elements include an uninterrupted 90-minute reading block, one-to-one tutoring for students who are struggling (concentrating on first graders), innovative approaches in preschool and kindergarten, emphasis on writing, assessment of student progress every eight weeks, and developing a strong family support network.

Combined with the developers' other instructional components (Roots & Wings), the model becomes a true whole school reform program. Roots & Wings includes two additional components—MathWings and WorldLab. MathWings is a constructivist mathematics program for grades 1–5 focused on higher order skills and metacognition. WorldLab is a social studies and science curriculum that emphasizes simulations and group investigations, also for grades 1–5. In sum, Success for All/Roots & Wings is a research-based WSR model which, when fully implemented, will meet the guidelines for reform adopted by the New Jersey Department of Education.

http://successforall.com

FIGURE 4.2. Description of the Success for All/Roots & Wings (SFA) program provided by the New Jersey State Department of Education.

different activities occurring simultaneously. A teacher is conducting a reading lesson with a group of six students at a large, round table. Seven other students are working on reading or mathematics assignments, and the materials in front of each child are of different types and from different levels of the curricula.

While two students are engaged in an experiment about light and optics at a science center, another is putting together a puzzle map of North America at a social studies center. Another student is at a desk tape recording a poem she has written, and yet another is curled up in the library corner

New Jersey State Department of Education

Community for Learning/ Adaptive Learning Environments Model (CFL/ALEM)

Community for Learning is a data-based, comprehensive K–12 program that focuses on high academic achievement and positive student self-perception. The program includes a site-specific implementation-planning framework that incorporates a schoolwide organizational structure, and a coordinated system of instruction and related services delivery. The focus is on breaking down artificial barriers within the school and across the multiple service providing agencies to ensure the healthy development and educational success of every student.

Implementation of the CFL program impacts three major areas of student outcomes:

- Improved academic achievement of all students, including and particularly those at the margins.
- Patterns of active learning and teaching processes that are consistent with the research base on effective practices.
- Positive attitudes by students and staff toward their school, and, most importantly, the expectation that every student has the capacity for educational success.

Findings from implementation studies in a variety of school settings to date show a positive pattern of change in a variety of student outcomes including reading and math, and attitudes about learning and their classroom and school environments when compared with students in non-program schools. Research findings also indicate that CFL families and communities become increasingly active in a wide range of school activities and in the decision making process.

http://www.temple.edu/LSS/csr.htm

FIGURE 4.3. Description of the Community for Learning/Adaptive Learning Environments Model (CFL/ALEM) provided by the New Jersey State Department of Education.

New Jersey State Department of Education

The Comer School Development Program (SDP)

The Comer School Development Program is a nationally recognized program, established in 1968 in two of the lowest achieving schools in New Haven by Dr. James Comer, a psychiatrist at Yale University's Child Study Center. This program focuses on bridging the gap between the home and the school by identifying and addressing the underlying problems of students and their families and involving all school staff, community agencies and parents in designing appropriate solutions to identified problems. The SDP is not a program, but a process for involving all stakeholders in the development of school plans that focus on improving: school climate, instruction, collaboration with local social and health providers, and parental involvement in the schools.

The SDP includes a governance and management team, student and staff support team and a parents program. The School Planning and Management Team (SPMT) is composed of teachers, representatives from the student and staff support team, parents, support personnel and the school principal. This team is responsible for guiding the school's improvement efforts which include the development of the school plan, periodic assessment of programs and student performance, staff development, and curriculum development and implementation. The Student and Staff Support Team, is composed of a guidance counselor, nurse, social worker, psychologist, speech therapist and special education staff. Their responsibilities include the development of strategies to help teachers solve students' behavioral and instructional problems, as well as establishing linkages with social and health agencies to provide students and their families with services. Finally, the parents' program or Parental Involvement Team plays an active role in schools by serving on various committees, including the SPMT, and by volunteering to work in schools.

Decisions by all team members are made by consensus, and include collaboration with all stakeholders and using a no-fault problem solving approach. The SDP requires approval and support of the superintendent and the board as well as hiring staff. The staff consists of a program facilitator, along with instructional and mental health staff.

As a result of the implementation of the SDP program in New Haven, Connecticut, students who had once ranked lowest in achievement among 33 elementary schools, by fourth grade had caught up to grade level. Furthermore, the researcher states that money and efforts expended for educational reform will have limited benefits to poor minority children unless the underlying developmental and social issues are addressed. Another source, Squires and Kranyik, report that the Comer program succeeds because it supports a change in the school culture and it focuses on child development.

http://info.met.yale.edu/comer/welcome.html

FIGURE 4.4. Description of the Comer School Development Program provided by the New Jersey State Department of Education.

reading a book. In a distant part of the room, four students are rehearsing a play, which they will present the next day.

A classroom assistant is circulating about the room. In a five-minute span, she checks one student's completed assignment, assists another who signaled for help, and interacts briefly with three others as she passes their way. Teachers continuously move about in all areas of the classroom, either responding to student requests or giving on-the-spot instruction, changing a prescription, or offering feedback and reinforcement to students. Each contact with a student is brief; when extended assistance is required, sessions are scheduled for a later time. Teachers scan the room to see where they are needed next. Each student has a work folder, containing completed work and an individualized prescription sheet to guide his or her activities.

It might seem like chaos, but it's not. Regular classroom teachers, special education and Title I teachers, paraprofessionals, and volunteer assistants work together in the same room toward a common goal—helping students learn. The rules and procedures are clear from the outset, so the room is active but rarely confused. A special education teacher can enter the room and meet with a student in one corner without interrupting the flow of activity or attracting any particular attention. Students and teachers all talk in low voices, creating a pervasive hum, but no one raises his or her voice. Although students occasionally walk from one place to another as they change tasks or get or return materials, the movement is purposeful, not distracting or disruptive.

An Hour in a Typical CFL Classroom:

9:45 a.m.

Student enters room, picks up her work folder and consults her prescription sheet. She sees that she is to work on math, and she moves to join a group of four students gathered at a small cluster of desks on the perimeter of the room. The teacher presents a new math lesson to these students and guides each one through a workbook practice exercise. She checks each student's work and gives them individual feedback. She marks the completed task on each prescription sheet, altering some to recommend work on areas of difficulty.

10:15 a.m.

One student needs additional instruction. She moves to a smaller group on the opposite side of the room to receive tutoring. Another pupil moves on to the next activity—independent work in the workbook listed on his prescription sheet. He struggles with some vocabulary words, so he flips over his "teacher call"—the purple side of a two-toned wood block—to signal he needs help. While he is waiting for assistance, he opens his wait-time folder and completes a worksheet using words that also appear in the story he is working on. The teacher arrives, helps him with his vocabulary, and makes sure he is ready to proceed on his own. If he needs more help, she might ask another student to offer peer tutoring, assign remedial activities such as additional worksheets, or schedule small-group or individual tutoring for a later time. Another student moves from this group to an individual meeting with a special education teacher who has just entered the room.

10:45 a.m.
A student who needs no additional help moves to the reading exploratory learning center for enrichment activities that reinforce what she has just learned. She can choose from activities listed on her prescription sheet, or the teacher will assign her a task, such as making a crossword puzzle with the vocabulary words from the last reading story or working on the computer identifying the main ideas in a story. The student might also be asked to be a peer tutor for another student.

Parts taken from *Adaptive Education Strategies: Building on Diversity* by Margaret C. Wang. Paul H. Brookes Publishing Co., Baltimore, 1992.

The features of CFL/ALEM intend to overcome the stereotypical image of urban children as not able to learn. The program also provides students with a means of becoming psychologically "resilient," that is, able to cope with the adversities of life effectively. Increased student independence is a key objective and a component of resiliency. To achieve these objectives, CFL/ALEM attempts to change practices associated with urban classrooms, including strict discipline that promotes passive compliance, the use of rote teaching methods that do not promote critical thinking, and dependence on the teacher as the center of knowledge instead of encouraging students to learn how to learn.

Implementation of CFL/ALEM required training by experts from Temple University's Center for Research in Human Development and Education. Temple trainers and facilitators provided initial training sessions for school faculty and administrators, one-on-one in-classroom guidance and evaluation, and periodic districtwide professional development days.

The New Jersey Core Content Curriculum Standards

Another component of the *Abbott V* elementary school mandates was the use in Abbott districts, as in all other districts in New Jersey, of the New Jersey Core Content Curriculum Standards (CCCS). This was a key component of the effort to fulfill the state constitutional "guarantee that regardless of residency, its children will receive a 'Thorough and Efficient' education" (New Jersey Department of Education, 1998, p. i). Formulated by a committee of citizens and educators and adopted in 1998 during Governor Christine Todd Whitman's administration, the CCCS defined "the results expected but do not limit district strategies for how to ensure that their students achieve these expectations" (New Jersey Department of Education, 1998, p. i).

The 1998 CCCS standards for Language Arts were

> **Standard 3.1** All students will speak for a variety of real purposes and audiences in a variety of contexts.
>
> **Standard 3.2** All students will actively listen in a variety of situations in order to receive, interpret, evaluate, and respond to information obtained from a variety of sources.
>
> **Standard 3.3** All students will compose texts that are diverse in content and form for different audiences and for real and varied purposes.
>
> **Standard 3.4** All students will read, listen to, view, and respond to a diversity of materials and texts with comprehension and critical analysis.
>
> **Standard 3.5** All students will view, understand, and use nontextual visual information and representations for critical comparison, analysis, and evaluation. (New Jersey Department of Education, 1998, p. 3-3)

Following each standard is a list of cumulative progress indicators that all students should be able to demonstrate by the end of fourth grade.

In 2002, during the administration of Governor James McGreevey, a revision of the CCCS aligned them with the standardized tests and other requirements of NCLB. The goal of the 2002 Language Arts Literacy CCCS was that "Students will read well and independently by the end of the third grade." The Language Arts standards were

> **Standard 3.1 (Reading)** All students will understand and apply the knowledge of sounds, letters, and words in written English to become independent and fluent readers, and will read a variety of materials and texts with fluency and comprehension. (New Jersey Department of Education, 2002, p. 8)
>
> **Standard 3.2 (Writing)** All students will write in clear, concise, organized language that varies in content and form for different audiences and purposes. (p. 20)
>
> **Standard 3.3 (Speaking)** All students will speak in clear, concise, organized language that varies in content and form for different audiences and purposes. (p. 32)
>
> **Standard 3.4 (Listening)** All students will listen actively to information from a variety of sources in a variety of situations. (p. 38)
>
> **Standard 3.5 (Viewing and Media Literacy)** All students will access, view, evaluate, and respond to print, nonprint, and electronic texts and resources. (p. 42)

A more detailed set of objectives for each grade level followed each standard than was provided in the 1998 CCCS.

The Elementary School Proficiency Assessment

In 1997, New Jersey instituted standardized tests for all students in the 4th, 8th, and 11th grades, and these tests formed another component of *Abbott V.* The fourth-grade test—originally the Elementary School Proficiency Assessment (ESPA), then revised in 2003 to become the New Jersey Assessment of Skills and Knowledge (NJASK)—was intended to measure knowledge of the CCCS. Another objective of the standardized test was to assess critical thinking processes with questions that emphasized problem solving, open-ended questions, and writing samples. Samples of the NJASK are available at http://www.nj.gov/njded/assessment/es/sample/njask.htm.

Bridge Street's Introduction to CFL/ALEM

Newark Board of Education delays in paying Temple University and difficulty in scheduling training sessions resulted in postponement of implementation of CFL/ALEM at Bridge Street School until January 2001. Although they were apprehensive about Whole School Reform, many teachers and administrators nonetheless expressed frustration over the bureaucratic fumbling.

To introduce CFL/ALEM, on March 22, 2000, the WSR facilitator from the Church Street School in Elizabeth presented a workshop to the entire Bridge Street faculty based on Church Street's experience with CFL/ALEM since November 1999. She explained the structure of CFL/ALEM and answered most questions to the teachers' satisfaction. For instance, many teachers worried about managing the rotation among learning centers. The facilitator reported her own experience: "When you do small group and peer instruction, the kids become accustomed to the timer going off every 20 minutes and rotating to the next lesson." She also reassured teachers that CFL/ALEM worked well, with statements such as "Any time there is a learning center it is cooperative learning. The research shows that cooperative learning is more effective than a teacher standing in front of the room lecturing." Another concern for many teachers was the use of prescription sheets—the main method for individualization of instruction.The facilitator assured them that it was not difficult to have a prescription sheet for each student, because "The whole class actually has the same prescription but each child does different activities. Temple requires that you level the class—that is, different kids need different types of activities even within language arts."

In the course of training, the facilitator briefly discussed all elements of CFL/ALEM and Church Street's experience with them. For example, she explained that "The teacher call device, a sign that a student raises to indicate that they require a teacher's assistance, is different than raising a hand because it does not disrupt the class or what the teacher is doing." She also noted that "The wait-time folder is different than seat work because it is used when a student finishes an individualized project. The work is on grade level, not individualized, and unlike seatwork, it is not graded. The intention is to increase time for learning."

According to the facilitator, after a few months and minor modifications, Church Street's experience with CFL/ALEM was positive. Even features such as self-scheduling worked well: "After a while the kids learn how to handle self-scheduling but you have to control it or they will all be at the computers all of the time." To reassure the teachers that the program was suitable for their classrooms, she noted that "The 'A' in ALEM is for 'Adaptive.' To me, when a program says it is adaptive *it is adaptive*."

The facilitator emphasized several times that "Abbott is a law that you have to follow, you don't have any choice." She said, for example, that *Abbott V* required using technology throughout the curriculum. A Bridge Street teacher then asked about the resources for carrying out CFL/ALEM, and the facilitator responded, "You should remember that the state of New Jersey is *loaded*." In response, the over 100 teachers and aides roared with laughter.

The Bridge Street teachers felt that Church Street's WSR facilitator had conducted the most interesting professional development workshop they had ever attended. It was apparent, however, from the teachers' questions that most still had important questions about the mechanics of CFL/ALEM and the changes required to implement it. Missing from the workshop was any discussion of the educational philosophy underlying CFL/ALEM.

Formal Training in CFL/ALEM

In November 2000, all teachers attended a week of training in CFL/ALEM led by a facilitator from Temple University. The training began with a film that demonstrated the typical classroom use of CFL/ALEM (similar to the Web site description quoted earlier). Training also included a presentation of the scientific studies that support CFL/ALEM, along with a brief mention of its educational philosophy.

Most of the training presented and discussed specific elements of implementing CFL/ALEM, including the use of teacher call devices and the purpose of wait-time folders. The majority of the time was spent focusing in detail on how to create learning centers. In fact, 50% of the workshop was devoted to "make-and-take" materials for learning centers. This required the teachers to split into grade level groups to brainstorm about what a learning center should be and make the materials for one—usually with construction paper, tape, and assorted objects such as drinking straws, paper cups, and tongue depressors. The entire group then reassembled, and teachers explained and demonstrated their learning centers. After a presentation, the teachers applauded their colleagues' efforts, and the facilitators always praised everyone.

An important topic of discussion was student self-scheduling and self-learning. The facilitator explained that self-scheduling was a requirement of the learning center scheme because, with five learning centers in each classroom, "The self-scheduling board is a way for kids to self-schedule their time at learning centers. Dr. Wang, who developed CFL/ALEM, believes that kids have to be responsible for their own learning. Self-scheduling works in tandem with the learning centers. If you implement one you have to implement the other or it makes no sense." She then asked, "Why self-scheduling? What are the assumptions behind it? Why do we want our students to be responsible? *They have to—it's a survival skill.* This takes time. For generations and generations kids have waited for us to tell them what to do. This is different." When asked by the facilitator, most teachers said that they already used learning centers and individualized instruction, but no teacher indicated that he or she employed self-scheduling or self-learning.

The facilitator explained that periodic classroom evaluation would rely on a Degree of Implementation (DOI) instrument that Temple University had developed to monitor the progress of teachers using CFL/ALEM. The evaluation categories, which reflected important dimensions of CFL/ALEM, were

1. arrangement of space and furniture,
2. creating and maintaining instructional materials,
3. establishing and enforcing rules and procedures,
4. managing aids,
5. record keeping,
6. diagnostic testing,
7. writing prescriptions,
8. monitoring and diagnosing,
9. interactive teaching,
10. motivating, and
11. developing student self responsibility.

Even with this list of expected behaviors that teachers would be judged on, the facilitators frequently emphasized that CFL/ALEM should be "adapted" to the needs of particular teaching styles and classroom situations. For example, one trainer said

> Nothing I'm telling you is "set in stone." There are parts of the model that you may not use and other parts that you can modify to meet the needs of your kids. The CFL Web site has different accommodations that people have come up with. It should be practical. The concept is to reduce down time in the classroom. Start with what you are comfortable with and work from there. CFL only makes what you are already doing more systematic.

Despite the emphasis on flexibility, several practices that emerged as central to CFL/ALEM, and not negotiable, were individualization of instruction, the use of learning centers, and the use of multiple instructional methods. To reinforce individualization as a key component of CFL/ALEM, the facilitators frequently admonished teachers to limit or stop whole class instruction.

The Temple University trainers did not have knowledge of *Abbott V*, the specific schools, or the local communities. They did know, however, that they were training teachers in a high-poverty, low-achievement urban school. After attending a training session, one vice principal commented, "CFL misses the point. There is still no parental involvement. Instead of Whole School Reform the school should be open every night and weekends to bring parents in and serve as a resource for the community."

The Bridge Street administration decided to use CFL/ALEM only for language arts in 2000–2001 and to add math in 2001–2002.

CFL/ALEM in Classrooms, Year 1

Mrs. Smith's First-Grade Class. Mrs. Smith, who earned an undergraduate degree from State Teachers College in 1968, was a veteran teacher who in 1995 decided that she would either develop a new, more personally satisfying and effective way of teaching, or she would leave teaching altogether.[8] Her classroom, which was filled with diverse interesting objects, was arranged into learning centers organized around the theme "Kids Under Construction." Each student had a hard hat and carpenter's apron to wear for special activities every day.

In a typical lesson, Mrs. Smith dressed as "Farmer Fred" and read a story to the students, who sat on the floor around her rocking chair. During the lesson, in which she talked and behaved like "Farmer Fred," she asked questions about the story, taught phonics when necessary, and had the children embellish the story as she wrote vocabulary words on a whiteboard easel. After the story, the students went to various language arts learning centers in the room and worked independently. Mrs. Smith either worked with a group or circulated through the room to assist.

After experimenting with several reading programs, Mrs. Smith selected guided reading. She had no reading groups, and she taught each student on at his or her own level using literature. She taught phonics, but not separately from teaching literature, and she did not use phonics drills. She explained, "I am not overly concerned with phonics because in a relatively short time, with a few exceptions, the kids learn them easily. My approach is like whole language but I use some phonics, too." Mrs. Smith did not use workbooks or seatwork.

Mrs. Smith emphasized that she set high standards and expected students to reach them. She observed that "I find Success for All's promise that by fourth grade all kids will be reading on grade level too low—they should be above."

On another day, for a reading lesson Mrs. Smith dressed as "Mrs. May," a goofy but lovable character with a southern drawl. With the assistance of the students, she wrote a story on a primary paper easel; the story ended with Mrs. May making a clay pot. The students were fascinated as the pot took shape.

Then, instead of giving clay to each student to make a pot—which is what they expected—Mrs. Smith spent 15 minutes working with letters, which the entire class made into words. After this, she distributed clay and told the students to make something of their own design. The interval of delayed gratification created intense student focus that resulted in a prime learning opportunity.

A February 2000 *Star-Ledger* article with the headline "Teacher Builds Up Kids' Ability to Learn" described Ms. Smith's innovative teaching, particularly her use of literature to teach reading. The article quoted the Bridge Street principal: "In September, some children in her class were reading at a kindergarten level and now they are reading at an upper second-grade level." Mrs. Smith said, "This is a sort of mission for me. These children need me. I want to give them experiences that they may or may not get at home. Teaching in Newark has been such a positive experience. You couldn't get me to leave." The principal put the article on a bulletin board outside her office. After a week, she removed it because several teachers had complained that Mrs. Smith received too much attention.

Although the Bridge Street administrators endorsed Mrs. Smith's instructional style because it produced high student achievement, they and official Board of Education policy differed with Mrs. Smith on fundamental issues. For example, a vice principal thought that "Phonics works better in Newark than in the suburbs because the kids do not come to school with a reading and language experience from the home." Board policy also endorsed an emphasis on phonics, seatwork, and workbooks to reinforce lessons.

Mrs. Lake's Fourth-Grade Class. Mrs. Lake, a graduate of a large midwestern university, had taught in Newark—her first teaching position—for 6 years before *Abbott V.* Although her husband urged her to get a job in a suburban school, Mrs. Lake liked teaching in Newark and felt that she made a more significant contribution there than she would have in the suburbs. However, in 1999, to test the job market she interviewed in a suburban district and was surprised to find that the focus on preparing students to pass the ESPA that was so prominent at Bridge Street was not important in the suburb.

Mrs. Lake did not know much about Abbott or Whole School Reform but thought that Abbott "Is a really bad thing because it makes all of the teachers in Newark look really terrible, which is not the case." In her opinion, Abbott funds did not improve classrooms in ways other than purchasing computers. In fact, as in previous years, she and other teachers spent their own money on classroom supplies.

Her classroom appeared disorganized. Desks haphazardly clustered around the room, stacks of books sprang up everywhere, students' desks overflowed with papers, and the doors to the coatroom were always open. This setting reflected Mrs. Lake's easygoing, warm relationships with her students, which were more important to her than rules and clear routines. The students responded to the loose structure with good behavior and genuine appreciation for Mrs. Lake.

Mrs. Lake's 23 students, like those in every classroom at Bridge Street, had diverse achievement levels. Most students were 2 years below grade level in reading, with a range of several students at pre-K and two students at grade level. Because of a change in district policy the year before, special education students were included in regular classrooms. As a result, one student in Mrs. Lake's class had an in-class tutor who helped him while Mrs. Lake taught a lesson.

A typical lesson found Mrs. Lake at the front of the room using an overhead projector to introduce a concept to the entire class. She then presented several examples and worked through a few more examples with the students, followed by students working individually on an assignment from the text. While the students worked, Mrs. Lake circulated through the class, answering questions and offering advice. She then reviewed the problems with the entire class and assigned another set of exercises for completion in class and an additional set for homework. Throughout the lesson, the noise was considerable, but it did not bother Mrs. Lake; she only reprimanded students when they disrupted the class or bothered another student. There was no individualization, use of small groups, or cooperative learning.

According to Mrs. Lake, the ESPA, which was administered in April, "is overemphasized by the central Board and takes too much class time for preparation." A large part of every day—at least 2 hours—involved review of previous ESPAs using commercially prepared review books, Newark Board of Education review tests, and practice tests from the New Jersey Department of Education.

In Mrs. Lake's view, the ESPA contained culturally biased questions, was too difficult for her students, and "creates failure for inner city students" because they predictably perform lower than suburban students. During a practice ESPA reading passage about kayaking, she said, "These kids *may* know what a kayak is, but they have *never been in one*. How can they relate to this story?" Another example was a reading passage on a practice ESPA about a Jewish grandmother who used Yiddish terms such as "Oy Ves Mir." Mrs. Lake, a Jew, complained, "How can my kids be expected to do well on this test? They don't know about Jewish grandmothers, let alone Yiddish expressions. They should have stories about things they know about. *They're being set up for failure!*"

Because of the extensive time spent preparing for the ESPA, Mrs. Lake and the other fourth-grade teachers did not implement CFL/ALEM during the second half of 2000–2001 as planned. In addition, several teachers delayed because, they argued, it was disruptive for the children to break the established school routine in mid-year. Ms. Lake promised, "In September 2001 I'll have CFL totally up and running."

Abbott V and CFL/ALEM Implementation Throughout the School, Year 1

Because of *Abbott V,* Bridge Street had a well-equipped computer lab and every classroom had five computers, but the computers were not connected to the Internet because the Newark Board of Education had exhausted its computer funds. As another consequence of *Abbott V,* the principal converted a classroom into a resource room for the Whole School Reform facilitator and teachers.

In the first 6 months, in addition to CFL/ALEM training taking place, a WSF facilitator began work, the School Management Team met, two preschool classrooms were started, and class sizes were adjusted to comply with the *Abbott V* elementary school mandate.

Work began on the court-ordered zero-based budget. This consumed a significant amount of the principal's time because she was not familiar with the software the state provided, and documenting every budget item took time. She observed that "It's too early to know if the budget process will make a difference in the school."

The WSR facilitator was an experienced literacy teacher who advocated reforms that focused on individualization of instruction. He complained, however, that "Too much paperwork is required by the central office," particularly concerning student evaluation, and that this reduced his and teachers' time with students. His opinion was that "Teachers are able to assess their kids just by what they do in the classroom." He also thought that CFL/ALEM would succeed in individualizing instruction more effectively than had previous programs. He asked, "Can change be accomplished in a short time? Yes, but it's a lot to expect from the teachers." In his view, despite its potential benefits, CFL/ALEM threatened teacher autonomy, would hasten teacher retirements, and would impede teacher recruitment.

A vice principal offered a more positive assessment: "CFL will be successful if it gets the teachers to individualize instruction and move away from rote teaching. But this might not be easy because the Board of Education has been requiring whole class instruction until now."

The expectation was that all classroom teachers would implement CFL/ALEM. However, only one second-grade teacher claimed to have fully implemented it. In fact, though, her control of everything in the classroom—including self-scheduling—and her use of harsh discipline and traditional pedagogy had no fidelity to CFL/ALEM and instead undercut its objectives.

By the end of the school year, most of the other teachers beginning to apply CFL/ALEM techniques in their classrooms. For example, most teachers had developed at least one learning center and posted self-scheduling charts. More advanced teachers filled out prescription sheets for students and had wait-time folders.

In faculty meetings and professional workshops, issues were discussed such as the appropriate number of learning centers, how to write prescriptions, the content of wait-time folders, and the recommended length of each lesson. The answers from facilitators and administrators were usually suggestions to encourage teachers to experiment and discover what worked effectively in their own classrooms. The facilitators and administrators infrequently used directives or invoked the *Abbott V* mandates to change teacher behavior.

Teachers also raised asked questions about how much time should be allocated to CFL/ALEM every day. The administration answered that 100 minutes a day should be devoted to it. However, the New Jersey Supreme Court and Temple University intended that the model be applied throughout the day and the week, not inserted occasionally as a special activity.

During the first year, many of these issues were irrelevant because most teachers did not use CFL/ALEM. Like Ms. Lake, the majority decided, with the acquiescence of the administration, to wait for the first full year of school to use CFL/ALEM. Others argued that the teaching methods they used were either superior to or the same as CFL/ALEM.

Further reducing the emphasis on CFL/ALEM, three times during the spring the Board of Education replaced the fourth-grade professional day for training in CFL/ALEM with workshops to prepare for the Elementary School Proficiency Test (ESPA), the state standardized test. This made the priorities of the Board clear to all administrators and teachers. One teacher observed, "We focus on the ESPA from pre-K."

Standardized Test Scores, Year 1

Since 1998, all fourth-grade classes in New Jersey have taken the ESPA. The results for the first 3 years for students who scored proficient at Bridge Street were

	1998–1999	1999–2000	2000–2001
Language Arts	44.6	33.9	57.9
Math	29.3	53.2	37.3

The faculty had difficulty understanding the meaning of these scores because of the fluctuation. However, although the scores were average and in some years above average for elementary schools in Newark, it was clear they had to improve.

Bridge Street and *Abbott V*, Year 2—2001–2002

The Superintendent Reflects on *Abbott V*

In a September 10, 2001, newspaper article, the second state-appointed superintendent of Newark's schools asked, "Whole school reform is a great idea! Right? So why, as we begin a new school term, are we still struggling four years after a court ruling and the issuing of state mandates?" (Bolden, 2001, p. 15). Her answer was that the state had not supplied enough money to implement *Abbott V* and that reconstructing a school system was difficult and time consuming under the best conditions. She concluded

> I am frustrated by a process that too often takes us off task. I am frustrated by the constant struggle as we are pulled in a dozen different directions. But I am also excited by an opportunity to do what hasn't been done before. We have the potential to make a significant difference. As a community, as a state, we must refocus on the goals we have set and go about the business of working together to achieve them. (Bolden, 2001, p. 15).

The Whole School Reform Facilitator Quits

In September 2001, the Bridge Street Whole School Reform facilitator resigned because he was frustrated with Temple University and with the Newark Board of Education. Among his complaints about Temple were that on several occasions Temple facilitators had forgotten to come to the school for faculty development workshops, and there was continuous facilitator turnover. The WSR facilitator happily returned to the classroom as a literacy teacher, where he felt he could benefit students.

Second Thoughts About CFL/ALEM

Soon after the school began, several teachers told a vice principal that they thought that CFL/ALEM was not an appropriate program for the school. When she asked what they would like to replace it with, they had no suggestions. She reassured the teachers that the administration would support them and that Temple would provide more training. Her view was that "The teachers want to do CFL the right way. They are very concerned with getting it right. But, we have to get it going. We'll work out the problems as they arise."

At the same time, the other vice principal observed that

> It is almost impossible to change teachers. You wouldn't believe how many times I've written-up certain teachers—*a pile of write-ups*—and they don't change. I never saw a teacher use the teacher call cards or the wait-time folder. Only a few teachers even tried any part of CFL. Some teachers set up one learning center at the beginning of the year and never change it and never use it. But, when I come into the room and ask them about CFL they tell me that they have a center. I write them up and try to get them to change and I talk to the assistant superintendent and principal about it. But they do nothing.

He then observed that a key problem with the change process was that the principal was not an effective "instructional leader" and that the burgeoning bureaucratic paperwork required by the central office and state reduced her time to lead the school.

Additional Training

Throughout the second year, Temple University facilitators visited classrooms and conducted training in CFL/ALEM on districtwide professional development days. A typical workshop would start with an explanation of the reasons for using learning centers and why creating different levels of activities for children of different abilities was important. Following this brief presentation, teachers would work in grade level groups to make learning centers. After an hour, the teachers would meet again to demonstrate the learning centers they had created.

After a few of these workshops, teachers grumbled among themselves that the sessions were useless. They preferred to spend time working individually or discussing issues of concern to them. During a break in one workshop, the negative reactions to the Temple facilitator were so pervasive that the principal reprimanded the entire faculty and urged them "to take advantage of the opportunity to improve the school." The faculty quietly endured the scolding without raising the concerns they had about the training or about CFL/ALEM.

The format was not significantly different for workshops conducted by the school WSR facilitator. Typically, the facilitator would give teachers handouts and rapidly read them, with little discussion. An example was a presentation of Howard Gardner's theory of multiple intelligences. After reading the list of multiple intelligences—including the new ones of "naturalist" and "spiritualist"—the facilitator asked if there were any questions. One teacher asked if she had to incorporate multiple intelligences into CFL/ALEM. The facilitator answered that she should use the theory when possible. However, privately several teachers admitted that they did not know how to incorporate multiple intelligences theory into their classrooms, that they were overwhelmed with new demands, and that they did not want additional complications.

The Focus of Training

The focus of training was mainly technical issues concerning implementation or classroom management rather than discussions of the educational philosophy underlying either *Abbott V* or CFL/ALEM. For example, there were lengthy discussions of how to use a laminating machine, how to construct a teacher call card, and how to use an Ellison machine to cut paper into shapes. The infrequent computer training focused on the mechanics of computers—how to log on to the World Wide Web and trouble shoot—rather than how to integrate computers into the curriculum.

Monitoring Implementation

In addition to training, Temple University and the WSR facilitator monitored the implementation of CFL/ALEM by observing classes with a checklist of items that comprised the Degree of Implementation instrument. Teachers, who in many cases received the results of evaluations months later, were supposed to use them to create an improvement plan.

Several times during the year, representatives of the New Jersey Department of Education visited the school. It was never clear to administrators and teachers whether the officials' role was to assist with, monitor, or enforce Abbott regulations. After a few visits, a vice principal concluded that the officials harmed the change effort because they created confusion. To avoid further confusion, to satisfy their requests for data he fabricated information.

CFL/ALEM in Classrooms, Year 2

Mrs. Smith's First-Grade Class. Although a vice principal expected her to use CFL/ALEM, Mrs. Smith's class was almost the same as it has been the previous year. A major change was improved learning centers leveled according to CFL/ALEM guidelines. Otherwise, Mrs. Smith made no adjustments in her teaching to accommodate CFL/ALEM—of course, she had developed similar methods independently—and continued to update instructional materials and refine her own teaching methods.

When a rumor spread that Success for All might become the districtwide model, Mrs. Smith said, "I would quit before I'm forced to use a model based on rote learning." (The district did not adopt a single model; see note 7 for a full breakdown of the models selected.) She also worried about the inability to implement CFL/ALEM throughout the school and doubted that instruction would improve without an appropriate and usable model.

Mrs. Smith frequently had individuals from other schools or districts visit her classroom. In addition, Joan Sibert, a professor of education from the local branch of State University, placed a student teacher in her classroom every semester. Once, after observing her student work with Mrs. Smith, Dr. Sibert commented that "Mrs. Smith is *'THE BEST'—a fabulous teacher—if only we could clone her!*"

One day Mrs. Smith commented that Dr. Sibert had written a "negative" book about Newark. Mrs. Smith, a White middle-aged suburbanite, said that friends and relatives often asked her, *"Even though they know who I am and what I do"*—'Can you teach *those children* in Newark how to read?'" Mrs. Smith said she could not understand why suburbanites and professors like Sibert perpetuated a negative image of Newark.

Mrs. Lake's Class. "CFL is dead. I haven't heard anything about it," said Mrs. Lake, who interpreted the slow appointment of a second WSR facilitator as the end of CFL/ALEM. In fact, there was no evidence of CFL/ALEM in Mrs. Lake's classroom, and she used the same teaching methods she had used the year before. The only differences were that the fourth-grade teachers departmentalized instruction by having students rotate among them for reading and math, and a few days after school started (much earlier than the year before), Mrs. Lake and her colleagues started to prepare her students for the ESPA.

The Second AFL/ALEM Facilitator

In early November 2001, a well-liked, affable African American second-grade teacher became the second WSR facilitator, and Mrs. Lake and the other fourth-grade teachers began talking with her about implementing CFL/ALEM. However, in mid-November, in addition to administering Board-mandated "benchmark" tests in math, language arts, and science, the Board required the fourth grade to review for a practice ESPA test. This pushed any thoughts about CFL/ALEM aside as teachers devoted substantially more time to decontextualized test preparation. As a result, the fourth grade became little more than a test preparation center until the May 2002 ESPA.

In April 2002, the WSR facilitator went on maternity leave, and the position remained vacant for the balance of the school year.

Abbott V and CFL/ALEM Implementation Throughout the School, Year 2

The administration wanted more teachers to implement CFL/ALEM but could not find a way to create change. For example, to encourage the use of learning centers, the vice principals constructed elaborate learning centers for literacy, earth science, and math in each hallway. However, only one second-grade teacher implemented learning centers, and most teachers continued to use traditional teaching materials and methods. When asked why more teachers were not using CFL/ALEM, a vice principal answered, "Well, it's Newark. What would you expect? That's just the way things are here."

In a tactical shift, in May 2002, instead of training all teachers, a CFL/ALEM workshop at Bridge Street invited only teachers from throughout Newark who were high implementers of CFL/ALEM. Only seven teachers attended the workshop; the Temple facilitators were not happy with either the revised strategy or the turnout. The other teachers—the low and non-implementers—attended a variety of workshops on topics as diverse as conflict resolution techniques, computers in the classroom, and methods for preparing students for the ESPA.

Mrs. Lake Departs

Mrs. Lake's husband, who worked for an investment bank, was transferred to Philadelphia in May 2002. Mrs. Lake, who reluctantly finished the year in Newark, took an elementary teaching position in a suburb in southern New Jersey for the following year. Before she left Newark she observed that "CFL/ALEM was the wrong program for my students. They need a program with more structure." Also, she felt the Board of Education was not competent: "It's as though they were never in a classroom." She recommended that to improve schools, the New Jersey Supreme Court, the State Department of Education and the Newark Board of Education "should have listened to teachers more."

More Tests

In early December, the Board initiated a set of "benchmarking" tests in math for all grades. The Bridge Street faculty complained about too many tests that took a significant amount of time from instruction. A vice principal observed, "We're supposed to individualize and do Whole School Reform but all they want to do is have us give 'benchmark' and 'achievement' tests. I hope that when he becomes governor, McGreevey changes this Whole School Reform thing." Many teachers shared this sentiment, and, for most, the testing program provided another convenient reason to delay implementing CFL/ALEM.

Standardized Test Scores, Year 2

The fourth-grade ESPA results for 2001–2002 were language arts 64.4% proficient and math 37.3% proficient. The improvement in language arts from 57.9% proficient the previous year was encouraging and was interpreted as a significant improvement. However, the math score was the same as the previous year, and the faculty could not understand why.

Bridge Street and *Abbott V*, Year 3/ NCLB, Year 1—2002–2003

NCLB, Year 1

In September 2002, although there was a general awareness of NCLB, the details of the legislation and what it would mean for Bridge Street were not clear to the administrators or faculty. For example, after attending a central office meeting devoted to NCLB, the principal was still vague on the details, other than "If a school doesn't improve in a few years the administration can be replaced."

A New Math Program

In September 2002, the Board initiated training for kindergarten and first-grade teachers in Everyday Math, an innovative approach to teaching mathematics developed by the University of Chicago. The rationale for selecting this program was its presumed alignment with the Core Content Curriculum Standards and the ESPA. The plan was to introduce it in all elementary grades over 2 years.

CFL/ALEM in Classrooms, Year 3

Mrs. Smith's First-Grade Class. Mrs. Smith attended all CFL/ALEM training and used the Temple trainer's ideas to level the materials in learning centers. Although her methods were more teacher-centered than the Temple model prescribed, her teaching became increasingly similar to CFL/ALEM. Because most other teachers did not even attempt to implement CFL/ALEM, Mrs. Smith, already considered an excellent teacher, continued to be the school's only innovator.

Mrs. Ondine's Fourth-Grade Class. Mrs. Ondine had departmentalized reading and math with Mrs. Lake during Mrs. Lake's time at Bridge Street.[9] Mrs. Ondine used learning centers more than Mrs. Lake but did not believe in the underlying principles and instructional methods of CFL/ALEM. Concerning pedagogy, she said, "I am not comfortable with constructivism. I believe in direct instruction and I think it's what these kids need."

Mrs. Ondine tried to incorporate preparation for the ESPA into every lesson. Her basic teaching method was whole class instruction followed by walking around the room helping students with exercises that reinforced the lesson.

Abbott Phase II

In January 2003, when James McGreevey became governor of New Jersey, a shift occurred in the relationship between the state and the Abbott districts. McGreevey's administration was the first to cooperate with the court to enforce the *Abbott V* mandates.

A short time after McGreevey took office, in another shift, the State Department of Education initiated Abbott Phase II, which refocused the *Abbott V* elementary mandates. It did not abandon the WSR models, but it did deemphasize them in favor of a preference for standards-driven classroom reform that emphasized the CCCS.

The principal's response to this redirection at Bridge Street was, "We already focus on the CCCS. This is not a new approach. The CCCS are good. But it's hard to get the teachers to go beyond the basics." The new librarian, formerly the WSR facilitator, evaluated Abbott Phase II with the observation that "WSR could be history by July."

The End of CFL/ALEM

Abbott Phase II required all schools to poll their faculty to determine if they wanted to continue with the original WSR model or change to another court-approved model. To prepare for the possibility of a new model, a professional development day was devoted to viewing videos of Success for All, The Comer School Development Program, and the Accelerated Schools Project.

Bridge Street conducted the survey in January 2003. On February 25, 2003, before announcement of the results, the Board of Education directed the six elementary schools in Newark that were implementing CFL/ALEM to terminate it immediately. The stated reasons were that CFL/ALEM did not meet the criteria of a scientifically valid program under the NCLB Act, was not data-driven, and did not have a method for assessing the progress of students.

Although few teachers had used CFL/ALEM, the termination edict produced a sense of relief. Several administrators, as well as many teachers, thought that the school would be better off without it. But the demise of CFL/ALEM created concern about what would happen next, and many teachers feared the Board would impose Success for All. Ironically, the poll indicated that most teachers had voted to continue CFL/ALEM—even though they didn't use it—because they disliked the other models and wanted to avoid retraining.

Bridge Street experienced another wave of relief a few months later, when the faculty learned that a Newark-developed WSR model would replace CFL/ALEM. In addition, the Board informed the administration that the state would provide up to $450,000 for 3 years of training for schools that did not have a WSR model. The principal applied for the funds to train faculty in the Bank Street College of Education Literacy program, which several schools in Newark already used successfully (Silin & Lippman, 2003).

NCLB Again

At a faculty meeting a few days after the termination of CFL/ALEM, the WSR facilitator and a union representative presented the details of NCLB to the entire faculty. The possibility of identification of a school as "in need of improvement" and the sanctions that accompanied it surprised many teachers. As with the introduction to CFL/ALEM, many teachers thought that enforcement of NCLB would be weak, but others were convinced that this time things would be different. In general, the faculty was concerned about what they perceived to be the negative aspects of NCLB, and most teachers did not think it would improve the school.

Toward the end of the workshop, confirming teachers' fears, the WSR facilitator announced that, like most elementary schools in Newark, Bridge Street was on the list of schools "in need of improvement." This created a heated discussion among the teachers, with accusations that some were holding the school back because they did not implement CFL/ALEM. Others countered that the training was ineffective and the program was not appropriate for the school.

The Superintendent Is Reappointed

In November 2002, the Commissioner of Education requested that the state advisory board consider candidates for the superintendent position in Newark. This shocked many people in Newark, because they assumed that reappointment of the superintendent was certain. After several months of turmoil, because of strong community support, the superintendent retained her position.

In early 2003, the superintendent felt optimistic because she detected "a shift from conflict to cooperation with the state." More important, in her view, the Department of Education shifted its emphasis from monitoring Newark's budget "toward more concern with teaching and learning."

Standardized Test Scores, Year 3

The 2002–2003 fourth-grade test, reformulated by the Educational Testing Service of Princeton and renamed the New Jersey Assessment of Skills and Knowledge (NJASK), produced scores for Bridge Street of 42% proficient in language arts and 23% proficient in math.

Both scores were unacceptable because they were significantly lower than the previous year's scores. Of course, for Bridge Street and the other schools that had scored lower, the issue was whether the new test was more difficult and had been scored more rigorously.

Because Bridge Street had not met adequate yearly progress (AYP) criteria under NCLB, the school was required to send a letter to parents advising them that their children could transfer to another school in Newark. Few parents inquired and no students transferred. One reason was that all of the schools near Bridge Street had failed to achieve AYP; the only option for Bridge Street parents was to send their children to a school a significant distance from home.

Bridge Street and *Abbott V*, Year 4/ NCLB, Year 2—2003–2004

The Newark Reform Model

The Bridge Street administrators decided to implement the Newark Reform Model. One element was Everyday Math, which had been in the lower grades and which all grades would eventually use. The other components of the model remained unspecified.

Bank Street Literacy Training

The state gave Bridge Street $450,000 for 3 years of Bank Street College of Education literacy training, which began for pre-K and kindergarten teachers in October. After an introductory meeting with the Bank Street trainers, the principal referred to them as "'60s people" to characterize their liberal philosophy of education, which she regarded as out of touch with current conditions in Newark and the United States.

NCLB, Year 2

The effect of NCLB on Bridge Street was to focus all activities in the fourth-grade on the NJASK. The goal was to raise scores to achieve AYP and avoid further penalties, particularly the label "in need of improvement" for a second year.

Early in the school year, the Bridge Street administrators visited several nearby elementary schools with higher NJASK scores than Bridge Street. They discovered that these schools had also not implemented a WSR model—no matter which model they had formally selected—and there was no evidence of more effective teaching. The major difference was that the schools "taught to the test" and tutored fourth-grade students intensively. In response, the Bridge Street administration increased the classroom time spent on test preparation and offered after-school tutoring and workshops for parents to learn how to prepare their children for the test. For 90 fourth-grade students, only 10 parents attended these workshops.

The first professional development workshop of the year for third- and fourth-grade teachers focused exclusively on the NJASK. During the workshop teachers blamed parents for not caring about their children, the administration for not providing enough support, lower grade teachers for inferior teaching and not retaining enough students, the state for changing the test, and each other for the low scores. Several hostile interchanges among the teachers at various points during the workshop remained unresolved.

CFL/ALEM in Classrooms, Year 4

Mrs. Smith's First-Grade Class. Early in the year, Mrs. Smith became seriously ill and was on medical leave for the remainder of the year. While recuperating, she applied for and became a district reading specialist for 2004–2005. Her assignment was four elementary schools in Newark, but not the Bridge Street School.

Mrs. Ondine's Fourth-Grade Class. According to Mrs. Ondine, there was an "extreme emphasis" on preparing students for the NJASK. Most of the students in her class were near grade level in reading, but several were as low as second grade. She reflected that "Suburban kids come to school with literacy skills. Many of our kids don't go to preschools and the skills they need are not developed in the home. There is no effective way to deal with kids who fall so far behind. I use a literature-based approach to reading and individualize it for each student. Sometimes, I have a slower kid work with a faster kid."

Concerning the NJASK, she said, "The NJASK is always in back of my mind. I use the NJASK rubric to grade writing. Each kid has two writing assignments a month geared to the NJASK. One is a picture prompt and the other is a poem prompt. We use the computer to revise the story to get it into publishable form in our class magazine."

Bank Street College of Education Training

Bank Street literacy training began in October for pre-K and kindergarten teachers and aides. Ten teachers and three aides, all African American women, attended the sessions on the Bank Street approach.

The first topic was the meaning and use of routines in pre-K and kindergarten classrooms. The Bank Street trainer, an African American female, stated, "Research says that children and parents should have routines built early in the year. Routines develop trust and a classroom community." She also explained that "Bank Street was not a scripted program like Success for All and not a curriculum. We use collaborative learning and learning centers and we try to make the children independent." Many features of Bank Street were similar to CFL/ALEM.

During a training session in January 2004, a kindergarten teacher questioned whether the Bank Street program was as effective as reading instruction methods used in the suburbs. "I visited a school in Edison last month," she said, "and they don't teach reading the way we do in Newark or how Bank Street does. It's completely different. I also observed a class in Piscataway and it was different. There was more emphasis on socialization in kindergarten and on letting children enjoy reading and waiting until they mature physically and mentally before introducing phonics and other drills. There was an emphasis on developmentally appropriate activities."

The Bank Street trainer responded, "If we look at programs in Short Hills or Summit we will probably see things that we would like to do here but we can't because of the different resource levels and administration. It is better not to do that because we can't use it. I have learned the hard way not to do anything that the administration won't support. It's usually not productive."

Privately the teacher expressed surprise at this response. In her opinion, because of political pressure, Newark introduced the mechanics of reading before children were developmentally ready, which created frustration and difficulty learning. In the suburbs she observed, learning to read was a gradual process. She also suspected that Bank Street had altered its program to fit what the Newark central office thought was appropriate for inner-city children. Several other teachers also questioned whether the training accurately reflected "The *real* Bank Street Literacy program."

Standardized Test Scores, Year 4

For 2003–2004, the NJASK scores were 61% proficient in language arts and 59% proficient in math. These scores were significantly higher than in the previous year, and Bridge Street met AYP. This was a considerable relief to the administration and faculty. One possible reason for the improvement was a significant increase in decontextualized tutoring for the test. Another reason, reluctantly admitted a vice principal who vocally opposed President George W. Bush and his education policies in the 2004 election, was that "NCLB made the teachers buckle down and do a better job. There was more focus by the teachers. It's hard to believe, but NCLB meant more to Bridge Street than did Abbott and CFL/ALEM."

Another vice principal thought that the test might have been easier and graded more leniently. She said, "The people in Trenton don't want to look bad. But it might also be that the kids and the teachers are getting used to the test."

Bridge Street and *Abbott V*, Year 5/ NCLB, Year 3—2004–2005

NCLB, Year 3

NCLB replaced the *Abbott V* elementary mandates as the guiding force in the Bridge Street School. Although all teachers claimed to use the CCCS, the main objective was to increase NJASK scores and, for the first time, the NCLB-mandated third-grade test. This was particularly important because the school wanted to retain AYP.

NCLB in the Classrooms, Year 5

Mrs. Ondine's Fourth-Grade Class. Although she did not like it, Mrs. Ondine continued to structure her classroom primarily to prepare students for the NJASK. As a result, her teaching methods became more traditional, which also accommodated the Board's increased emphasis on monitoring student progress. For example, as a way to improve the literacy scores of the NJASK, the Board required submission to it every month of a sample of each student's writing. Mrs. Ondine's response was to have students use specific rules that would raise their scores on the NJASK. For example, the rubric for the writing section of the test gave more points to good openings and closings of paragraphs than to punctuation. Accordingly, she paid less attention to the use of commas and periods.

She and the other fourth-grade teachers also taught test-taking skills, including how to eliminate multiple choice answers, budget time, work under pressure, and check answers. She accepted as reasonable spending more time on these strategies because the test was increasingly important. However, she observed that "The Board and everyone else—for example CFL/ALEM—encourage us to individualize because they say that every student has their own learning style. Yet, they ignore differences when they give everybody the same curriculum and standardized tests."

NCLB and Reform Throughout the School, Year 5

Work continued on incremental change in a number of areas. For example, training for pre-K and kindergarten teachers proceeded, and first-grade teachers began training in the Bank Street Literacy program, which emphasized best practices.

The fifth grade began implementation of Everyday Math, and the fourth grade began using a new Harcourt Brace reading program selected by the district. There was no evidence of CFL/ALEM, and the WSR facilitator became a literacy coach.

One day in November an unannounced and unexpected shipment of $50,000 in new books arrived for the library. The librarian, who had discarded many books that were almost 100 years old, was ecstatic and said, "Whoever selected these books did an excellent job."

The District Reform Model

For a professional development day in March 2005, the district sent three central office trainers to Bridge Street to introduce the district WSR model. The model was a variation on CFL/ALEM that emphasized individualization, diagnostic testing, multiple intelligences, and learning centers. The trainers used the term "guided reading" and presented an approach similar to Mrs. Smith's. At one point, a trainer emphasized that "Good curriculum comes first, but we have no control over curriculum these days." The philosophy underlying the model never became an issue and the teachers listened without overt criticism.

The Superintendent Is Reappointed, Again

In June 2005, the Commissioner of Education reappointed the superintendent to a third 2-year term beginning in July 2006. The *Star-Ledger* editorialized that higher expectations should apply for her third term. The editor wrote that

> She inherited and fixed a $70 million deficit that never should have happened on the state's watch. During her tenure, school scores have gradually improved, particularly in the lower grades. Those are the reasons she needs to stay. . . . But there are also too many deficiencies that are just plain shameful this far along into the state takeover and her tenure. . . . Many complex problems affect urban education. But around the country there are examples of schools that find ways to overcome those problems. Newark has to find the way. ("Expect More," 2005, p. 8)

Standardized Test Scores, Year 5

The standardized test scores for the fourth grade in 2004–2005 were 55.7% proficient in language arts and 69.2% proficient in math, including 15.4% who scored advanced proficient. Language arts scores dropped a little over 5%, and math improved just over 10%.

NCLB, Year 3

Of the 71 schools in New Jersey required to undergo "restructuring" according to NCLB in 2005–2006, 14 were in Newark. Although this development did not directly affect Bridge Street, which because of a low score in language arts received a Year 1 "early warning" for 2005–2006, it raised questions in Newark concerning resource allocation and new programs (Mooney, 2005d).

Analysis of the Bridge Street School

Legitimacy and the Eco-Cognitive Framework

The dynamics of legitimacy explain the development of the changes at Bridge Street and their impact on student learning. After a long period of incremental change that had failed to improve student outcomes, the state takeover of Newark attempted to create short-term radical change. This was the initial source of delegitimation because it challenged the entire school system but did not improve it.

Abbott V eroded legitimacy further by threatening to reduce teacher autonomy even more than the state takeover. Responding to the externally initiation of change, teachers challenged the court's legitimacy because they felt coerced. The state further undermined the legitimacy of *Abbott V* when the McGreevey administration introduced Abbott Phase II. Administrators and teachers interpreted this shift as official acknowledgment that the reforms were not working.

At almost the same time that the Board of Education terminated CFL/ALEM, NCLB re-established change through coerced legitimacy. NCLB differed from the state takeover and *Abbott V* because it could penalize individual schools and the district. When nearby schools improved test scores because of intense preparation and NCLB sanctions were enforced, the change to intensive rote test preparation further narrowed the curriculum and the type and meaning of education.

Another major shift occurred after the punctuation created by the end of CFL/ALEM. The reversion to gradual change represented by the Bank Street Literacy program and the Newark Whole School Reform model contributed to relegitimating educational change from the perspective of the teachers.

The eco-cognitive framework, a core element of the school's culture, influenced all major decisions during CFL/ALEM and NCLB implementation and contributed to the rejection of CFL/ALEM. The distinction between education appropriate for urban and education suitable for suburban students eliminated the central components of CFL/ALEM of self-scheduling and self-selection, as well as "constructivism" or any teaching method associated with it, such as peer learning.

An important example of the eco-cognitive process was the rejection by the Bank Street trainer of the suggestion to explore reading techniques used in suburban schools. In the taken-for-granted world of social class and race distinctions in a segregated social structure, it was natural for her to think that Bridge Street could not learn from or emulate suburban schools.

Ironically, in most instances, the eco-cognitive legitimation was benevolent in its intent. The distinction between urban and suburban students protected urban students from pedagogic techniques and programs that teachers considered not appropriate or beneficial. Self-scheduling and self-learning would result in chaotic conditions in classrooms, and standardized tests "set students up for failure."

Changes in Classrooms

The result of the nonlegitimacy of external coercive change and the eco-cognitive framework was that the *Abbott V* funding equalization and elementary reforms had no impact on the deep structure of classrooms. Only Mrs. Smith's class experienced change in most deep structure components. However, the changes were not the result of either reform program but were primarily the self-generated reconstruction by Mrs. Smith of her teaching practices.

Although NCLB was also external and coercive, it created a punctuation that terminated the *Abbott V* mandates and exerted more impact on classrooms. NCLB approached classrooms indirectly with the assumption that standardized tests would create curricular and pedagogic reform. Instead, the meager attempts to implement, and the ultimate rejection of, CFL/ALEM temporarily challenged and dismantled deep structure assumptions. This process created a vacuum, which the eco-cognitive framework and the NCLB emphasis on tests filled with test preparation.

Another major change with potential long-term consequences was the use of standardized tests to motivate students. As a result, an emphasis on learning as intrinsically valuable or for occupational attainment became an abstract extrinsic motivation to perform well on the test (Deci, Koestner, & Ryan 1999; Ryan & Deci, 2000).

A Typology of Bridge Street Teachers

The Bridge Street teachers' responses to *Abbott V* and NCLB varied based on the interaction of their values and behaviors. Mrs. Smith, who was marginal to the school culture because she pursued her own agenda, displayed *self-motivated value-driven* change. Her values, which explicitly rejected social class and race distinctions, resulted in behavior change independent of, but similar to, CFL/ALEM. Her students acquired reading and math skills often significantly above grade level, learned how to work independently as well as collaboratively, and experienced an attempt to develop intrinsic motivation.

Mrs. Lake, who exhibited *covert active resistance* to change, was skeptical of *Abbott V* and promised to change but never did. Her values and behavior reflected the benevolent eco-cognitive framework; she tried to protect her students from outside forces that would make them fail. Her students learned how to prepare for standardized tests, which reinforced extrinsic motivation to learn. They also learned that school is fun in a minimally disciplined environment.

More willing to conform to external change than Mrs. Lake, Mrs. Ondine engaged in *selective incremental* change. Instead of uncritically adopting CFL/ALEM, she selected elements she thought would fit the needs of her students within the benevolent understanding of urban students. Because of her narrowly focused test preparation, students learned that education was a set of skills required to execute a specific task to satisfy organization goals.

Although two teachers successfully resisted CFL/ALEM, all three teachers experienced significant change. Mrs. Smith improved all dimensions of her classroom continuously. Mrs. Lake and Mrs. Ondine changed primarily because of the emphasis of NCLB on standardized tests. In fact, they experienced externally initiated coercive change; they would not have voluntarily focused their instruction on test preparation and periodically but unsuccessfully resisted it.

Changes in the School

At Bridge Street, because of passive leadership, teachers influenced what changed more than did the administration. The inability of the principal and vice principals to change teachers in response to the federal, state, and district actions produced a pattern of "unanticipated incremental change."

The punctuation created by the failure of CFL/ALEM, followed by its formal discontinuation, terminated the *Abbott V* elementary school mandates except for the court-ordered funding increase. Then, during NCLB, mediated by the eco-cognitive framework, the evolutionary processes of selection and retention returned the school to familiar local remedies and incremental change.

This occurred even though the reform process centralized decision making in the federal government and eventually recentralized it in the district. An important outcome of centralization was that NCLB, through the state and district, changed the nature, type, and pervasiveness of the organizational control system by measuring academic achievement exclusively with standardized tests and instituting corrective actions.

Despite the centralization of policy decisions, teachers retained an important source of power because they were able to reject or modify the reforms.

Most important, the legitimacy of the urban–suburban bifurcation created conditions that reproduced and relegitimated a specific form of urban education and was the basic source of power for the teachers.

Conclusions

Abbott V and NCLB did not develop the capacity to change, and the Bridge Street administration had no theory or method to increase the likelihood of successful change. For example, the administration could have used Mrs. Smith as a model for other teachers. However, under these conditions, model teachers often decrease change. Richard Elmore (2004) noted that

> The existence of exemplars, without some way of capitalizing on their talents, only reinforces the notion that ambitious teaching is an individual trait, not a professional expectation. (p. 25)

More important, over 5 years, Bridge Street experienced a complete change cycle. With the critical exception of the continuation of standardized tests, the implementation of the Newark-developed Whole School Reform program returned the school to local conceptions of education. One reason for the development of the Newark WSR program was the inability of either *Abbott V* or NCLB to improve test scores. But the primary cause was the nonlegitimacy of the external changes, which modified their potential effectiveness because of the influence of the eco-cognitive framework.

Ultimately, administrators and teachers defined a situation intended to improve the school as one that instead created conditions that would result in less effective education. *Abbott V* and NCLB imposed coercive change, which contributed to the perpetuation of a self-fulfilling prophecy (Merton, 1948; Weinstein, 2002) that urban students required a distinctive type of education. During the change process, the eco-cognitive framework validated and reinforced the notion.

Although teachers retained control over their classrooms to some extent, their race- and class-based decision making contributed to the failure of *Abbott V* and to NCLB changing the meaning and purpose of urban education. They rejected *Abbott V* and reluctantly accepted the NCLB focus on standardized tests, which narrowed the curriculum throughout the school, restricted teaching techniques to rote drill, and changed student motivation.

Based on 2004–2005 standardized test scores, which marked 2 consecutive years of failing to achieve AYP, the Newark school district confronted the prospect of NCLB sanctions, including state takeover.

CHAPTER 5

The College Avenue School

The Normal Appearance of Change

The Social Context of Education: Elizabeth

Elizabeth, a colonial city, until after World War II was a major industrial center. Like Newark, it experienced an influx of African Americans and Latinos at roughly the same time that its industrial infrastructure began a steady decline that continued into the 21st century (Newman, 1988). However, because of its strategic location, access to major highways, a nearby airport, a large unskilled labor pool, and comparatively inexpensive industrial real estate, Elizabeth remained a significant distribution center, with several of the largest and highest volume warehouse operations in the country.

In 2005, after years of decline, its port became one of the busiest in the United States because of the vast increase in Chinese imports (Marsico, 2005). In addition, during the past 10 years, discount shopping malls that attract suburban shoppers have opened on the highways that dissect Elizabeth.

Ethnic Enclaves

The most important result of the migration and dismantling of traditional industries was the exit of the White middle class to the suburbs. The racial and ethnic groups that now populate Elizabeth live in segregated neighborhoods. Italian, African American, Jewish, and several increasingly larger Latino sections have distinctive ethnic restaurants, bars, and retail stores. Among the service businesses are the Honduras Athletic Club and storefronts advertising cheap airfare and telephone rates to Central and South America. The main business street, which features bargain-priced merchandise, is an agglomeration of locally owned stores but few national retail chains.

An important reason that recent immigrants from Central and South America find Elizabeth attractive is its inexpensive housing compared with nearby suburban communities and gentrified neighborhoods in other cities.

Although the neighborhoods vary greatly in appearance—ranging from small apartment buildings to large illegally subdivided houses—they are all urban in character; none successfully emulate the manicured lawns, architecture, and land use of the suburbs. For many families, as it was for earlier immigrants, Elizabeth is a starting point for relocating to the suburbs to fulfill the American dream.

Mixed Perceptions

Elizabeth still suffers from the perception by suburbanites that it embodies the ills of urban America. "I have a friend who said to me, 'Aren't you afraid to live in Elizabeth?'" said Sally Newkirk, 54, who moved to Elizabeth with her husband in 1985 and lives along a park near the city's western border. "It's not like that. When I came here, there used to be a lot of cars stolen in this area. Now I don't see that" (quoted in Strunsky, 2002).

But Elizabeth does have many of the problems of American cities. For example, in June 2005, 100 federal agents and local police arrested 13 members of a Latino street gang whose members were illegal immigrants from Colombia, El Salvador, and Honduras. The gang used violence and drug trafficking to control a neighborhood (Martin & Ryan, 2005). Despite periodic flare-ups of violence and gang activity, as in Newark, suburbanites distinguish the safe parts of Elizabeth—where they shop or patronize restaurants—from the dangerous areas.

The Education Problem

Concerning education, a *New York Times* article titled "Prosperity Beckons: For Elizabeth, Once Down on Its Luck, a Dynamic Time" (Strunsky, 2002), which described recent improvements in Elizabeth such as the shopping mall and the economic activity at the port, concluded,

> But for all of Elizabeth's improvements and potential, even its biggest boosters say long-term prosperity depends on a struggling public school system that while showing signs of improvement, continues to perform well below the state as a whole. (Section 14, p. 1)

Elizabeth's Population

The 1990 population of Elizabeth was 110,000. There were 22,000 African Americans (20% of the population) and 72,000 Whites (65% of the population). Latinos, at 43,000 or 39% of the population, identified themselves as being of either Black or White racial origin. The 1990 median family income was $28,000.

In 2000, the population of Elizabeth was 120,500. The 24,000 African Americans composed 20% of the population, and the 67,000 Whites made up 56%. Latinos of both races totaled 60,000, or 50% of the population. The median family income was $35,000, and 4,500 families (21,000 individuals) were below the poverty level. The unemployment rate was 7.4%, 0.3% lower than the average for Abbott districts.

The county population was 65.5% White, 21% African American, and 20% Latino. The county median income was $55,300, and 8.4% of the population had income below the poverty level. As in the case of Newark, the income inequality between Elizabeth and the suburbs in the county was extreme. Also, as in Newark, most of the suburbs had a very small percentage of minority families.

The Elizabeth School District

In 2000, the Elizabeth School District had a total enrollment of 20,000 students. Twenty-five hundred students were White, 4,800 were African American, and 12,700 were Latino. In 2002, 72% of the students were eligible for free or reduced-price lunch, which was 10% higher than all Abbott districts. The high school graduation rate was 64.5%, slightly lower than the 66.9% rate for all Abbott districts.

Elizabeth had 2,100 full-time teachers with an average experience of 11 years. The average teacher salary was $48,700, which was lower than the state and Abbott district averages. However, because of *Abbott V* funding and new contracts, the 2005 starting salary was $44,500, which made Elizabeth competitive with the suburbs. Most of the teachers were White, but the presence of Latino professionals in schools was increasing.

The Elizabeth school district had 18 elementary schools, 6 middle schools, and 1 high school with 5,300 students. The district had 27 buildings with an average age of 62 years, and the Abbott district building age was 61 years. Despite their age, and with the exception of a few leaky roofs, the school buildings in Elizabeth were in very good repair.

During the first 7 years of *Abbott V*, as Table 5.1 shows, the average annual per pupil expenditure in Elizabeth was $10,855, compared with $9,495 for the state. This was an average increase for Elizabeth of 14.3% over the state average.

The College Avenue School Community

Compared with other neighborhoods in Elizabeth, the College Avenue community was relatively prosperous. It was near State University and adjacent to a stable mixed working- and middle-class town with a predominantly White population. An important part of the neighborhood was a modern Orthodox

TABLE 5.1. Elizabeth Per Pupil Expenditures Compared With State Average Expenditures, 1997–1998 Through 2004–2005

	Elizabeth	State Average
1997–1998	$ 7,768	$ 7,958
1998–1999	8,385	8,194
1999–2000	12,828	8,692
2000–2001	9,901	9,236
2001–2002	10,992	9,688
2002–2003	10,992	10,273
2003–2004	13,299	10,709
2004–2005	12,681	11,215
Average	$10,855	$ 9,495

Source: New Jersey Department of Education.

Jewish community whose members observed the Sabbath and dressed distinctively but not as traditionally as Hasidic Jews.

While the Jews' impact on the local economy and culture was significant, and the houses they lived in surrounded the school, the Jewish families had no contact with Elizabeth's public schools because their children attended a Yeshiva. College Avenue's student population, which came primarily from a different neighborhood across a major street, shifted from predominantly Cuban in the 1980s to a mix of recent immigrants from Central and South America.

The College Avenue Elementary School

The College Avenue School opened in 1916. Over the years, it had several additions, the largest in 1957. Despite its age, the school was in impeccable condition with large, well-lit, comfortable classrooms. Overcrowding was the only major problem, and the Abbott school construction program planned to replace College Avenue with a larger modern facility by 2007.

Over the main entrance to the College Avenue School—as in all elementary schools in Elizabeth—a banner read, "First Cohort Whole School Reform." Other visible results of the *Abbott V* mandates included five computers in every classroom and adequate supplies and instructional materials.

In 2003–2004, almost 60% of College Avenue's students reported that Spanish was the primary language spoken at home. Fifteen percent of the students were African American, and the few White students were refugees from Bosnia and Herzegovina. The student mobility rate for 2001 through 2004 was 21%, whereas the state mobility rate for the same period was 13%. In 2003, 65% of students attending College Avenue received free or reduced-price lunch.

Except for an African American music teacher and three Latina teachers, the 45 administrators, teachers, and aides in the school were White. Most schools in Elizabeth had similar teacher demographic characteristics and did not reflect the racial and ethnic composition of particular students or communities.

College Avenue Before *Abbott V*

Before the *Abbott V* mandates, College Avenue was among the highest achieving elementary schools in Elizabeth. Residents of the largely Cuban neighborhood that its student body came from, which was across the street from the Jewish community, viewed Elizabeth as a transitional step to suburbia. With faith in the social mobility opportunities provided by education and hard work, many families succeeded in moving to nearby mixed working- and middle-class suburbs. By the mid-1980s, students from most countries in Central and South America had replaced the Cubans. With the change in student population, College Avenue's test scores declined to slightly above average for Elizabeth's elementary schools.

The school had a traditional administrative structure, curriculum, and classroom organization. According to the principal, "I tried to create a loving environment for the kids." With a display of every gift from College Avenue's students during his 20 years as principal, his comfortable office symbolized his administrative style. The principal's accessible, warm leadership earned respect among parents and loyalty from the teachers.

College Avenue and *Abbott V*, Year 1—1998–1999

Selecting a Whole School Reform Model

As in the Bridge Street School, the faculty felt they had insufficient information for selecting a Whole School Reform (WSR) model. They also felt pressured by the principal to select the Community for Learning/Adaptive Learning Environments Model (CFL/ALEM) because he had expressed a preference for it at a faculty meeting.[1]

The principal thought that CFL/ALEM was appropriate for the school because "It tries to create a nurturing community within the school and a way to reach out to the community which is what the school needs to do to help create internal nurturing." He also observed that "CFL/ALEM is similar to what we are already doing and won't require much change." In a districtwide meeting for administrators, he learned that the expectation was that after 3 years of CFL/ALEM a school should be able to continue the reform process without assistance from Temple University.

Initially, he was not clear about the goals of *Abbott V* other than, "It is implied that the test scores should go up. There is a lot of emphasis on the

ESPA [Elementary School Proficiency Assessment]. But no one has ever mentioned a percent that they should go up."

The principal knew at the beginning of the *Abbott V* elementary implementation that he planned to retire in a few years. Reflecting a short-term view—but a realistic one under the circumstances—he frequently said that he was taking Abbott "one day at a time." Early in the change process, he delegated responsibility for managing *Abbott V* to the WSR facilitator.

Formal Training

In January 1999, the faculty trained in CFL/ALEM for a week. The plan was to implement it fully in September 1999.

The training was similar to that described in Chapter 4. It included the same video, along with written materials that presented the features of CFL/ALEM. There was also little discussion of the philosophy of CFL/ALEM and a brief presentation on multiple intelligences. As at Bridge Street, approximately 50% of the training was devoted to "make-and-take" activities for learning centers.

With a few minor exceptions, the teachers were cooperative and did not challenge the Temple University facilitators. Most questions concerned technical issues and practical details for using the program. During the first 6 months of training, there was rapid turnover of Temple personnel; teachers complained that the trainers contradicted each other.

The Approach to *Abbott V*

College Avenue's principal emphasized that the superintendent wanted to follow the *Abbott V* mandates and rules strictly, and these rules guided most of the early reform effort. When mandated class size reduction was not possible because of space constraints, the superintendent authorized the salary of a second teacher for the classroom to comply with the court order. Another rule specified that all classroom computers had to be turned on all day.

For the principal, one of the most demanding requirements of *Abbott V* was the zero-based budgeting process. Budgets were solely the responsibility of the principal. After review by the central office (but no substantial changes), budgets were sent directly to the New Jersey Department of Education, which would then negotiate with the principal. Thus, the budget consumed months of the principal's attention.

CFL/ALEM in Classrooms, Year 1

Mrs. Jordan's and Ms. Jones's First Grade. Because College Avenue had no empty classrooms, to meet the court-mandated class size reduction to 21 students for the first grade, Mrs. Jordan's class had 35 students and two teachers.

In a typical lesson, the students' desks, clustered tightly in the middle of the room, faced Mrs. Jordan as she taught phonics using the chalkboard. Fifteen minutes into the lecture, the first graders fidgeted; at 20 minutes there was uncontrollable twitching.

To refocus the students, Mrs. Jordan, a teacher for 15 years, asked a question. A third of the students raised their hands; many jumped out of their seats pleading, "I know, I know!" or "Me, me, me!" If a child gave the incorrect answer, Mrs. Jordan did not comment but went to the next student until she received the correct answer.

After a half-hour lecture followed by questions, Mrs. Jordan assigned two pages from a workbook for the students to complete at their desks. Ten minutes later, she called on students to tell the class their answers. Again, if a student gave the wrong answer, she called on another until the answer was correct.

During the lecture Ms. Jones, the second teacher, observed the lesson, graded papers, roamed the class to monitor or assist students, and performed clerical tasks. Mrs. Jordan and Ms. Jones never communicated during the lesson and did not use team teaching.

There was scant evidence of CFL/ALEM in Mrs. Jordan's classroom. Although signs labeled learning centers, there was little material in the centers and students never used them. In addition, there was no attempt to vary the format of instruction—by using small groups, collaborative learning, or individualization, for example.

Mrs. Jordan was determined and explicit about her approach to teaching. A professional development day in March 1999 was a workshop by the WSR facilitator on how to individualize instruction for CFL/ALEM by creating different levels for students with different needs. During the workshop Mrs. Jordan grouped her class based on standardized test scores. However, the next week she taught the entire class without any attempt to individualize instruction. She explained that she believed that children in first grade should not be broken into ability groups because "they should be provided with an equal chance to learn."

Elaborating on her approach to teaching, Mrs. Jordan volunteered that "My friend who teaches in Chatham was amazed at how extensive the vocabulary of the children in Elizabeth is when I showed her the books they read and samples of their writing." When asked if children in Chatham—a wealthy White suburb in a nearby county—have equally extensive vocabularies, she replied, "I don't know. They use whole language there and it's hard to know. Whole language works well in the suburbs but not here. These children need phonics and more drill with vocabulary than whole language provides."

When they entered first grade none of Mrs. Jordan's and Ms. Jones's 35 students knew how to read. By March, only three were nonreaders—even though most were below grade level—and one of them was in the process of referral to a special education class.

Mr. Byram's and Ms. Vann's Fourth Grade. Mr. Byram earned a B.A. in political science from a highly regarded university in the south and became an elementary teacher through an M.S. teacher certification program at State University. The College Avenue School management team hired him in 1999 under the authority provided by the *Abbott V* elementary mandates, and the principal regarded Mr. Byram very highly.

Like Mrs. Jordan, to meet the court's student–teacher ratio requirement, in 1998–1999 Mr. Byram had a co-teacher for his class of 35 students. Ms. Vann, who had student-taught at College Avenue and graduated from State University the previous May, spent most of her time on administrative chores or roving the class helping students while Byram lectured to the entire class. Mr. Byram and Ms. Vann never used team teaching.

The only evidence of CFL/ALEM in Mr. Byram's classroom was a "Science Center" poster over a few science books arranged on a table. His teaching method was to lecture to the entire class using a loud voice—yelling as if he were a coach on an athletic field—as he moved back and forth at the chalkboard or walked around the room. He never individualized instruction and after a lecture assigned the same textbook or workbook pages to all students, had them do several examples, and then reviewed them with the entire class.

Byram used rote teaching. For example, during a multiplication lesson in which students mechanically solved problems on the chalkboard, Mr. Byram yelled, "I don't care if you don't know what you're doing. I just want you to get the right answer. That's what's important for the ESPA." Mr. Byram had participated in CFL/ALEM workshops and, when asked, demonstrated learning centers that incorporated constructivist pedagogy.

To prepare students for the writing section of the ESPA, the day before a practice test Mr. Byram worked on indentation. Although this was a problem with many students' writing, it was particularly important for the ESPA because failure to indent would lower scores. To motivate the students, Byram warned that he would dock 15 minutes of computer time for anyone who failed to indent on the practice test. He also offered rewards: "If you take your time tomorrow and write good paragraphs with a least three sentences in each, you'll get more time at the computer."

Mr. Byram genuinely cared about his students and often treated them as an audience for his sophisticated jokes. He seldom used harsh discipline and permitted a fair amount of noise before asking for quiet. In return, the students appeared to like and usually obeyed Mr. Byram.

Although Mr. Byram mentioned the ESPA as early as September and focused on preparing students for it, he was not as absorbed with the test as many of his fellow fourth-grade teachers. In January 1999, however, like all fourth-grade teachers in Elizabeth, the district ordered him to focus exclusively on ESPA preparation until the test in May. At this time, to prepare for the ESPA, the principal reallocated the music and art teachers as well as administrators to tutor students for the ESPA.

Abbott V and CFL/ALEM Implementation Throughout the School, Year 1

The administration and faculty thought of College Avenue as "the last suburban school in Elizabeth." Their mission was to protect College Avenue from the encroachment of the city. Several teachers, however, felt the battle was being lost because an influx of immigrants from Central and South America had appeared to reduce parent support for education, with more students entering school unprepared.

Implementation of *Abbott V* and CFL/ALEM for most teachers meant setting aside a table or two in their classrooms for learning centers—which they seldom or never used. There was no use of prescription sheets, wait-time folders, self-scheduling, or any of the other elements of CFL/ALEM. The Temple University program was a concern only when a Temple facilitator visited the school.

The major change created by *Abbott V* in its first year at College Avenue was not restructuring classrooms, but teaching to the test and the use of test preparation tutors.

College Avenue as a Model for CFL/ALEM

At the end of May, because the principal and the superintendent regarded College Avenue as having implemented CFL/ALEM more extensively and successfully than any other school in Elizabeth, the principal organized a visitation day for anyone interested in observing CFL/ALEM. Twenty educators from outside Elizabeth attended, including several from Newark and 10 from affluent White suburban districts who wanted to see if CFL/ALEM would benefit their schools.

The presentation involved the principal, the Whole School Reform facilitator, and a representative from Temple University. They described the program, showed the video of CFL/ALEM in action, and answered questions.

Short visits to three classrooms followed the presentation. Mrs. Jordan's class, more disorganized than usual because of her ever-fidgeting students, presented no evidence of CFL/ALEM during the visit. Another class also displayed teacher-controlled activities and minimal use of CFL/ALEM. The last classroom used learning centers that the teacher assigned for each student.

The visitors from the suburban districts were not impressed with CFL/ALEM or the classroom visits. The teachers from the urban districts, whose schools had not yet selected a Whole School Reform model because they were in the second cohort of Abbott implementation, were less judgmental but wanted to know more before making a commitment to the program.

Standardized Test Scores, Year 1

Elizabeth changed from annual administration of the California Achievement Test to the TerraNova standardized test for all grades except the fourth, which took the ESPA. The change occurred because, in the view of administrators, the TerraNova test aligned more closely with the ESPA and New Jersey's Core Content Curriculum Standards.

For the 1998–1999 ESPA, 56.8% of College Avenue's students were proficient in language arts and 58% were proficient in math.

College Avenue and *Abbott V,* Year 2—1999–2000

A New Implementation Timeline

At a faculty workshop before school started, the WSR facilitator presented a new timeline for CFL/ALEM implementation. Each teacher received the following schedule, which would produce full implementation of CFL/ALEM by the end of the year.

September 30, 1999: Teachers will have implemented:
- For all disciplines:
  - Prescriptions
  - Work Folders
  - Wait-Time Folders
  - Teacher Calls
  - Student Progress Charts
  - Learning Centers
  - Self-Scheduling Boards
  - Self-Scheduling Forms
- Leveled Prescriptions for Language Arts and Math
- Leveled Learning Centers for Language Arts and Math

December 31, 1999: Teachers will have implemented:
- Leveled Prescriptions for Science, Social Studies, and Health

April 30, 2000: Teachers will have implemented:
- Leveled Learning Centers for Science, Social Studies, and Health

At this workshop, the principal announced that the results of the ESPA: "We went up 10 points in math but the language arts section was lower."

The scores, however, were not final because the state was regrading the test because scores in all districts were low. He observed that "If they had only been low in urban districts this wouldn't happen. But the suburbs went down, too."

The principal also told the faculty that he had attended a workshop during which people from around the country presented strategies for improving test scores. Some states had improved test scores by 20% over several years by using tutors. He said this affirmed his decision to use tutors and that he would expand tutoring by reassigning more special subject teachers and structuring tutoring with pre-tests and post-tests. An important goal was to identify more accurately children in the third and fourth grades who would benefit from tutoring.

The WSR facilitator discussed the use of test scores to identify each student as having achieved mastery, partial mastery, or nonmastery. The purpose of this discussion was to use test scores for diagnostic purposes, and not to locate students who were unlikely to improve and others who could pass with extra help. The facilitator commented on this possibility and said, "This would be triage, and it is not the policy of Elizabeth." The principal then said, "We are going to tutor different kids each month and the focus will be the CCCS. We are not going to label certain kids as needing a permanent tutor."

Another issue discussed at the workshop was the use of the Core Curriculum Content Standards. The WSR facilitator had attended a meeting of the Board and a "strong suggestion" from an assistant superintendent was "to focus tightly on the limited objectives of the CCCS."

Toward the end of the meeting, the WSR facilitator said, "One criticism is that we are 'teaching to the test.' *But they want us to teach to the test.* It's OK. The test is where we want kids to focus. 'Computation' is out as a skill and 'thinking' is in. Of course, thinking is more difficult to teach, but let's teach to the test."

The principal then observed, "The ESPA is good because it gives students something to strive to accomplish. When I was in school, I wanted to do well on the PSAT and the SAT. They provided a challenge and I felt good when I did well on them. However, I am not entirely comfortable with 'teaching to the test.' Education is broader and includes life skills as well as things measured by the ESPA."

CFL/ALEM in Classrooms, Year 2

Mrs. Jordan's and Ms. Jones's First Grade. This year Mrs. Jordan used learning centers on occasion. She directed the students to the centers because the same individuals always wanted to use the computers. She did not implement any other CFL/ALEM practice. For example, because she did not believe in it, Mrs. Jordan intentionally did not level activities. In fact, many of her lessons were below grade level—either pre-K or kindergarten level.

There was no attempt to collaborate with Ms. Jones, and the teachers continued to perform separate activities in the classroom. Basically, Mrs. Jordan's teaching style remained the same as the year before. However, teaching was more demanding because her students were the first cohort to attend kindergarten under the Board of Education mandated High/Scope kindergarten program. Her opinion was that High/Scope was "too child centered" and did not prepare students either socially or intellectually for first grade.[2]

Mr. Byram's and Ms. Vann's Fourth Grade. Mr. Byram's and Ms. Vann's classroom also did not change significantly. Byram and Vann occasionally divided the class in two, which Byram referred to as "our style of CFL." They both taught the same reading lesson, using materials published by Scientific Research Associates. Byram, more than Vann, asked lower level skill questions about the reading material, such as names, dates, and places, rather than questions requiring the higher level critical thinking skills that the ESPA measured.

This year, for math, three ability groups rotated among the fourth-grade teachers for instruction. Other than this, Byram, Vann, and the other fourth-grade teachers made no effort to individualize or level instruction according to CFL/ALEM practices. For all other subjects, including infrequent science lessons, Mr. Byram lectured the entire class. In fact, most of Byram's teaching—Ms. Vann taught less than Byram and spent most of her time on clerical tasks—from the beginning of school prepared the class for the ESPA.

At the end of the year, Ms. Vann requested a transfer to another, "more creative" classroom for the following year. In 2000–2001 she taught third grade.

Abbott V and CFL/ALEM Implementation Throughout the School, Year 2

The major impact of *Abbott V* on the College Avenue School was preparation of the zero-based budget. Because of a change in software supplied by the New Jersey Department of Education, the budgeting process was not any smoother the second year than it had been the first, and it was not finished until mid-November.

Most teachers put the various signs and charts that CFL/ALEM required in their rooms but did not use its techniques. When they did use learning centers, it was for one class period per day, not throughout the day, and usually only one day each week.

The WSR facilitator said, "I love CFL because it is an instructional model that does not dictate what teachers have to do. Teachers are free to use their judgment concerning curriculum and time. For example, if an objective takes an hour to teach they can use an hour. Similarly, if it takes only 15 minutes, that's what they use."

The principal observed that "CFL is pretty well implemented throughout the school. I think that it has improved the collegiality of the faculty. I also think that the skills taught through CFL and the ESPA are life-long skills."

At CFL/ALEM workshops, teachers always behaved as though they either had or would implement it. But, when the principal left the room, the teachers complained bitterly about Temple University, the CFL/ALEM trainers, and the district for insisting that they use it.

The most vocal criticism was for CFL/ALEM in general. Teachers said that it was "nothing new" because they had used learning centers for years prior to CFL/ALEM and tried to individualize instruction as much as possible. They all agreed that student self-scheduling and self-selecting of learning centers were unrealistic. One asked and answered, "What would the scores on the TerraNova and the ESPA look like if we let them do that? They would be a disaster."

Another factor that affected implementation of CFL/ALEM at College Avenue was the announcement in February by the principal that he would retire in June 2000. Most teachers assumed that a new principal would want to do things differently. As a result, most calculated that investing time and effort in CFL/ALEM was not a good bet.

Monitoring CFL/ALEM

In addition to the Temple University and school WSR facilitators visiting classrooms, a person from the Elizabeth central office performed a district implementation check several times each year. Beginning in February 2000, through an informal arrangement, the teachers notified each other of the inspector's presence by having a student go from room to room with the message, "Mrs. Cardy lost her keys. Can you give her a ride home?" If they had enough time, teachers changed their lessons to make it appear they were using CFL/ALEM.

Standardized Test Scores, Year 2

The ESPA language arts scores for 1999–2000 were 61.9% proficient, and the math score was 71.5% proficient. These scores were considerably higher than those the year before. The principal had difficulty explaining why the test scores had increased. It was not clear to him what effects to attribute to CFL/ALEM, test preparation, or increased tutoring. He also thought that scoring problems affected the results.

College Avenue and *Abbott V*, Year 3—2000–2001

A New Principal

From a Board of Education approved list of three candidates, the school management team selected a new principal, who began work in August 2000. He was different from his predecessor in many ways. He had a Ph.D. in English Literature, had taught at a university, and had worked as an elementary classroom teacher and administrator—but never as a principal—in Newark and another Abbott district. Interpersonally, compared with his predecessor, he was much less outgoing and warm and presented himself as a somewhat aloof professional.

Although he understood that College Avenue was, by Elizabeth's standards, a successful school, his intention was to use *Abbott V* to create significant change. He viewed the court's mandates positively, because "They took pressure off local educators who often found themselves wrongfully accused of pushing their favorite reform agenda."

As of December 2000, however, aside from the symbolic change of transforming the principal's office from a cozy den to a corporate office, and improvements to the teachers' lounge, there was little evidence of change in the school. However, some teachers detected a change in the culture of the school but could not specify what it was.

Redefining CFL/ALEM—Individualization

In January, after observing all classrooms, the principal decided that a gradual approach to change would be most effective. He viewed CFL/ALEM as an appropriate program for College Avenue, "because it built on what they were doing and fit well with the school," but he had no interest in implementing its components. Instead, he redefined the objective of reform as increasing individualization of instruction and CFL/ALEM as one method to achieve it; any attempt to address the specific needs of a student was evidence of reform and implementation of CFL/ALEM.

The principal wanted to improve ESPA scores and was aware that identifying students with scores that were near passing and tutoring them intensively would be a successful strategy. But he rejected triage and continued the tutoring program developed by his predecessor. He was also concerned that the ESPA could become the sole focus of the school.

To align Elizabeth's curriculum with the CCCS, the Board of Education introduced Everyday Math, a constructivist approach to math, into several elementary schools, including College Avenue. At the same time, the Board mandated use of the Open Court reading series.[3] The principal had no objections to either program and, to increase their use, had all other math and reading books removed from classrooms.

CFL/ALEM in Classrooms, Year 3

Mrs. Jordan's First Grade. The principal ended team teaching. He recognized that the second teacher functioned primarily as a clerk and that eliminating teams would significantly cut the budget. However, with Board approval, this increased the student–teacher ratio above the *Abbott V* mandates.

The absence of a second teacher in Mrs. Jordan's class meant that she had to devote more time to grading papers and clerical tasks. It did not affect instruction because team teaching had never occurred and, despite the principal's preference for individualization, Mrs. Jordan continued to lecture to the entire class.

Mr. Byram's Fourth Grade. Mr. Byram felt the new principal was entirely different than his predecessor and worried about what his plans were for the school. As of December 2000, however, except for putting a daily schedule of lessons on the chalkboard, which the principal insisted that all teachers do, there were no changes in Mr. Byram's teaching.

He sensed that a phasing out of CFL/ALEM was under way because of what he regarded as the redefinition of what a learning center was and the expansion of the meaning of individualization. He observed that "The way the new principal sees a center creates more freedom for the teachers. A workbook page is now considered a learning center." He speculated that CFL/ALEM would end by the start of the next school year. Mr. Byram predicted that "The ESPA will be history next year, too."

Abbott V and CFL/ALEM Implementation Throughout the School, Year 3

Implementation of Everyday Math and Open Court was a major issue, and teachers attended training for both programs. The faculty welcomed the principal's interpretation of CFL/ALEM as a mechanism for increasing individualization of instruction. The result was that few teachers used any element of CFL/ALEM and felt no pressure to do so. Although only a few were performing individualized instruction, most intended to implement it soon.

Standardized Test Scores, Year 3

The 2000–2001 ESPA score in language arts was 74.1% proficient and in math 65.9% proficient. The language arts score increased 12 percentage points, whereas the math score decreased almost 6 percentage points from the previous year.

College Avenue and *Abbott V*, Year 4—2001–2002

The principal's major goals were to reorganize the schedule to provide more preparation time for teachers and to find additional ways to support them. During the year, he observed classrooms and taught literacy in every grade level, to demonstrate effective teaching.

He also discovered that the central office was not helpful, because "There aren't a lot of people there who know what's going on in the schools." He maintained positive relationships with the superintendent but lowered his expectations for support and buffered the school from what he considered the harmful interference of the central office.

CFL/ALEM in Classrooms, Year 4

Mrs. Jordan's First Grade. The new policy for CFL/ALEM was to permit more flexibility concerning whether to use learning centers, self-scheduling, or wait-time folders. The Temple University trainer, who visited Mrs. Jordan's class a few times during the year, accepted the redefinition of individualization.

Still, Mrs. Jordan's approach to teaching did not change; she continued to lecture the entire class. As before, there was little, if any, evidence of CFL/ALEM in her classroom and she no longer used learning centers.

To prepare students early in their schooling for standardized tests, for the first time, the board decided to administer the TerraNova test to the first grade. In response, Mrs. Jordan devoted time to prepare the students with test-taking skills such as filling in answer bubbles.

Mr. Byram's Fourth Grade. To Mr. Byram's relief, the new principal was "very laid back" and he no longer worried about his intentions. One important change was that the central office had developed computerized self-teaching materials for ESPA preparation. This further reduced Byram's teaching of other subjects and eliminated concern with the CCCS.

The students, who regarded Mr. Byram as a somewhat unpredictable friend or uncle—he was interpersonally approachable, though at times he could exercise impersonal authority—did not overtly object to the hours of computer-based test preparation. Although many had computers at home, using a computer in school was still a novelty.

Abbott V and CFL/ALEM Implementation Throughout the School, Year 4

The policy of individualization coupled with flexibility eliminated all conventional implementation of CFL/ALEM. Teachers could now do anything if it conformed to the broad definition of individualization of instruction.

Standardized Test Scores, Year 4

On the 2001–2002 ESPA, the language arts score was 69.4% proficient. Only 52.1% were proficient in math, which was a drop from 65.9% proficient the previous year and the second straight decrease in math scores.

College Avenue and *Abbott V*, Year 5/ NCLB, Year 1—2002–2003

Abbott Phase II

Several major changes occurred in 2002–2003. First, the state discontinued zero-based budgeting, and the central office prepared a budget that the school had to accept. This was a response to a $7 billion state budget deficit and the unwieldiness of the school budgeting process. Second, Abbott Phase II shifted from the Whole School Reform model as a change strategy to standards-driven reform that focused on the Core Content Curriculum Standards.

The most important change for College Avenue was that the principal concluded that no teachers had ever implemented CFL/ALEM and that "Very little change has occurred because of Whole School Reform." Based on this conclusion, he continued to focus on implementing Everyday Math and Open Court, as well as individualization of instruction and test preparation.

NCLB, Year 1

Although the expectation of the Bush Administration was that implementation of NCLB in 2002 would create significant change, it had little effect on the College Avenue School. Instead of implementing the *Abbott V* mandates, the first principal, through the tutoring and test preparation programs, had inadvertently anticipated a means, if not a school reform, to satisfy the basic standardized test requirements of NCLB. In addition, the ESPA test scores at College Avenue were comparatively high, and the faculty was not concerned with NCLB sanctions. The principal, however, wanted to improve test scores to guard against penalties from NCLB.

CFL/ALEM in Classrooms, Year 5

Mrs. Jordan's and Mr. Byram's Classrooms. Mrs. Jordan's and Mr. Byram's classrooms did not change except for "intensification" of test preparation in the fourth grade. This consisted of more time spent on decontextualized drill and computer-based practice tests during class. For students who volunteered, the Board of Education offered after-school test preparation.

Abbott V, CFL/ALEM, and NCLB Implementation Throughout the School, Year 5

More teachers became skeptical of *Abbott V*. They were aware that Governor-Elect McGreevey was rethinking Abbott and hoped he would abandon it or develop a program that would fit the needs of their school. The result was even less interest in reform, because the expectation was that whatever had already changed—which was not much—would probably change again the next year.

Standardized Test Scores, Year 5

Although, as in previous years, the precise cause of the scores remained mysterious, because of the low math score the year before, math preparation had become the focus of preparation for the NJASK. The strategy paid off. While the 2002–2003 language arts score improved modestly to 73.1% proficient, the math score of 72.2% proficient was a 20% increase over the previous year. As a result, College Avenue achieved Adequate Yearly Progress under NCLB. The improvement in test scores at College Avenue was unusual because this was the first year of the NJASK, a revision of the ESPA, and many schools either scored the same as the year before or experienced significant decreases.

College Avenue and *Abbott V*, Year 6/ NCLB, Year 2—2003–2004

The Principal Reflects

The principal viewed Whole School Reform and CFL/ALEM as having never been implemented, no longer supported by the state, and, in effect, terminated. In his view,

> The pendulum swings in education and in the state. The pendulum has now swung to a position that is pre–Whole School Reform. In fact, the state created a lot of confusion. But the positive part of WSR is that over the past few years it drew attention to the issues of urban education and made the districts, schools, and teachers examine what they are doing. To some extent, the attention given to the problems created some level of change and improvement.

In his opinion, NCLB created more change in the school than did *Abbott V*. The NJASK became the focal point for the school—particularly the fourth-grade teachers—and peer pressure created change because the teachers did not want to let the school down. The fifth grade did not experience the same pressure as the fourth, and their TerraNova scores did not improve significantly.

CFL/ALEM in Classrooms, Year 6

Mrs. Jordan's First Grade. Mrs. Jordan's classroom operated the same way as in previous years. Because most of her students learned how to read by the end of first grade—even if not at grade level—she had a reputation as a good teacher.

Mrs. Jordan observed that the population of the school was growing and changing as more students from other parts of Elizabeth enrolled illegally in College Avenue because of its high test scores. In her view, these students were not prepared to work near or on grade level.

She also noted that the school had seven reading tutors and thought that "they really made a difference." As an example, she cited a Haitian student who made significant progress with the tutors, but she observed that "If she had support from home, she wouldn't need the tutor." Finally, Mrs. Jordan liked Everyday Math. The students enjoyed using manipulatives and the individual chalkboards. The only difficulty was that assessment took considerable time.

Mr. Byram's Fourth Grade. Mr. Byram's teaching style did not change or vary, and he no longer mentioned CFL/ALEM. With the implementation of NCLB, preparation for the NJASK test intensified. This year, more frequently than before, he and the other third- and fourth-grade teachers used commercially produced computer drills and practice tests, along with paper and pencil practice tests.

Mr. Byram did not like Everyday Math. He said that "All of the fourth-grade teachers I know use it selectively. Most supplement it with NJASK drill books. Chicago math teaches kids four ways to do division. We're lucky if they can learn one way. Come on, you have to be realistic."

Mr. Byram completed an administrator's certificate program at State University and began to look for an assistant principal position in either Elizabeth or suburban districts in northern New Jersey. By May Mr. Byram had several job prospects, and in fall 2004 he became an elementary school vice principal in a suburban district.

Abbott V, CFL/ALEM, and NCLB Implementation Throughout the School, Year 6

CFL/ALEM was still "in the air" but not used in any meaningful way in the school. Its transformation into the idea of individualization was complete. However, as in previous years, most teachers used traditional lectures and ability groups for reading and math.

Standardized Test Scores, Year 6

Scores for the 2003–2004 NJASK in language arts increased almost 12%, to 82.8% proficient and an additional 2.0% advanced, for a total 84.8% passing. Math scores were 14.1% proficient and 77.8% advanced—91.9% passing—just under 20% better than the previous year. The College Avenue School achieved Adequate Yearly Progress for the second consecutive year. Mr. Byram observed that "We did as good on the NJASK as many suburban schools."

The Principal Leaves

Because he was concerned with restricting his career opportunities if he worked exclusively in Abbott districts, the principal accepted the position of superintendent/principal in a small town in the western part of New Jersey. He started work in July 2004.

College Avenue and *Abbott V*, Year 7/ NCLB, Year 3—2004–2005

The Third Principal

In the 2004–2005 school year, two Latinas became the principal and vice principal of College Avenue. Because the school had achieved AYP for 2 consecutive years and the central administration regarded it as a success story, the new principal continued the policies of her predecessor.

She was aware that the school did not implement CFL/ALEM. Because of this, she planned to become familiar with the teachers before deciding what role, if any, CFL/ALEM would play. Her immediate focus was to improve the use of Everyday Math and to continue the tutoring and test preparation programs.

Another change was that centralized decision making by the Board of Education increased. In addition to selecting instructional programs and textbooks, the Board now issued directives for every teacher, such as to put a list of spelling words on classroom walls, and to post a parent-friendly weekly schedule in each room and send it home.

CFL/ALEM in Classrooms, Year 7

Mrs. Jordan's First Grade. Mrs. Jordan's class remained the same as it had from the beginning of *Abbott V.* Of course, each year the individual issues children presented differed, and Mrs. Jordan had more discipline problems than usual. Although she continued to enjoy teaching, she also started to think about retiring in a few years.

Abbott V, CFL/ALEM, and NCLB Implementation Throughout the School, Year 7

Although awareness of *Abbott V* remained, there was no attempt to implement any components of CFL/ALEM. The major concerns were test preparation and using Everyday Math and Open Court reading.

Standardized Test Scores, Year 7

Standardized test scores for language arts in 2004–2005 were 76.9% proficient plus 5.8% advanced, for a total of 82.7% passing. In math 42.3% were proficient and 44.1% were advanced, for a combined 86.4% passing. Initially, College Avenue was on the NCLB "early warning" list because of higher passing standards. After an appeal, however, it made AYP again.

Analysis of the College Avenue School

Legitimacy and the Eco-Cognitive Framework

Compared with other schools in Elizabeth, prior to *Abbott V* College Avenue performed well on standardized tests, and the faculty interpreted the scores as good enough not to require major changes. The Supreme Court mandate, particularly the Whole School Reform model, was regarded as not legitimate because it was not needed.

The major reason for the nonimplementation of the *Abbott V* elementary reforms, however, was that the first principal agreed with the assessment that changes were unnecessary. Under pressure to introduce and manage change to improve test results, his agenda became to *appear* to obey the *Abbott V* mandates but not to implement them. Responding to external pressure, he decided to improve student test performance and instituted changes to raise standardized test scores.

Underlying this response was that the eco-cognitive framework *created invidious distinctions*. The idea that College Avenue was "the last suburban school in Elizabeth" separated it from the rest of the city by defining other neighborhoods and schools negatively. This further reduced administrators' and teachers' ability to identify with *Abbott V*; in their view, it targeted schools in more distressed neighborhoods than the one College Avenue served. In fact, the demographic profile of College Avenue students was the same as that of other students in Elizabeth.

Similarly, Mrs. Jordan's acceptance of the appropriateness of suburban students learning to read with whole language and her students' need for phonics was an invidious distinction.[4] Mr. Byram frequently attributed inferior intellectual capacity to his students, relative to suburban students, and accepted that rote learning was the most effective way to teach them.

Ironically, despite the differentiation of students on the basis of the eco-cognitive framework, because the school was in a comparatively prosperous neighborhood the faculty thought that College Avenue students should strive for high achievement. A way to attain this goal, along with avoiding criticism for not implementing CFL/ALEM and achieving Adequate Yearly Progress, was to turn the school into a test preparation center.

Changes in Classrooms

Resistance to *Abbott V* was not organized and explicit but was part of the school's culture. Teachers did not resist the change efforts of the first principal, but willingly participated in his subtly communicated plan not to implement the reforms.

The redefinition by the second principal of reform as "individualization" eliminated any incentive to implement CFL/ALEM. Instead of exerting leadership, even after he correctly deciphered the school's recent history, he acquiesced to the culture of passive resistance and reinforced the view that change was not necessary. But fundamental change did occur in all classrooms—in the shift to year-long test preparation.

A Typology of College Avenue Teachers

Although most College Avenue teachers used passive resistance to avoid the *Abbott V* mandates, Mrs. Jordan demonstrated *overt active resistance* to change. Her belief that inner-city children needed a different type of education than suburban children let her disregard the changes. On specific occasions, her resistance was covert because she actively engaged in training for change but did not implement it.

Most students in Mrs. Jordan's class learned how to read by the end of first grade, but not at grade level. They also learned that school involved long lectures that were not responsive to their developmental stage. They learned very little about individual decision making, responsibility, or collaboration.

Mr. Byram used *covert passive resistance* to avoid CFL/ALEM. He never vocally opposed it, but pretended that *Abbott V* did not exist. The leadership style of the first two principals made this a successful tactic.

Students in Mr. Byram's class learned that school was about preparation for an important test in the distant future. In fact, most of Mr. Byram's instruction was not even teaching to the test but rather tutoring and practicing for the test.

Changes in the School

The characterization of College Avenue as having engaged in "the normal appearance of change" refers to the construction of what, on the surface, looked like adherence to *Abbott V.* Considerable activity was devoted to *Abbott V* and CFL/ALEM, but it was invariably rhetoric instead of action.

At the same time, however, at the beginning of the change process, the first principal found a solution for the external demands for improved education by preparing students for standardized tests. By the time NCLB arrived, the school was proficient in test preparation and, under pressure from the central office, devoted even more resources for it. The comparatively high scores and achievement of Adequate Yearly Progress reinforced the correctness of the test preparation regimen.

The second principal accurately observed that "NCLB created more change in the school than did *Abbott V.*" However, the adoption of the test preparation strategy was a response to external demands for improvement in the absence of an understanding of either what would be an appropriate change or how to manage such a change.

The eco-cognitive framework legitimated the expedient approach to reform and reproduced the type of education suitable for students who could only learn through rote teaching. The focus of NCLB fit the predispositions of the administrators and faculty and reinforced their understanding of the social class and economic requirements of urban education. Ultimately, the changes created more teacher control over students, not the student responsibility for their own behavior that CFL/ALEM envisioned.

Conclusions

Externally triggered change promoted skepticism and resistance among the administration and teachers. The change process became an exercise in satisfying external demands for change. Yet the change initiated by the first principal to focus on standardized tests was a punctuation that altered the deep structure and created revolutionary change. However, the eco-cognitive framework remained intact, because extensive preparation for tests was part of the framework that teachers and administrators considered an appropriate education for poor minority urban students.[5]

A significant outcome of the reform attempts is that the school did not develop a capacity to change. Instead, most teachers learned that passive compliance with the principal reduced and subverted the leadership skills necessary to articulate a new vision of education and the ability to execute it.

In addition, the changes legitimated control by the federal government over local education. This happened even though the administration and faculty had successfully resisted the New Jersey Supreme Court's attempt to control their school. It is possible that this sequence of events set a precedent that only external coercive change would be effective in the future.

In summary, College Avenue experienced a revolutionary change despite trying to avoid change. Instead of implementing *Abbott V* mandates, the school changed by systematically redirecting most efforts to test preparation instead of basic education. NCLB contributed to this shift by focusing on accountability. The change did not improve the educational opportunities for the Latino and African American children who attended College Avenue but instead narrowed their academic preparation.

The Change Cycle: Ending and Beginning

In May 2005, because of a perceived failure of leadership, the Elizabeth Board of Education appointed a new superintendent. It became uncertain what elementary instruction would consist of for 2005–2006. Chapter 7 describes the changes that affected all public elementary schools in Elizabeth.

CHAPTER 6

The Church Street School

Immediate Sustained Rigid Change

The Church Street School Community

The main business district of this Elizabeth neighborhood is across the street from the Church Street School. Most of the stores have signs in Spanish, and travel agencies, phone call centers, and check cashing services cater to the Latino population. Directly across the street from the school an employment agency with a sign reading "Agencia de Trabajos—Trabajo Inmediato" (Employment Agency—Immediate Work) specializes in finding legal and illegal Latino workers temporary jobs in nearby factories and warehouses, including Liz Claiborne, Petco, and Barnes & Noble. From the school windows, at 8:00 a.m. and 3:00 p.m. workers can be seen queuing and hurriedly boarding vans for short-term low-paid work.

Residents of the community view this type of work with disdain and prefer to find more secure, higher paying work in local factories, warehouses, and retail stores. Although regular work for illegal immigrants is often difficult to find and legal residents are periodically unemployed, because Elizabeth and nearby towns have many large warehousing operations, manual labor jobs are relatively plentiful, along with seasonal work in construction and landscaping.

In general, the economy of the Church Street School neighborhood—which had a 2000 median family income of $34,000—remains fragile, despite benefiting from the recent surge of inexpensive imports and the creation of jobs at the nearby port (Fishman, 2005; Kogut, 2003; Sassen, 1991). Globalization could marginalize unskilled workers further, with negative consequences for the local economy.

The houses in the neighborhood are modest and well kept, with small gardens in the front yards. Narrow alleyways separate the houses, many of which have either tarpaper or aluminum siding. There are no vacant lots or abandoned buildings, and signs of growth appear occasionally, such as several two-family houses built recently and other houses undergoing remodeling.

The Church Street School

The principal of the Church Street School emigrated from Guatemala to the Church Street neighborhood when she was 11 years old. She often pointed out that she was the only faculty member who still lived in the community, observing that "Even those who grew up and were educated in Elizabeth have left for the suburbs."

As a student in Elizabeth, she experienced tension between the Latinos and African Americans and, according to her, the conflict between them never ended. In fact, throughout the school year she received telephone calls from Latino parents who requested transfers to the Church Street School after discovering that they had inadvertently moved to a neighborhood where their children had to attend a school with too many African American students. Although it was against Board of Education policy, she usually tried to facilitate a transfer.

The principal, who had earned her undergraduate degree and several Master's degrees and professional certificates from State University, spent her entire professional career in Elizabeth schools as a teacher of English as a second language (ESL), a guidance counselor, and in various administrative positions. Church Street was her first position as principal.

Church Street Before *Abbott V*

Until 1997, the Church Street School was a Catholic elementary school. Instead of closing it because of declining enrollment, the Archdiocese sold it to the Elizabeth Board of Education. Church Street opened as a public school in September 1997, with 200 students.

All of the teachers in the new school transferred from within Elizabeth. They had a common socialization into the Elizabeth school system, but because the school was new, a distinctive organizational culture had not developed before *Abbott V.*

Early in the first year of Church Street, after careful research, the principal and faculty selected texts appropriate for their students and formulated what they considered to be an innovative program. However, because it was before *Abbott V,* which a year later provided funds for new books, they selected instructional materials from the Elizabeth resource base, which in some cases was several editions out of date.

The Church Street Student Population

In September 2000, a large addition opened. It had no innovative architectural features to facilitate educational programs but did provide 10 large classrooms and a spacious, well-stocked library. That fall, 200 sixth-, seventh-, and eighth-grade students transferred from nearby overcrowded schools. The addition also relieved overcrowding in the elementary grades, which permitted the reduced class size mandated by *Abbott V.*

Ninety-three percent of the 400 K–8 students in the Church Street School were the children of recent immigrants from Central and South America, with the largest percentage from El Salvador. Most of their parents were agricultural workers who came to the United States to improve their economic opportunities. There were very few African American students in the school. Seventy-five percent of the students were eligible for free or reduced-price lunch. The student mobility rate was 26%, compared with 13% for the state, and 27% had limited English proficiency.

In 2003–2004, of the 42 faculty 6 were Latina, 2 were Latino, none were African American, and the majority were from various White ethnic groups. The vice principal was a male of Italian descent, and the aides, security, and other ancillary workers were Latino.

Church Street and *Abbott V,* Year 1—1998–1999

Selecting a Whole School Reform Model

Many teachers who transferred to Church Street when it opened had come from schools that used Success for All (SFA). In fact, most teachers transferred to Church Street because their experience with SFA was negative—it was scripted and rigid, and it did not produce higher standardized test scores.

The principal thought that all of the court-approved Whole School Reform (WSR) models were irrelevant for Church Street. In her view, instead of implementing a WSR model, it would have been preferable to involve parents more in their children's education and to help the community cope with the issues of being immigrants. In fact, the principal received a $3,000 grant for parent training and started a community-based program with the school social worker.

She also thought that the WSR programs mandated by *Abbott V* were too expensive. She cited as an example that to use the Community for Learning/ Adaptive Learning Environments Model (CFL/ALEM), Church Street had to spend $8,000 for travel expenses for Temple University trainers and $38,000 on materials during the first year.

Despite the principal's concerns, as required by *Abbott V,* the faculty voted to implement CFL/ALEM, primarily as a reaction to negative experiences with Success for All. There was no strong belief among the administrators or faculty that CFL/ALEM would significantly change the school. But it met the requirement of *Abbott V* and appeared to be an acceptable program.

Training in CFL/ALEM

In late August and early September 1998, the Church Street faculty trained in CFL/ALEM. However, because of overbooking of the Temple University facilitators, CFL/ALEM implementation did not start until November 1998.

An important difference in the formal training session conducted at Church Street, relative to those at the other three schools, was that the WSR facilitator emphasized at Church Street that teachers had to comply with *Abbott V* because "*It is the law.*" Although there was little discussion about what it meant to obey or disobey a court order, the teachers appeared to accept that their control over the reforms was limited.

Although the principal wanted to improve standardized test scores, she did not attempt to manage the emerging elements of the school to form a culture of change. Instead, her skepticism that CFL/ALEM could improve student achievement led her to put compliant and effective teachers in the fourth grade to boost student performance.

CFL/ALEM in Classrooms, Year 1

Mrs. Martin's First Grade. One of two first-grade teachers at Church Street, Mrs. Martin, who had taught in Elizabeth for 7 years, was an enthusiastic person who clearly liked children and teaching.[1] Her Master's thesis at State University, where she also earned an undergraduate degree, was on how CFL/ALEM worked for children with special needs. She was married shortly before she began teaching at Church Street and relocated from Elizabeth, where she went to high school, to an upper middle-class suburb near the Jersey shore.

Mrs. Martin used CFL/ALEM learning centers, and she assigned students to rotate to each one once every day. Although it took considerable time for her to settle the students into each learning center because they asked many questions about the new activities, she did it without excessive effort to control students' behavior. With students at three or four learning centers, the class often became noisy, but Mrs. Martin endured the minor chaos. After 20 minutes, the students rotated to the next learning center and the question and noise cycle resumed.

Her attitude toward CFL/ALEM was, "I'm done with training for CFL. It was a lot of time and effort to change and I learned everything there is to know—and I do it." In fact, she was one of the few teachers in the school who used features of CFL/ALEM such as teacher call cards and wait-time folders. However, she never used self-scheduling, self-selection, or peer learning and only used CFL/ALEM for an hour each day instead of throughout the day.

Of the 21 students who entered Mrs. Martin's class, only three had reading skills. Mrs. Martin, like many of the teachers in Elizabeth, blamed the pre-K High/Scope program for the low number of readers. She estimated that by the end of the year 60% would be reading. As it turned out, by June all but three students—two of whom Mrs. Martin identified as candidates for special education—were able to read, but only about half were at grade level.

Mrs. O'Dell's First Grade. In 1998–1999, Mrs. O'Dell's first grade, which was directly across the hall from Mrs. Martin's room, was a bilingual classroom. Mrs. O'Dell, who had taught for 5 years in a middle school in Elizabeth prior to her arrival at Church Street, was a graduate of State University and life-long resident of Elizabeth until 1996, when she married and moved to a nearby suburb.

To implement CFL/ALEM she used learning centers each morning for reading instruction. For 90 minutes, students rotated among four learning centers that had activities such as workbook pages on phonics, listening tasks, and computer-based lessons. Another center was a reading group in which Mrs. O'Dell worked with a group of five or six children. The students used teacher call cards, but Mrs. O'Dell was usually too busy with the reading group to acknowledge them. When they were finished with an assignment, students used wait-time folders.

Each time students rotated among the learning centers Mrs. O'Dell spent a great amount of time scolding to control them. In fact, the 20-minute rotations seldom went smoothly. For example, computer problems—which occurred every day—ranged from students using the wrong program to Mrs. O'Dell rebooting the computer. By the time she returned to the reading group, only 10 minutes remained for instruction.

Mrs. O'Dell did not attempt to have students self-select learning centers or self-schedule their time. She exercised tight control over all student activities. Consequently, the rotation among learning centers, instead of reducing teacher control, increased it. Similar in function to seat work, the learning centers occupied students who were not working with Mrs. O'Dell in the reading group.

In the five reading groups, Mrs. O'Dell emphasized phonics (e.g., "When a vowel makes a long sound what does it do? It says its name.") had students read orally individually and collectively, and asked factual questions about the story. Although the class was bilingual, all instruction was in English and students never spoke Spanish.

Like Mrs. Martin, whom she often consulted, Mrs. O'Dell expected 60% of her students to be reading by the end of the year.

Ms. Fadora's Fourth Grade. Church Street was Ms. Fadora's first teaching job after graduating from a small private liberal arts college. When she student-taught in a suburban school, Ms. Fadora used a variety of teaching methods, including learning centers and constructivist techniques that, according to her, "are not as useful in this school because the kids here need more concentration on basic skills." Ms. Fadora also noted that "When I was student teaching I never had to raise my voice. I try not to raise my voice with these kids but sometimes I have to."

As a new teacher, Ms. Fadora was concerned about meeting the expectations of the principal and other faculty. Adding to the pressure she felt as a novice, fourth grade had become more important and more stressful than other elementary grades because of the emphasis on the Elementary School Proficiency Assessment (ESPA).

Ms. Fadora reserved time for CFL/ALEM after lunch 3 days each week. She told students, who sat in clusters of four desks, which learning centers to go to and had them rotate among them after 20 minutes. She did not permit talking above a whisper and, if the class became too noisy, she stopped all activities until the students were silent. Because of her soft voice she seldom yelled but instead clapped three times to get the students' attention. On occasion, to establish order, she threatened to keep a student after class or dock the entire class from gym or another special activity.

Ms. Fadora attended several workshops on preparing her students for the ESPA. According to her, "They emphasized ways of teaching that were appropriate for the test but did not tell us to 'teach to the test.'" During the year, Ms. Fadora increasingly used commercially prepared test preparation books and practice tests provided by the central office. Although she felt pressured by the ESPA—"A lot of emphasis is put on the ESPA in this school . . . the principal *really* stresses it"—she tried to maintain a balance between test preparation and the standard curriculum. Even when preparing for the ESPA, instead of using rote teaching, Ms. Fadora asked students to explain their answers. However, as the ESPA approached, in response to pressure from the principal and central office, she spent more time on decontextualized test preparation and used rote teaching methods.

In a typical lesson, Ms. Fadora had six students sit on a rug at the front of the room for reading instruction. She would read a section of a story from an anthology aloud and then ask students to read sections. Because by fourth grade the expectation was that students were able to read, Ms. Fadora did not conduct formal lessons in the mechanics of reading.

However, because for many students' English was either a second language or not the primary language spoken at home, more than half of the students read phonetically. Instead of letting them struggle to pronounce a word, or teach phonics, Ms. Fadora immediately corrected them. When she asked a question about the story—usually names and places or what a character did—these students were unable to answer; their fragmented phonetic oral reading made comprehension impossible.

While Ms. Fadora taught a reading or math group at the front of the room, the other students worked on assignments at their desks or on computers. She never had more than three groups at once and, although one section of the room was "The Science Center" and another "The Social Studies Center," students never used them.

At least once a day, Ms. Fadora lectured the class for an hour on some topic, or alternated between lecturing and having students answer questions about a story or solve math problems at the chalkboard. At Church Street workshops, the Temple University CFL/ALEM facilitators always discouraged the use of whole class instruction.

Ms. Fadora's relationship with her students was professional. With a few exceptions, during the day she was very low-key and seldom displayed enthusiasm or disapproval.

Abbott V and CFL/ALEM Implementation Throughout the School, Year 1

The lower elementary grade teachers varied substantially in their use of CFL/ALEM, with most using it either at specific times during the day or occasionally. No teacher used CFL/ALEM throughout the day or with all of the features its developers intended.

Teachers above fourth grade used traditional departmentalization of classes. Because the eighth grade also had a state standardized test, there was considerable pressure on eighth-grade teachers to improve student performance.

The principal thought that two teachers did not perform satisfactorily and, after several discussions and classroom observations, they were not able to improve. Both received negative evaluations and took jobs in other school systems.

Standardized Test Scores, Year 1

Scores on the 1998–1999 ESPA for the Church Street School were 35% proficient in language arts and 35% proficient in math. These scores were among the lowest in Elizabeth and were difficult for the school administrators to interpret and accept as valid indicators of their students' achievement. The principal deflected immediate concern because the students who took the test had transferred to Church Street from other schools in Elizabeth. Supporting the theory that Church Street wasn't responsible for the poor performance, the second-grade students, who began their education at Church Street, performed well on the annual TerraNova achievement test.

Church Street and *Abbott V*, Year 2—1999–2000

CFL/ALEM in Classrooms, Year 2

Mrs. Martin's First Grade. Only one student had reading skills in September. By June 2000, all but two of Mrs. Martin's students were reading either at or close to grade level. Mrs. Martin viewed this as a successful year.

Throughout the year, she used the elements of CFL/ALEM that she had selected the previous year. Her classroom management skills improved significantly, reducing discipline issues during the rotation among learning centers. Usually a very positive person, Mrs. Martin complained several times during the year that she did not like to try to translate into Spanish for parents: "I don't know Spanish and they should learn English. Everybody should be required to learn English."

Mrs. O'Dell's First Grade. Mrs. O'Dell's class continued the pattern that had developed the previous year. Although she used the basic idea of learning centers, they usually served to occupy students when she worked with reading groups, and she preferred to use "direct teaching." Wait-time folders and teacher call cards were present but were used infrequently. The preparation involved with rotating among learning centers continued to require almost half of the 20 minutes allotted to each rotation.

During the year, Mrs. O'Dell did not change much but remained among the highest implementers of CFL/ALEM in the school. Like Mrs. Martin, she succeeded in teaching reading skills to most of her students.

Ms. Fadora's Fourth Grade. Because of low standardized test scores the previous year, pressure to improve ESPA scores increased. More time for decontextualized test preparation included multiple practice tests each month supplied by the central board. Unlike many of her colleagues, Ms. Fadora continued to teach thoughtfully during what the board intended to be rote test preparation.

On May 4, 2000, the first day of the ESPA, Ms. Fadora, the principal, and two special education teachers supervised the test. The principal was particularly nervous; as students worked, she paced up and down the rows of desks.[2] She reported that she was "OK" the week before, but as the test date approached, she worried, "The district expects a 10% increase over last year and they could reward or punish me by transferring me to another school that is better or worse."

Abbott V and CFL/ALEM Implementation Throughout the School, Year 2

Preparing the budget occupied the principal and the WSR facilitator until November. There were occasional workshops on various CFL/ALEM topics, and the Temple facilitator visited the school once a month to observe classes.

Most classrooms, however, did not implement CFL/ALEM or used it in a limited way. Mrs. Martin, Mrs. O'Dell, and Ms. Fadora used CFL/ALEM more than the other teachers did.

Standardized Test Scores, Year 2

The 1999–2000 ESPA scores were 20% proficient in language arts and 43.3% proficient in math. This was a 15% drop in language arts from the previous year and an increase of a little over 8% in math. The language arts scores were very disappointing to the principal and teachers.

Church Street and *Abbott V*, Year 3—2000–2001

CFL/ALEM Training

As part of a workshop immediately before school began in September 2000, the WSR facilitator observed that "As we go along, the people from Temple are modifying things. For example, they are open to changing some of the forms." Concerning the Core Curriculum Content Standards, she announced that Elizabeth's policy was to "Look at the district guides and do only those. Don't waste time on all of the state objectives in the CCCS. They won't be on the test."

CFL/ALEM in Classrooms, Year 3

Mrs. Martin's First Grade. In 2000–2001, Mrs. Martin's students entered school with more skills than the previous class had; almost all students had rudimentary reading skills. She was not certain whether the High/Scope program had adjusted to meet the needs of the specific student population or if she was lucky. But she was still critical of High/Scope: "It doesn't have enough structure and it doesn't coordinate well with CFL/ALEM, which is more structured. The transition is difficult for many kids when they find out that first grade is not play. Play as learning is OK but High/Scope emphasizes play too much." Another issue was that her class began with 17 students but by October 15, because of transfers from other schools, the class had 26 students, which "is too many kids to teach reading to effectively."

Early in the year, Mrs. Martin complained that she was increasingly uncomfortable with parents' requests that she speak Spanish in class and be more sensitive to the needs of Latino students. Concerning CFL/ALEM, Mrs. Martin said that the Temple consultant, meetings with the principal, the WSR facilitator, and observations by central office monitors, which were always very complimentary, did not help her become more effective.

Mrs. O'Dell's First Grade. In fall 2000, Mrs. O'Dell became a tutor for sixth, seventh, and eighth grades. In this position, she assisted students with low standardized test scores to understand a lesson while the teacher was teaching it in the classroom. The year before, tutoring in Elizabeth had been a student pull-out program, which meant that while students received extra help they missed regular instruction. The use of triage based on test scores refined a practice that had been in use before the emphasis shifted to preparation for standardized tests.

Ms. Fadora's Fourth Grade. Mrs. Fadora continued to use CFL/ALEM for 1 hour each afternoon. As in the previous year, the morning routine was literacy instruction for a small group working with Ms. Fadora while two other groups did seat work or used the computers for writing assignments.

Compared with other teachers, Ms. Fadora frequently used computers as instructional tools. For example, early in the year typical assignments had students transcribe handwritten essays into Microsoft Word or look up various topics with a search engine. By November, Mrs. Fadora had students using computers more creatively—for writing assignments for 20 minutes each morning. For instance, selected students either kept a journal or wrote stories on a topic that interested them.

In January 2001, the central office issued a directive that all fourth-grade teachers were to focus on the ESPA. Ms. Fadora complied, and her classroom became a test preparation center.

Abbott V and CFL/ALEM Implementation Throughout the School, Year 3

Little changed despite periodic CFL/ALEM workshops intended to create change. The workshops covered basic topics—for example, how to level a learning center—but in more depth than during the initial training.

Whenever a new teacher arrived—either at the beginning of the year or as a replacement for a teacher on maternity leave—the principal told the teacher that he or she would receive CFL/ALEM training. But training never happened and the teachers did not complain.

Standardized Test Scores, Year 3

The 2000–2001 ESPA language arts score was 75% proficient, a 55% increase over the previous year. It was not clear why this occurred and the administration and faculty, while somewhat pleased, understood that the score was not reliable. The ESPA math score was 40% proficient, and this slight decrease from the year before was within expectations.

Church Street and *Abbott V*, Year 4—2001–2002

Mrs. Martin Leaves Church Street

In September 2001, Mrs. Martin began working as a second-grade teacher in an upper middle-class suburban community. In addition to working closer to home, she was tired of dealing with the issues of parents' demands that she use more Spanish in class.

Ms. Gordono, who had previously taught fifth grade in Church Street, took over Mrs. Martin's class. The principal proposed that she delay CFL/ALEM until December, when she was accustomed to first grade. Ms. Gordono was not enthusiastic about CFL/ALEM because it was "too child centered and our students need structure." She never implemented any elements of the Whole School Reform model.

Mrs. O'Dell Becomes the WSR Facilitator

In fall 2001, when the original WSR facilitator took a job as a teacher trainer in the district office, Mrs. O'Dell became the Church Street WSR facilitator. The position of facilitator was important because her responsibilities were to train new teachers in CFL/ALEM and to support veteran teachers. In addition, the school was in its third year of implementation, and Temple University facilitators visited infrequently based on the expectation that the school, under the guidance of its facilitator, could improve implementation.

Mrs. O'Dell liked her new job and said that the principal was "committed to CFL/ALEM for the long term." She had planned to observe all teachers to evaluate their implementation of CFL/ALEM. However, the principal suggested that she "hold off until further notice."

CFL/ALEM in Classrooms, Year 4

Ms. Fadora's Fourth Grade. The major change this year in Ms. Fadora's class was that she used her selected features of CFL/ALEM throughout the day. According to her, she had implemented CFL/ALEM fully—except for self-scheduling and self-selection of learning centers, because "I can't find a way to fit it into the time frame of all of the activities during the day." Ms. Fadora seldom met with the Temple University trainers or the WSR facilitator.

Ms. Fadora felt that her use of CFL/ALEM, application of the Core Content Curriculum Standards(CCCS), devoting 45 minutes every day to test preparation, and frequent administration of ESPA practice tests provided appropriate instruction for her students. The major difficulties were that students were at different levels in the subjects studied, and most read well below grade level.

A significant change this year was the introduction of Everyday Math by the Board of Education. Mrs. Fadora was optimistic because the students enjoyed using manipulatives and the program aligned with the math section of the standardized test. She was aware that several of her previous students missed proficiency on the standardized test by only a few points. In her view, Everyday Math would probably boost test scores for this type of student.

Ms. Fadora summarized her year with the observation that "Things must be going 'OK.' I'm still a fourth-grade teacher."

Abbott V and CFL/ALEM Implementation Throughout the School, Year 4

To improve ESPA scores, the principal reassigned the other fourth-grade teacher to sixth grade and transferred a third-grade teacher to fourth grade. Instead of using CFL/ALEM, the new fourth-grade teacher focused on test preparation. In addition, in October, the school began offering after-school enrichment classes for the TerraNova, the ESPA, and the Grade Eight Proficiency Assessment.

Standardized Test Scores, Year 4

The 2001–2002 ESPA language arts score was 69.2% proficient, and the math score was 34.6% proficient. Again the language arts score, although similar to the year before, appeared to be high, and there was concern over why it was so difficult to improve the math score.

Church Street and *Abbott V*, Year 5/ NCLB, Year 1—2002–2003

CFL/ALEM in Classrooms, Year 5

Ms. Fadora's Fourth Grade. The December 10, 2002, *Elizabeth/Hillside Gazette Leader* contained an article headlined "Elizabeth Students Enjoy 'Everyday Math'" that featured Mrs. Fadora's class. After the superintendent praised the University of Chicago for developing a high-quality program, the article quoted the principal of Church Street:

> The United States Department of Education has identified this program as one of the 10 most exemplary and promising. The curriculum inspires both

> teachers and students to break through the traditional mathematics barriers and to explore math concepts that aren't usually taught at their grade levels.

She also noted that Everyday Math created a better alignment with the ESPA than the previous math curriculum and that it covered many Core Content Curriculum Standards.

Ms. Fadora remained enthusiastic but wary of Everyday Math because her students did not know "the basics." However, she used it with her version of constructivist teaching methods. As a precautionary measure, she continued extensive rote drill in math to prepare for the NJASK. She and the other fourth-grade teacher also used computer drills and practice tests to prepare for the language arts section of the NJASK.

Although she had a larger class than the previous year—a peak enrollment of 25 students—that made managing the class difficult, her assessment was that "The kids have made a lot of progress this year. I do the best I can."

At the end of the year, Mrs. Fadora received a Master's degree in counseling from a nearby Catholic university. She said the coursework had helped her understand her students better and that she eventually wanted to become a guidance counselor.

Abbott V, CFL/ALEM, and NCLB Implementation Throughout the School, Year 5

In the principal's view, Abbott Phase II, which gave the school the opportunity to change to another Whole School Reform model, was irrelevant. "Even if we wanted to change we can't because the budgets are frozen and there would be no money for training in the new program," she said. "We are staying with CFL/ALEM even though it and WSR aren't working out as they're supposed to. Test scores are not improving."

Mrs. O'Dell transferred to a position in the central office training department, and the WSR facilitator position remained vacant until September 2003. Because of teacher turnover, the reduction of Temple University visits to Church Street, and and the lack of an WSR facilitator, training in CFL/ALEM ended.

Standardized Test Scores, Year 5

This was the first year for the NJASK. In language arts 53% of the Church Street fourth-grade students scored proficient; 36% scored proficient in math. The language arts score dropped significantly from the previous year, and the math score was roughly the same.

Church Street and Abbott V, Year 6/ NCLB, Year 2—2003–2004

Church Street and NCLB

The principal observed, "All that NCLB has done is create more paperwork, more rigidity, and it holds the school and teachers accountable. All that 'accountable' means is that we have a lot of tests. The philosophy of NCLB is fantastic, but the reality is too much paperwork and rigidity."

Although all parents received notification that they could transfer their children from Church Street because it did not achieve Adequate Yearly Progress (AYP), none did. The principal observed that "There is nowhere for them to transfer because all of the schools are either overcrowded or also scored low on the test."

CFL/ALEM in Classrooms, Year 6

Ms. Fadora's Fourth Grade. Ms. Fadora became more comfortable with Everyday Math but continued to prepare students for the standardized test with drills and practice tests. This year, the central office introduced the Houghton Mifflin Open Court reading series, which focused on basic skills and used a more traditional pedagogy than did Everyday Math. Ms. Fadora thought the new reading series was acceptable and hoped it would improve literacy scores. Her opinion was that Everyday Math and Open Court were positive changes because they aligned the Elizabeth curriculum with the CCCS and the NJASK. Because of this, although she did not stop decontextualized test preparation, she felt less pressure to teach to the test.

Somewhat contradictorily, however, Ms. Fadora observed that

> NCLB is a nightmare. It doesn't take into account the individual needs and performance levels of the kids. Individual kids show progress on their own terms, but still don't meet the AYP. For example, one girl started the year reading 14 words per minute and by the time of the test read 40 words per minute but the test expects 140 words per minute. She will fail the test, but on her own terms, she is a success. I follow the district curriculum, which I think has improved, but the kids still don't do well on the tests. I don't know why.

Ms. Fadora also had reservations about CFL/ALEM. In March 2004, she visited the elementary school she had attended in a nearby upper middle-class suburb. She reported that "The kids there still sit in rows, don't do any cooperative learning or use learning centers and yet they score 95% or above on the NJASK. I really doubt that a program like CFL/ALEM matters much."

Abbott V, CFL/ALEM, and NCLB Implementation Throughout the School, Year 6

New teachers did not receive training in CFL/ALEM but were trained in Everyday Math and Open Court reading. This diminished the importance of CFL/ALEM and shifted more effort to test preparation throughout the school.

Standardized Test Scores, Year 6

On the second administration of the NJASK, the fourth-grade students scored 71% proficient in language arts and 61% proficient in math, which included 9.8% that were advanced proficient. Because of the significant gains over the previous year, the school achieved AYP.

Church Street and *Abbott V*, Year 7/ NCLB, Year 3—2004–2005

Ms. Fadora Becomes a Guidance Counselor

In September 2004, Ms. Fadora took a position in the guidance department of a nearby suburban high school.

Abbott V, CFL/ALEM, and NCLB Implementation Throughout the School, Year 7

The departure of Ms. Fadora ended the use of CFL/ALEM in classrooms. Test preparation supplanted any attempt to change teaching methods or innovate in any way.

Standardized Test Scores, Year 7

The 2004–2005 NJASK language arts score was 64.3% proficient, with 2.4% scoring advanced. The math score was 62.2% proficient, which included 13.3% scoring advanced. Because of an increase in the NCLB standards, however, Church Street did not achieve AYP and landed on the "corrective action" list. This, of course, disappointed and concerned the principal, who thought that she and the faculty had improved instruction significantly.

Analysis of the Church Street School

Legitimacy and the Eco-Cognitive Framework

The principal of Church Street viewed her mission as the socialization of immigrant students from Central and South America into American society.

This created tension with *Abbott V* because, although CFL/ALEM had a component that stressed socialization based on the concept of resiliency, it emphasized academic achievement.

Initially, many teachers viewed *Abbott V* as more legitimate than did the principal. However, the emphasis on the legal aspects of *Abbott V*, while legitimating the court mandates, resulted in rigid adherence to a selection of CFL/ALEM components—only elements congruent with teachers' understanding of their students' needs—rather than its full program. Throughout the implementation of CFL/ALEM, the principal did not actively undermine it but displayed little enthusiasm. Instead of overt organized resistance, predictable and routine organizational processes such as teacher turnover and inertia reduced its implementation.

The limited implementation of CFL/ALEM reflected the social class and particularly race distinctions that were part of the principal's worldview. She sought to protect Latino students from African American students by enforcing the geographic boundaries between them. While the eco-cognitive framework at Church Street acknowledged differences between urban and suburban students, on occasion it focused more on the differences between Latino and African American students.

Although the principal did not articulate what she considered the appropriate educational program for Latino students—other than nurturing and protecting—she rejected CFL/ALEM or any WSR model. She also disagreed with the emphasis on testing in NCLB, but the directives from the central office were impossible to ignore because they affected her career prospects.

Changes in Classrooms

The acceptance of externally coercive legitimacy resulted in rigid implementation. All three teachers attempted not to deviate from what they understood as the CFL/ALEM program. For example, Mrs. O'Dell continued rotating among learning centers despite the classroom management problems and interference with learning that it created. In Ms. Fadora's class, many times students worked productively at the computer or became absorbed in an oral story, but the lesson ended abruptly after 20 minutes.

As discussed, the teachers who used CFL/ALEM implemented limited versions of the model. They never attempted student self-scheduling and self-selection as prescribed by the Temple University trainers. Also intentionally absent were activities that used constructivist pedagogy, with the exception of the district-mandated Everyday Math.

New teachers, who did not attend the initial CFL/ALEM training, brought their own teaching styles to Church Street. Most of them believed that urban students needed drill in the basics and thought that CFL/ALEM was not appropriate.

A Typology of Church Street Teachers

Structural coercive change characterizes Mrs. Martin's and Ms. Fadora's behavior. Mrs. Martin implemented CFL/ALEM mechanically; she never fully accepted the need for it but did not resist, and her enthusiasm for teaching enhanced her performance. Students in Mrs. Martin's class learned reading skills and that school could be an interesting and friendly place.

Ms. Fadora also fits this pattern because, although she overcame her initial resistance to CFL/ALEM and her students benefited from it, she never fully accepted its educational philosophy. In fact, for Ms. Fadora, CFL/ALEM was legitimate only to the extent that the school expected her to use it. In addition, the central office undermined her use of CFL/ALEM and possible acceptance of it by increasing the emphasis on test preparation. As a result, Ms. Fadora's students learned lessons in bureaucratic precision when they rotated smoothly among activities and prepared for a standardized test; only occasionally were they taught in a more creative way than through rote drill.

Mrs. O'Dell exhibited *structural coercive reverse change.* Even though Mrs. O'Dell's version of the program was simplified, it seldom functioned as planned. Despite the disorganization created by the struggle to implement CFL/ALEM, her students learned how to read and experienced school as a moderately chaotic environment.

Changes in the School

One cause of the rigidity was that Church Street was a new school. Without an established organizational culture, CFL/ALEM emerged as a key element in a framework for organizing the school. Another factor was that the principal did not intervene to support CFL/ALEM or modify it to fit the needs of the students.

Finally, in addition to understanding *Abbott V* as a law, the absence of a principal who actively intervened to manage the instructional program created uncertain expectations among the teachers. Those who implemented CFL/ALEM used rigid compliance to avoid criticism.

The central feature of Church Street that did not change was the mission to protect students from the negative encroachment of urban life. But the culture of nurturance was fundamentally incompatible with the CFL/ALEM philosophy of empowering students to control major aspects of their learning.

Conclusions

Church Street illustrates the legitimating role of the eco-cognitive framework through the powerful influence of passive leadership. The principal of Church Street delegitimated *Abbott V* from the beginning by rejecting it as a solution appropriate for her school. Her nonsupport affected most teachers' classroom behavior, including the few teachers who implemented it and strictly followed the elements of CFL/ALEM they had selected.

Unlike College Avenue, where the principal initiated test preparation before NCLB, under Church Street's conditions of passive leadership, the coercive enforcement of NCLB created by the Elizabeth central office was a more powerful change trigger than the New Jersey Supreme Court Abbott mandates. However, NCLB reaffirmed a concept of education that constricted exploration of new teaching methods. Consequently, because of the inability to develop a more compelling vision and practice of education than existed under *Abbott V*, student achievement did not improve significantly. Even intensive test preparation was ineffective.

The Change Cycle: Ending and Beginning

The changes in Elizabeth late in the 2004–2005 school year described in Chapter 7 formally ended CFL/ALEM throughout the district and created uncertainty for 2005–2006 among the Church Street faculty.

CHAPTER 7

The Park Avenue School

Chronic Resistance to Change

The Park Avenue School Community

The Park Avenue School is in the lowest income neighborhood in Elizabeth. Once a fashionable part of town, the area gradually lost its allure and, in the 1960s, went downhill rapidly as a desirable place to live when an elevated section of a major interstate highway isolated it from the rest of the city. Eroding property values further, in the 1970s, it became the site of Elizabeth's largest public housing project. In the 1980s, the expansion of a nearby international airport created constant jet traffic directly over the neighborhood and school.

Typical of many old urban areas in New Jersey, the neighborhood has taverns scattered throughout. Somewhat less typical, the Post Office across the street from the school has 2-inch-thick plexiglass above the counter to protect the clerks. The Elizabeth newspaper reports frequent bar fights and robberies in the neighborhood.

In 2000, affordable townhouses replaced some of the dilapidated, crime-ridden projects. Other positive forces are a Haitian church and several Latino congregations. These churches and a civic organization organize residents to improve the social, cultural, and economic conditions of the community. Indicative of urban problems, however, a large Catholic Church and elementary school that borders a park in the center of the community are struggling to stay open.

A few blocks from the Park Avenue School, the port has become one of the key economic engines of Elizabeth. However, the positive economic effects of the port had only a minor effect on the Park Avenue neighborhood, which has the highest unemployment rate in the city and a 2000 median family income of $26,555.

The Park Avenue community is visually different from the College Avenue and Church Street neighborhoods. The housing immediately around Park

Avenue is in poor repair, people mill about idly on street corners, men ride bicycles for transportation, and the neighborhood's general appearance immediately places it lower in the social and economic order. Although not as economically depressed and physically deteriorated as the Newark community the Bridge Street School serves, the Park Avenue neighborhood resembled it more than other neighborhoods in Elizabeth.

The Park Avenue School

With 900 students, Park Avenue is the largest elementary school in Elizabeth. Built in 1974, it is one of the newest schools in the city, and it has an indoor swimming pool, a library open to the community after school and on weekends, and a community health clinic. Although the school is in an economically distressed community, it is in excellent physical condition. The classrooms are large and well stocked with books and other instructional materials.

At the time of the study, the community and student population was predominantly African American, with a growing Latino population. Eighty-one percent of Park Avenue's students received free or reduced-price lunch. The student mobility rate was 30%, and 23% of its students had limited English proficiency.

Of the 120 teachers in the school, 80% were White and the remainder was split evenly between Latinas and female African Americans. Many of the teachers had worked at Park Avenue for over 20 years, and a few had been there since the school opened.

Park Avenue Before *Abbott V*

During the 5 years preceding *Abbott V*, Park Avenue had the reputation as a school that was out of control. The principal was ineffective, and the Board of Education had tried unsuccessfully to correct the situation. For example, one solution was to divide the school into three houses, each with a vice principal. This produced minor improvements.

Three years before *Abbott V*, Park Avenue tried to implement the Comer School Development Program, which became one of the New Jersey Supreme Court approved Whole School Reform (WSR) models. According to most teachers, the Comer program did not significantly change conditions, but several teachers thought that it was improving the school and would have succeeded if more teachers had participated. The Comer program was not in use when *Abbott V* began.

The principal of Park Avenue at the start of *Abbott V* was a 40-year-old African American woman who previously was a vice principal in Park Avenue. She had successfully distanced herself from the previous principal (who did not have the respect of the faculty) by being personable, ubiquitous, and action oriented. She graduated from the Elizabeth public school system and, like many teachers in the school, received her undergraduate and graduate education at State University. When she married, she relocated to a nearby mixed working- and middle-class suburb.

Her view was that "Being brand new is a help. The other principals have had culture shock. It's easier for me because Abbott is the only way that I know. For instance, zero-based budgeting was not easy but I didn't have to struggle any more than the other principals. To me, it's the only way to do a budget."

Park Avenue and *Abbott V*, Year 1—1998–1999

Selecting a Whole School Reform Model

Park Avenue's teachers vocally opposed all of the WSR models. They believed that to improve student achievement the school needed strict enforcement of the disciplinary code and increased emphasis on basic skills using traditional teaching methods. One veteran teacher expressed the prevailing sentiment: "If the parents would get more involved and if the students would pay more attention, there would be improvement."

Nevertheless, they had to select a model from the court-approved list, and the faculty voted for the Community for Learning/Adaptive Learning Environments Model (CFL/ALEM). According to the principal, "The superintendent did not force us to use CFL/ALEM and the teachers made the choice." Many teachers, however, reported that they had read only a short description of the WSR models, and felt pressured and rushed, and that they selected CFL/ALEM in reaction to the negative experiences of colleagues with Success for All. They settled on CFL/ALEM because it was similar to how they already taught and, in their view, it provided more structure than the other models.

The principal was aware of a sharp division between the older and newer teachers over the selection of CFL/ALEM. Her assessment was that the benefit of Whole School Reform and CFL/ALEM was "having control over the school. We know what we need and we are now able to make decisions that the district made before. The central office listens and is usually supportive. I like the control and I think that the staff likes the control. For example, we can now select and purchase our own reading materials. Before, everything was given to us by the central office."

Training in CFL/ALEM

During CFL/ALEM training at Park Avenue, teachers frequently vocally objected to the program. At a 4-hour voluntary Saturday training session attended by 30 teachers but no administrators, the conflict was intense. The Temple University trainer, an articulate, personable African American male, reviewed the basic elements of CFL/ALEM. The teachers listened politely but, when he finished, several teachers suggested that the training would be more effective if, instead of just talking about the CFL/ALEM principles and methods, he used them during the workshop.

The trainer explained that he had previously used CFL/ALEM techniques with adults but did not think it was appropriate for the Park Avenue faculty. The teachers explained at length why his answer was unsatisfactory, and the remainder of the workshop was a contentious discussion focused on the purpose and appropriateness of CFL/ALEM. The tense exchanges between the faculty and trainer did not systematically examine the issues, set the stage for a different type of training, or generate methods for improving student achievement, but simply aired teachers' grievances. After an hour of heated exchanges, the workshop ended with a tension-filled agreement to disagree.

Despite this type of opposition, the Temple trainer remained enthusiastic about CFL/ALEM. He viewed it as important because "It empowers the students. But for the students to be empowered the teachers have to be able to become empowered by their leadership and be willing to let the students become empowered." In his opinion, CFL/ALEM was appropriate for Park Avenue because research demonstrated that it could improve test scores in 1 year if fully implemented.

The Park Avenue WSR facilitator observed, "One of the hardest things is for teachers to give up control. The kids are OK with it but the teachers are reluctant to give it up. To some extent, this is because this school has not tested well and there remains an emphasis on basic skills."

CFL/ALEM in Classrooms, Year 1

Mrs. Argent's First Grade. Mrs. Argent was the first-grade teacher most willing to experiment and change. In fact, the other first-grade teachers, like most Park Avenue teachers, opposed *Abbott V* and CFL/ALEM and made meager attempts to implement the reforms.

Mrs. Argent, who grew up in an upper middle-class New Jersey suburb and graduated from a "pretty crummy" college in South Carolina, attributed her willingness to experiment with new methods to being a young, relatively new, teacher. "I try everything in CFL and then determine if it's OK for my class. The 'A' in ALEM stands for 'adaptive'. But, I have never used the self-scheduling because my kids need direction. I have to tell them what to do."

Mrs. Argent used learning centers when the students were well behaved. When a behavior problem arose, she spent considerable time scolding the students directly involved. This usually escalated to reprimanding the entire class. Then, as punishment, and a control mechanism, whole class instruction replaced learning centers.

By comparison, her colleagues—some of whom had taught for 26 years in the school and frequently reminded the principal of their long tenure—continuously resisted CFL/ALEM because, they said, "Years ago I tried the same things and they just didn't work." These teachers preferred to teach and reteach basic skills using time-tested methods—phonics, extensive drilling, and three ability groups for reading and math, for example—in a classroom with extensive control of students centered on the teacher as the source of knowledge. Mrs. Argent was critical of these practices and was irritated by her colleagues' unwillingness to change.

At the beginning of every year, however, Mrs. Argent joined the other first-grade teachers to argue that CFL/ALEM should be delayed until the students had adjusted to school. Another reason to delay CFL/ALEM was that the High/Scope preschool program focused too much on play and not enough on the skills needed to succeed in first grade. "Because of this," one teacher explained, "we have to spend the first 2 months of school teaching pre-K and K skills."

In response, the principal insisted that all teachers use CFL/ALEM from the first day of school. To accommodate the principal's directive, all teachers' classrooms displayed CFL/ALEM features—self-scheduling charts, signs for learning centers, and the computers turned on—but did not use them.

In October, at a weekly grade level meeting, several teachers vocally opposed CFL/ALEM and claimed that to use it they needed full-time teaching aides. The principal told them that there were no funds for aides and reiterated that "The central office and I are committed to CFL/ALEM and you should accept it and use it." Even though she occasionally agreed with these complaints, Mrs. Argent viewed the objections as excuses. Her colleagues did not want to change. She observed, "They blame every failure on everything but themselves."

Mrs. Monrose's Fourth Grade. In 1999, Mrs. Monrose, a veteran teacher, earned an M.S. in communication arts from State University, with a specialization in writing. Her thesis was an examination of the effectiveness of a technique for teaching writing to elementary students developed by a professor in Kansas.

Mrs. Monrose, who was in her early fifties and White, grew up in the public housing project a few blocks from the Park Avenue School and, at the age of 10, moved to a nearby White middle-class suburb. As a product and escapee of the projects, she felt a deep commitment to the neighborhood children and believed that they needed "structure and discipline in school to compensate for the disorganization in their home and community life."

As a member of the school management team, Mrs. Monrose opposed CFL/ALEM because "It is not suitable for these kids. These kids need more structure because of their home background. It probably works better in suburbs where control is not an issue."

She bet that in a few years the state would recognize that *Abbott V* reforms—particularly the WSR model—had failed and would introduce new reforms. In her view, the new reforms would also fail. Because of her conviction that the court and state could not improve urban education, along with her negative assessment of all reforms, she ignored WSR and persisted with her own teaching methods. Her overall assessment was that "WSR is too much change too fast. It's overwhelming and very demanding. All of the teachers feel that the change has been too rapid and too extensive."

Yet Mrs. Monrose saw some benefits from *Abbott V*, including reduced class size—"I now have 20 students and before I had as many as 35. This allows me to individualize more." She also liked the five computers purchased for her classroom with Abbott funds.

A typical lesson in Mrs. Monrose's class had two ability-graded groups working on either worksheets or textbook assignments at their desks while she taught another group in the back corner of the room. The groups then rotated so that each group worked with her. She had no tolerance for noise or for students who were not working hard. During a lesson, she frequently yelled from across the room, "*FOCUS* TAISHA . . . *FOCUS* ALFONSO."

When a monitor from the Elizabeth central office observed Mrs. Monrose in February 1999, she had student prescription sheets available for inspection, signs on the walls identifying learning centers, and charts for student self-scheduling and self-selection, indicating that she individualized lessons. These displays were "to keep the administrators happy."

Abbott V and CFL/ALEM Implementation Throughout the School, Year 1

The principal observed that "Everything is geared to the Core Content Curriculum Standards and the ESPA [Elementary School Proficiency Assessment]. We no longer try to teach using rote techniques but emphasize higher level thinking skills and multiple intelligences. You can't teach to the test because the ESPA now measures higher order critical thinking skills."

Concerning how implementation of WSR was progressing, the principal said, "I know that the teachers feel overwhelmed by all of the changes. Next year will be better, we'll be over all of the brainstorming and trial and error, and the third year will be even better. The teachers need to spend effort to learn the new approach because the approach to teaching has to change. There is progress toward a new understanding of what has to be taught; we have to emphasize the learning *process*, not facts."

Standardized Test Scores, Year 1

The scores for the 1998–1999 ESPA were 18.3% proficient in language arts and 21.7% proficient in math. These were among the lowest test scores in Elizabeth and the state. The superintendent, principal, and the newer teachers had expected improvements in test scores to result from Whole School Reform, but most teachers were resigned to low scores as normal.

Park Avenue and *Abbott V*, Year 2—1999–2000

CFL/ALEM in Classrooms, Year 2

Mrs. Argent's First Grade. Mrs. Argent did not change her classroom routine from the previous year. She used learning centers selectively instead of throughout the day and, if there were behavior problems, she reprimanded the entire class and stopped the rotation among the learning centers. She never attempted to use self-scheduling or self-selection, although several workshops during the year focused on these aspects of CFL/ALEM.

In May 2000, a central office WSR monitor visited Mrs. Argent's class. He came to the classroom unannounced to observe her implementation of CFL/ALEM. He was particularly interested in student prescription sheets, how Mrs. Argent used them, and how they correlated with the Elizabeth curriculum. Mrs. Argent reported, "My paperwork is good and there were no problems with the observation."

Mrs. Monrose's Fourth Grade. Mrs. Monrose did not change her classroom organization or teaching methods. She justified continuing the same approach and noted, "My ESPAs were the highest in the fourth grade last year." Although Mrs. Monrose's class scores were high for Park Avenue, compared with Elizabeth as a whole and with statewide scores they were extremely low. As a result, in November, the principal directed all fourth grades to shift to intensive rote preparation for the ESPA.

In January, with the curriculum restricted to test preparation by the Board of Education and the principal, Mrs. Monrose said, "I set very high standards for my students." But she also thought that the expectation to cover the entire Elizabeth curriculum guidelines was not realistic because "My kids started the year slowly in math, and to cover it all we now have to rush. But because of the time pressure and focus on ESPA it's not really being taught. It will affect how they do on the ESPA."

For the next year, the fourth-grade teachers planned to rotate classes, with each teacher specializing in a subject. According to Mrs. Monrose, "We did this years ago. It takes a lot of work but it should help and the principal likes it."

Abbott V and CFL/ALEM Implementation Throughout the School, Year 2

Temple University trainers and the Park Avenue WSR facilitators held workshops throughout the year on various aspects of CFL/ALEM. The most frequent topics were how to write individual prescriptions and methods for leveling the instructional materials in learning centers.

The principal continued to advocate CFL/ALEM, and the central board monitored classrooms for compliance. But, for the most part, teachers remained adamant—covertly and overtly—in their opposition to CFL/ALEM. For example, most teachers continued to teach lessons to the entire class, despite the CFL/ALEM emphasis on small group and cooperative learning.

Standardized Test Scores, Year 2

The 1999–2000 ESPA scores were 19.8% proficient in language arts and 30% proficient in math. The 8% gain in math was encouraging, whereas the virtually identical score in language arts from the previous year led to intensified efforts to improve the reading program.

Park Avenue and *Abbott V*, Year 3—2000–2001

CFL/ALEM in Classrooms, Year 3

Mrs. Argent's First Grade. Although she had experienced behavior problems with individual students in previous years, in 2000–2001 Mrs. Argent frequently had difficulty controlling several students in her class. To solve the problem, she requested that several children be evaluated by the school's child study team. In addition, she routinely used extensive control techniques directed at the entire class, including having the students put their heads on their desks, shutting out the lights, and threatening detention. This control ritual often took 15 to 20 minutes and had little enduring effect on student behavior.

Following the elementary reform mandates concerning the selection of teaching materials and techniques, a committee of first-grade teachers selected a Houghton Mifflin reading series with a 2001 copyright. Six weeks later, Mrs. Argent and the other teachers concluded that the textbook did not focus on phonics sufficiently for the needs of their students. They decided to replace it but, because it was expensive and had not been used long enough to be evaluated properly, the principal decided they should continue to use it. The teachers used the book but supplemented it with phonics worksheets and drills.

Mrs. Monrose's Fourth Grade. In Mrs. Monrose's opinion, a third of the 23 students in her 2000–2001 class required Ritalin because they suffered from attention deficit hyperactivity disorder (ADHD). When asked why so many students had this disorder, she explained that "The teachers in the lower grades either missed it or just didn't care." Other teachers in Elizabeth also thought that some of their students required Ritalin, but not as many as Mrs. Monrose.

When informed in January 2001 by the central office that fourth-grade classes would have to spend additional time on ESPA preparation, Mrs. Monrose was visibly upset. She felt that the "intensification" of ESPA drilling was a waste of time that should be devoted to basic education. Nevertheless, she drilled her class for the ESPA, using examples from the previous test.

As a result, Mrs. Monrose introduced topics and concepts that she would not have taught because, in her view, the technical language of science was beyond her students' ability. Illustrating this, during an ESPA drill in science that covered lists of scientific terms, she said, "These kids know what 'erosion' is—they see it every time it rains and the water washes away some dirt. They just don't know the term or how to connect the concept 'erosion' with the event." However, because the drill was decontextualized, Mrs. Monrose taught the terms as isolated concepts that did not demonstrate the logic or purpose of science.

Abbott V and CFL/ALEM Implementation Throughout the School, Year 3

To create a schoolwide culture focused on reading improvement, in September 2000 the principal initiated Drop Everything and Read (DEAR). The DEAR program required all classes to have every student read silently from 11:00 a.m. to 11:15 a.m. Even nonreaders were required to hold and look at a book. Many teachers thought that DEAR wasted time, and they refused to participate. Eventually, the principal enforced DEAR by having vice principals "write-up" teachers who did not comply.

Training in CFL/ALEM continued. At a Saturday workshop, the Temple University trainer focused on self-scheduling and distributed a handout titled "Establishing and Managing Adaptive School Learning Environments: The Self-Schedule System." This document, written by Dr. Margaret Wang, developer of CFL/ALEM, outlined the logic of CFL/ALEM and research that supported it.

Drawing on Dr. Wang's paper, the trainer said that the goal of CFL/ALEM was "to have kids come in on Monday, pick up a prescription sheet and without your help, be able to work for 4 or 5 days by themselves." The teachers were openly hostile and argued that it would not work because their students needed structure. An African American teacher said, "The problem is that the kids don't have much self-discipline." The trainer countered that "CFL is not an 'open' classroom and it actually is very structured. The essence of self-scheduling is to make them optimally independent. Another benefit of this is to free you up to work with small groups to create an enhanced learning environment which is much more effective than having to work with the entire group."

This explanation was not persuasive, and several teachers offered additional reasons for using learning centers only a few times each week and why self-scheduling could not work. Toward the end of the discussion, a teacher said, "I heard that there will be only one more year of CFL and then the state will make us use Success for All." The implication was that CFL/ALEM training was a waste of time.

Implementation of CFL/ALEM and the other court mandates for elementary grades varied throughout the school. For example, the school management team met monthly, but teachers reported that it did not affect them. Similarly, considerable time was devoted to the zero-based budget, but teachers claimed that it did not improve their classrooms and that they continued to spend their own money on instructional materials.

At the end of the year, the principal noted that an important change had occurred in the school culture. In her view, "The school is changing from the orientation in prior years that the teachers come first to one in which the students come first. There is still some resistance to this, but it is changing." Finally, she observed, "There is also increased awareness that reading is the most important task in the school. Without reading, the rest doesn't work."

An article in the May 31, 2001, *Elizabeth/Hillside Gazette Leader* announced that the 14 schools in Elizabeth that used CFL/ALEM had received a $120,000 grant from Temple University to identify and use the special talents of "high implementers." The superintendent noted that

> The implementation of whole school reform in any school is an all-encompassing and involved process. Every aspect of a school's program must be evaluated and major changes are often made in the way a school operates. The 14 schools currently involved with Temple's model have made gigantic strides in the last several years toward putting all the elements of this model into practice. (quoted in Runge, 2001, p. 3)

Standardized Test Scores, Year 3

On the 2000–2001 ESPA, 45% of the students scored proficient, a 20% increase over the previous year. However, the 25.5% proficient score on the math section was a 5% decrease from the previous year. Although encouraged by the increase in literacy, most teachers understood that annual fluctuations did not necessarily mean enduring improvements and acknowledged that both scores were still very low.

Park Avenue and *Abbott V*, Year 4—2001–2002

CFL/ALEM in Classrooms, Year 4

Mrs. Argent's First Grade. In September 2001, Mrs. Argent assessed her new class as having been significantly more socialized into the routines of school and academically prepared than the preceding class. She, and the other first-grade teachers, "grudgingly" attributed this change to the fact that these students had been the first class to experience 2 years of preschool in the High/Scope program.

This change motivated Mrs. Argent to experiment with more elements of CFL/ALEM in 2001–2002, including extensive use of learning centers. However, she and the other first-grade teachers continued to reject a nonphonics approach to reading and thought that DEAR wasted time.

At the beginning of the year, a Temple facilitator identified Mrs. Argent as a "high implementer" of CFL/ALEM and expected her to serve as a mentor/coach for other teachers. During the year, several teachers consulted her about how to set up learning centers but did not follow her advice.

In May, Mrs. Argent interviewed for an elementary position in a middle-class suburban school district. The interviewers were interested in her experience with CFL/ALEM. The job did not materialize, and she planned to return to Park Avenue.

Mrs. Monrose's Fourth Grade. Mrs. Monrose felt increasing pressure for her students to improve on the ESPA. The central office continued to pressure fourth-grade teachers to align all teaching to the ESPA. Mrs. Monrose did this with drills, practice tests, and a variety of test-related computer programs. Increasingly, test preparation displaced the Core Content Curriculum Standards (CCCS) as the explicit curriculum. Although the ESPA presumably measured the CCCS, test preparation focused on the CCCS subset that the central office thought would appear on the test.

As in previous years, the focus on the ESPA aggravated Mrs. Monrose because she believed that her students needed to learn "the basics." She was willing to teach and reteach the basics until every student demonstrated mastery.

Except for the display of CFL/ALEM signs, Mrs. Monrose did not use the program. In fact, if she had wanted to use CFL/ALEM, the time devoted to test preparation would have prevented it. To Mrs. Monrose's surprise, a Temple trainer selected her as a "high implementer" of CFL/ALEM. She accepted the recognition but was not happy to serve as a mentor.

Abbott V and CFL/ALEM Implementation Throughout the School, Year 4

The previous summer, a group of teachers aligned the district curriculum with the Core Content Curriculum Standards and the Houghton Mifflin reading series. The expectation was that this would improve classroom teaching and raise ESPA scores. However, most teachers continued to resist change of any type. When necessary to satisfy an administrative order or classroom observation, they falsified CFL/ALEM implementation.

Standardized Test Scores, Year 4

The ESPA scores were language arts 31.1% proficient and math 19.2% proficient. The drop in both scores from the year before was discouraging. The principal was not able to explain the scores and said, "We have done all that we know how to do and yet there isn't much to show for it. Realistically, all that we can do is try to focus more on literacy and math. It might be a matter of more time."

Park Avenue and *Abbott V*, Year 5/ NCLB, Year 1—2002–2003

CFL/ALEM in Classrooms, Year 5

Mrs. Argent's First Grade. This year, Mrs. Argent's class was poorly prepared for first grade because, she reported, "Most of them had a kindergarten teacher who follows the High/Scope program too carefully and doesn't teach academic skills but only sticks with the play emphasis of High/Scope. I've had to spend three months teaching things that they should have come to first grade with. My best students went to private daycare before coming to first grade."

At a workshop in December, Mrs. Argent heard that the incoming governor, James McGreevey, was planning "to get rid of Whole School Reform. But I hope not. I've worked very hard on it. But most teachers here would like to see it go." Because of the students' lack of preparation—not the possibility of the elimination of WSR—Mrs. Argent delayed using learning centers or other CFL/ALEM techniques until February. And, when she did use CFL/ALEM, she reverted to whole class lectures if there was any disruptive behavior.

In March, on several occasions when she had to work with a small group to administer a diagnostic test, Mrs. Argent used self-scheduling because the principal insisted on it, and she experienced some success. On occasion, however, self-scheduling devolved into chaos, which triggered prolonged reprimands.

Mrs. Argent also increased her use of Everyday Math, not only because the district mandated it but because she and the students enjoyed it—particularly the use of manipulatives. Nevertheless, she supplemented Everyday Math with rote drills in the four mathematical functions.

She noted that NCLB increased pressure for all students to perform better on standardized tests and that "We are now all teaching to the test, and I don't think it's a good idea."

Mrs. Monrose's Fourth Grade. In September 2002, Mrs. Monrose told the researcher, "After three years of observing my class you must understand by now how I teach," and ended her participation in the study reported here.[1]

Abbott V, CFL/ALEM, and NCLB Implementation Throughout the School, Year 5

In September, the principal observed, "The funding and resources are now in place. If test scores don't improve it is either something in the classroom—that I am unaware of at this point—or the parents have to be involved more. It's hard to know what the missing piece is."

Implementation of *Abbott V* and CFL/ALEM did not change significantly in classrooms from the previous year. Although Abbott Phase II permitted a school to change to another WSR model, the principal and superintendent wanted to retain CFL/ALEM and continued to insist on full implementation in classrooms.

In February, to comply with Abbott Phase II, the school management team sent a questionnaire to each teacher asking if CFL/ALEM should continue, be modified, or be replaced by another model. The overwhelming response was that CFL/ALEM should be retained unmodified. At a faculty meeting in March, the principal told the teachers, "If you don't use CFL I am willing to accept your resignation and help you transfer to another school." However, no teacher resigned, and she did not find ways to enforce use of the program.

To monitor reading instruction, the district supervisor and the principal requested that all teachers use the end-of-chapter tests in the Houghton Mifflin reading series. The principal also stressed that every teacher had to use computers every day with as many students as possible. Another change was that, because of funding limitations, class size could exceed the *Abbott V* mandate of 21 students.

It took considerable time for the administration and teachers to understand the requirements and implications of NCLB. At a faculty meeting, the WSR facilitator announced that "If test scores don't improve over several years, teachers could be fired or transferred, the school disbanded, or the state or a private company could take it over." The severity of these corrective actions shocked most teachers.

Finally, when the principal reflected at the end of the year on what had changed, she said that her most significant accomplishment was that "More teachers now think that all kids can succeed." Looking forward to the next year, she commented, "I think that President Bush is totally committed to education reform and this will help Park Avenue and Elizabeth."

The Principal Leaves

In mid-June, the principal announced that she would become the head of training at the central office. Although many teachers greeted her departure with a sense of relief, Mrs. Argent felt "betrayal" that she left in the middle of the changes.

Standardized Test Scores, Year 5

This was the first year for the New Jersey Assessment of Skills and Knowledge (NJASK), which many teachers expected to be more difficult than the ESPA. In language arts 26.8% of Park Avenue's students were proficient, and in math 15.6% were proficient.

Park Avenue and *Abbott V*, Year 6/ NCLB, Year 2—2003–2004

A New Principal

A female African American vice principal became Park Avenue's acting principal in September 2003. She continued the policies of her predecessor, particularly insistence on full implementation of CFL/ALEM. She left Park Avenue in December to become the principal of an elementary school in Elizabeth with 450 students.

In January 2004, an African American woman became the principal of Park Avenue. She had previously been a classroom teacher and a central office administrator in Newark, had worked at the New Jersey Department of Education, and immediately before Park Avenue, was the vice principal of an elementary school in an Abbott district. Several younger teachers had high expectations that she would revitalize CFL/ALEM; veteran teachers hoped that she would be receptive to their problems with the Temple program.

CFL/ALEM in Classrooms, Year 6

Mrs. Argent's First Grade. NCLB did not affect the first grade as directly as it did the 4th, 8th, and 11th grades, which all had high stakes tests. However, the central board was aware that because of NCLB all grades would eventually take high stakes tests. In response, to prepare all students the board introduced the TerraNova achievement test into the first grade.

To prepare first-grade students for the test, the Park Avenue administration changed the format of routine tests. For example, the Friday morning spelling test—in which the teacher said a word, used it in a sentence, the students wrote it, followed by the teacher repeating the word—became a multiple choice test to resemble standardized tests. For example:

Teacher: *MAKE*. I *make* time to do chores after school. *MAKE*.

Circle the correct answer:
1. meke 2. miku 3. mak 4. make 5. make 6. mkee 7. mke

Mrs. Argent strenuously objected to this approach, observing, "I can't tell whether they can spell the word or are making a good guess. And it's just not right to put more pressure on these kids at their age to do well on tests."

An important change was the selection by the central office of the Open Court reading program for use in all elementary schools in Elizabeth. Mrs. Argent thought that Open Court was appropriate and effective because "Since the kids did not come with good reading skills this year, the emphasis on phonics in Open Court has really helped. It's only October and all of the kids know the alphabet, and some know how to read. That's pretty good for this type of neighborhood. They should have used this program a long time ago."

In November, Mrs. Argent said, concerning NCLB, "They are 'freaking-out' about getting the test scores up. We were told again that if the test scores don't improve significantly we could all be transferred. This is a low-performing school, and people are starting to get worried."

Abbott V, CFL/ALEM, and NCLB Implementation Throughout the School, Year 6

The central office's selection of the Open Court reading series was an important change because, like the adoption of Everyday Math, teachers did not take an active part in the decision. In fact, many teachers thought that Everyday Math and Open Court did not fit well together or with CFL/ALEM. These programs stressed whole class instruction and decreased opportunities for individualization.

Most teachers felt pressure to teach to the test and teach test-taking skills for both the annual TerraNova test and the NJASK. All teachers attended workshops on how to improve student performance on standardized tests, and the school offered after-school and Saturday tutoring for the NJASK.

Standardized Test Scores, Year 6

The second year of NJASK yielded scores similar to the first year. In language arts 31.4% of the students demonstrated proficiency, and in math 15.1% were proficient. These scores were again among the lowest in Elizabeth and in the state.

Park Avenue and *Abbott V*, Year 7/ NCLB, Year 3—2004–2005

CFL/ALEM in Classrooms, Year 7

Mrs. Argent's First Grade. Because Everyday Math and Open Court required considerable time, and their pedagogic approach did not fit with CFL/ALEM, Mrs. Argent used learning centers infrequently. In addition, the new principal emphasized that everything in the classroom should be geared toward the TerraNova and NJASK, further pushing aside CFL/ALEM.

Mrs. Argent's experience with Open Court was still positive, and she and the students enjoyed Everyday Math. However, compared with the previous year, the achievement level of the class started lower and, although students made significant gains, learning required great effort.

Abbott V, CFL/ALEM, and NCLB Implementation Throughout the School, Year 7

According to many teachers, the new principal and new vice principals did not enforce student discipline. In the opinion of the teachers, under the previous administrators the school was more organized; the increased disorganization adversely affected the ability to teach.

More important, the new principal had not developed innovative educational programs or found a way to increase the use of CFL/ALEM. Her primary concern was to improve test scores, and she concentrated test preparation on the third and fourth grades, which had high stakes tests. For example, all administrators and special subject teachers tutored third- and fourth-grade students.

Some teachers hoped the new principal was still learning about the school and would take a more active role in discipline and promoting change in 2005–2006. In fact, she had floated the idea of restructuring the school by locating all grades together in an effort to improve discipline. This type of structure, according to veteran teachers, when used in 1994–1995 had failed to improve either discipline or academic achievement.

In April 2005, a team from the New Jersey State Department of Education visited the school because it was on the list of 79 schools in the state identified as a "low performing" Abbott school and was classified by NCLB as in need of "corrective action." The purpose of the visit was to help the administration and faculty develop ways to improve the school's academic performance. Team members observed classes and interviewed teachers.

Standardized Test Scores, Year 7

The 2004–2005 NJASK score for language arts was 37.9% proficient, and for math 21% proficient with 1.2% scoring advanced. These scores did not meet Adequate Yearly Progress (AYP), and NCLB labeled Park Avenue as requiring "restructuring." After an appeal to the New Jersey Department of Education, the school received 1 more year to improve to avoid restructuring.

Analysis of the Park Avenue School

Legitimacy and the Eco-Cognitive Framework

The challenge to the legitimacy of the *Abbott V* elementary mandates in Park Avenue was overt, strong, and sustained. Most teachers thought that the New Jersey Supreme Court did not understand the problems of the school. They also did not accept NCLB but, because of pressure from the central office and genuine concern for the future of their school—and worry over where they would be teaching next if test scores did not improve—they implemented the test preparation strategies. The emphasis the central office placed on tests remained nonlegitimate, but the sustained coercion overruled teacher concerns.

Despite direct attempts to force teachers to use CFL/ALEM, DEAR, and the Houghton Mifflin reading series, the principal succeeded in achieving only reluctant compliance from a few teachers. The issues of trust and legitimacy evolved into continuous negotiation of responsibilities and, eventually, distrust between the administrators and teachers.

The eco-cognitive framework was prevalent in Park Avenue and influenced the selection and retention of all educational programs and methods. Most teachers believed that the educational program should reflect the economic and social conditions of the community, and they were unwilling to change this viewpoint.

The attitude of the teachers was not conscious racism or overt social class bias, but rather their understanding of the harsh realities of their students' lives. The idea that students needed discipline, structure, and "the basics" was taken for granted by most teachers. It severely limited attempts to use CFL/ALEM. In fact, Mrs. Argent was often the only person to consider trying a new teaching technique.

Changes in Classrooms

Only a few teachers implemented any element of CFL/ALEM. The primary changes in classrooms resulted from the board mandate to use Everyday Math and Open Court reading to align the curriculum with the standardized tests. The alignment process demonstrated that NCLB was more powerful than *Abbott V* because it triggered the use of new programs. More important, NCLB restructured classrooms into test preparation centers.

A Typology of Park Avenue Teachers

Mrs. Argent demonstrated *voluntary reverse change*. She had no support for using CFL/ALEM from her colleagues; the principal supported her efforts but with occasional reprimands. However, the major problem was that Mrs. Argent continuously encountered, and in many instances created, classroom management difficulties when she used CFL/ALEM. The changes usually produced negative student behavior, which interfered with instruction and derailed implementation of CFL/ALEM.

Mrs. Argent's students learned that school was a place in which adults expend great effort to control children. The major cognitive achievement of the students was that, three or four exceptions, they learned near-grade-level reading skills.

Mrs. Monrose engaged in *overt active resistance to change*. Ironically, she was willing to use new techniques that she had learned at State University and rotate classes with other teachers, but she would not attempt to apply any of the court mandated methods. This behavior suggests that self-initiated change was acceptable but coercive change was not. Nevertheless, NCLB succeeded in coercing Mrs. Monrose into intensive decontextualized test preparation.

In Mrs. Monrose's class, students learned a constricted curriculum that focused on the basics and on how to prepare for a standardized test. If NCLB had not required Mrs. Monrose to move beyond the basics, she would have been content to spend the year recycling them until every student demonstrated proficiency.

Changes in the School

The major change at Park Avenue during the study period was creation of test preparation as the major goal for the school. This was accompanied by reinforcement of the related issues of control and resistance to change.

Teachers continually worried about "losing control" over their students. Indeed, Mrs. Argent and Mrs. Monrose, as did most teachers, spent a great deal of time and effort controlling their students. One reason for the difficulty was that the school was large and provided opportunities for discipline problems. For example, the walk from classrooms to the cafeteria or the library was long and presented many opportunities for student misbehavior. Another factor in the discipline problems was that teachers responded to the fact that the neighborhood visually displayed a loss of control—it was not neat and tidy like other neighborhoods in Elizabeth, even if they were low income, and it did not give the impression of order found in suburban communities. Finally, to some extent, the fear of loss of control increased teachers' feelings of professional marginality.

Ultimately, whatever the other reasons for concern about losing control—the negation of professional authority—in addition to having a court and the federal government impose reforms on the school, the CFL/ALEM method itself posed a threat to teacher control. The idea that teachers would let students determine important elements of learning made no sense to the teachers because of their own understanding of conditions at Park Avenue.

The teachers' resistance to change was related to loss of control because, in addition to being a tactic for retaining control, many teachers sincerely believed that the curriculum and pedagogy they used were appropriate. In their minds, the problem was the lack of cooperation from the students and their parents. Thus, for the majority of the teachers the diagnosis that *they* had to change was incorrect. Instead, from their perspective, students and their families had to change.

Conclusions

The principal at Park Avenue made a genuine effort to implement CFL/ALEM but did not succeed. Teacher resistance was strong and organized and, compared with other schools, the teachers frequently demonstrated and created conflict. Resistance was part of the culture of the school, institutionalized in the eco-cognitive framework and fear of losing control. The principal's direct approach to change was ultimately not effective because she forcefully confronted the resistance, instead of removing barriers to change. Further, she did not stay on the job long enough to manage the changes she envisioned.

Teachers like Mrs. Monrose, who predicted that Whole School Reform would fail, constructed a self-fulfilling prophecy (Merton, 1948). The fulfillment of the prophecy created conditions that would make the next phase in the evolution of the school less likely to produce successful change.

The Change Cycle: Ending and Beginning

The Superintendent Is Dismissed

In early May 2005, the Board of Education dismissed the superintendent. The timing was controversial because the termination occurred before the end of the school year and his contract, with a $200,000 annual salary, expired a year later, in June 2006.

The president of the board said that the departure was by mutual agreement and that the decision was because of consistently low scores on standardized tests and discipline problems in the schools. He continued, "After ten years to address problems in the district the board has decided to go a different way to address those problems. We're moving forward, we're not looking backward" (quoted in Golson, 2005, p. 27).

The superintendent complained that he had been fired without discussion or warning. He argued that during his 10-year term, 14 of Elizabeth's 17 elementary schools had improved their literacy scores and 9 of the city's 10 middle schools had improved their math scores. "It is easy to highlight poor test scores in a school district of Elizabeth's size and high poverty." He continued, "Our kids simply need more time and support to achieve" (quoted in McNamara, 2005, p. 1).

A May 19, 2005, editorial in the *Elizabeth/Hillside Gazette Leader* questioned the timing and motives of the firing:

> Apparently, test scores have not improved to the board's liking and so, they unanimously voted last week to give the superintendent a year off. That's the reason they gave publicly. But Elizabeth's test scores have always been among the weakest when compared to other school districts in the County. Why get rid of him now? And if this agreement was as mutual as the school board has implied, why not allow him to serve out the remaining year of his contract, rather than collect a paycheck, funded by taxpayers, for a year? ("More Than Just," 2005, p. 4)

The New Superintendent

The Board of Education appointed as acting superintendent for the 2005–2006 school year a Latino male graduate of Elizabeth High School who had earned his B.A. and M.A. degrees from Ivy League universities. The acting superintendent had visited Park Avenue frequently when he was an assistant superintendent and, in the opinion of many teachers, understood the school and the problems the teachers confronted. It was not clear to them, however, what new programs, if any, he would introduce.

The Elizabeth Reform Model

The acting superintendent began to address the teachers' concerns when he announced in early June 2005 that all Whole School Reform models in Elizabeth would end immediately. Starting in 2005–2006, pending state approval, Elizabeth would implement a WSR model based on the most successful elements of the court-approved models.

Most teachers were uncertain what a new model would include. A WSR facilitator speculated that it would incorporate elements of CFL/ALEM, particularly the use of learning centers and prescriptions to individualize instruction. In her view, a compelling reason for introducing a new model was to end a failed change cycle. She observed, "The new 'alternative' model would return to the fundamentals of reading, writing, and arithmetic, and some variation of CFL/ALEM is appropriate for that."

In late June, a few days before the end of school, uncertainty about the new model remained. Teachers worried that if the model was unveiled during the summer, assuming that it was significantly different from the previous model, it would require time for training before school started in September.

In July 2005, the Board of Education announced plans to involve faith-based organizations in the schools. In August 2005, the New Jersey Department of Education announced that according to NCLB eight schools in Elizabeth, including Park Avenue, were in the "restructuring" phase. Before the announcement, the acting superintendent had replaced three principals, but not the principals of Park Avenue, College Avenue, or Church Steet. He also announced that in 2005–2006 all schools would have 90-minute blocks of uninterrupted math and language arts instruction and more assessments.

Early in the 2005–2006 school year, the New Jersey Department of Education announced that because of 2 consecutive years of failing to achieve AYP, the Elizabeth school district was subject to NCLB sanctions, including restructuring or abolition.

In September 2006, schools began implementing the Elizabeth-formulated "E3," a districtwide elementary Whole School Reform program. The program focused on three major components: language arts, mathematics, and social emotional learning. An important feature of the new system was that from kindergarten through eighth grade all elementary students in a grade level would use the same instructional materials. This meant that when students transferred within Elizabeth their instruction would continue uninterrupted.

The basic instructional mechanism for language arts and math would be 90-minute blocks daily. For both subjects, instruction would begin with 30 minutes of whole group instruction in a particular skill. Then the class would break into small groups that would rotate in 15-minute intervals among four learning centers. Teacher tutors would work with classroom teachers to individualize instruction in the small groups.

The third component of the program was social emotional learning, which would "ensure that the school community rallies around the student and fosters each student's development by providing all necessary academic, social, and emotional supports."

The Whole School Reform facilitator's speculation about the future had been correct. A variation of CFL/ALEM was the foundation for the next wave of Elizabeth's school reform.

PART III

Explaining the Revolution

CHAPTER 8

What Changed?

Why Separate Cannot Be Equal

The NCLB Revolution

Over 3 years, No Child Left Behind changed the purpose of urban education in the schools described in this book from providing a broad education in all elementary subjects to preparing students narrowly to score higher on standardized tests. This more restricted curriculum focused on information expected to be on the tests.[1] For example, even though Newark and Elizabeth purchased new instructional material, its purpose was more efficient and effective test preparation.

Through interaction with the eco-cognitive framework of educators, NCLB created a new type of education in urban schools that was significantly different from that in suburban schools.[2] Further increasing the inequality of separate schools, NCLB also reinforced the eco-cognitive framework as the basic belief system of the schools. In addition, NCLB changed the distribution of power in urban education by replacing local leadership with federal leadership, and it instituted a new organizational control system based on standardized test scores and, when necessary, external intervention to improve them.

The Key Questions

To explain this revolutionary change it is necessary to answer the questions that guided this book, by using cross-site comparisons to identify changes common to the districts and the schools (Miles & Huberman, 1994). These questions are

- How did *Abbott V* and NCLB affect the learning and classroom behavior of low-income students in racially segregated urban elementary schools?

- After 7 years of *Abbott V* and 3 years of NCLB, why had these unprecedented urban education reforms failed to close the achievement gap?
- Can separate schools be equal?

Major Common Findings

The most significant findings across the two districts, the four schools, and all classrooms cluster into the following categories: macro-change, implementation, organizational outcomes, change in classrooms, and educational outcomes.

Macro-Change

Court and federal reforms replaced local reforms. Previously, the districts, schools, and teachers had attempted periodic internally initiated incremental change, and, in some cases, this continued during *Abbott V* and NCLB. One result of the external reforms was that court and federal leadership replaced local leadership, because both reforms imposed solutions that challenged or bypassed the authority of superintendents and principals.

However, the court (through the state) and the federal government did not facilitate or monitor the change process effectively. In fact, confusion over state and federal roles in local education contributed to resistance and to only partial implementation of the reforms. Federal, state, district, and school leadership was also ineffective because of inexperience in managing complex large-scale change.

A result of weak leadership at all levels was that, over 7 years, the change triggers evolved from external coercive reform initiated by *Abbott V* and NCLB, to a mixture of local district-initiated noncoercive reorientation and the punishment measures of NCLB. The dominance of NCLB over *Abbott V*, and the pressure experienced by districts and schools to avoid NCLB sanctions, shifted the initiative for change and the development of programs from the schools to the districts, primarily, in attempts to comply with federal law.

Implementation

Newark and Elizabeth approached *Abbott V* differently, and implementation varied within the two districts. Newark delayed implementation for multiple reasons and never fully supported it. When an opportunity came to end application of the Community for Learning/Adaptive Learning Environments Model (CFL/ALEM), the Newark central office replaced it with a local version of Whole School Reform (WSR). Initially, Elizabeth attempted to implement *Abbott V* with fidelity. However, teachers subverted WSR with various types of resistance. As a result, implementation varied within and across schools, and application of CFL/ALEM ranged from nonuse to selective partial use. No teacher used all of its elements (see Erlichson et al., 1999; Erlichson & Goertz, 2001; Supovitz & May, 2003).

Implemented reforms and other "best practices" did not diffuse within schools. Although teachers attended CFL/ALEM workshops, grade-level meetings, and forums for sharing teaching techniques and experiences with CFL/ALEM, there was very little emulation of successful teachers (Sarason, 1996).

Also affecting implementation was the fact that multiple change models existed in each school. Reforms initiated by principals before and during *Abbott V*, elements of *Abbott V*, district-initiated changes, and NCLB competed for attention and time. Even though state and federal reforms replaced local reforms for a few years, the multiple change models created conflicting objectives and adversely affected management of the reforms.

The effect of NCLB on *Abbott V*, particularly the Whole School Reform model, was termination of a faltering change. In addition to other obstacles to implementation of CFL/ALEM, the emphasis on standardized tests reduced time for it and narrowed the curriculum for all teachers. As a result, only a few teachers in each school used any elements of CFL/ALEM after NCLB.

Finally, the key reason for the failure to implement CFL/ALEM was that the various school cultures did not undergo the transformation into cultures of innovation. The eco-cognitive framework, the central element of these cultures, with few exceptions, prevented, modified, or subverted any type of substantive change.

Organizational Outcomes

The difficulties encountered in the *Abbott V* reform process made administrators and teachers skeptical of reform. Yet, after the failure of *Abbott V*, teachers participated in NCLB because of its coercive nature. Even though they lost a significant amount of control over their classrooms, teachers retained power to a certain extent because of the inability of principals (as well as the district and the state) to create voluntary change or to force change. NCLB coerced change, but teachers reshaped its intention when possible—to preserve some of their own power.

In most schools, teacher resistance overwhelmed administrative attempts to change. Teachers who did not change contributed to the failure of *Abbott V*. They understood from previous experience that, whether the reforms were successful or not, new fads and fashions in education would eventually replace the current reforms. This is not unique to education; managerial fads and fashions are also common in business organizations (Abrahamson, 1991).

Change in Classrooms

The change the reforms created affected specific activities in classrooms, whereas other behaviors remained the same. For example, grouping students for instruction did not change. Almost all teachers rejected the CFL/ALEM emphasis on individualization and collaborative teaching. Educators in Elizabeth discussed triage, but it was not district policy and was used infrequently (Booher-Jennings, 2005).

However, one significant change that did develop was that the materials and activities through which the curriculum was taught became progressively more aligned with a selectively reduced version of the Core Content Curriculum Standards and standardized tests. Nonetheless, their use varied significantly, and many teachers preferred direct teaching instead of constructivist techniques, even for Everyday Math. In Elizabeth, adoption of the Open Court reading series was a rejection of whole language or balanced approaches to reading instruction.

Beginning with *Abbott V*, but increasing under NCLB, the evaluation system that teachers used to assess student learning was the standardized test. In fact, the standardized test influenced all assessment activities. For example, when the Newark central office ordered teachers to submit a monthly writing sample for each student, it was to prepare for the New Jersey Assessment of Skills and Knowledge (NJASK).

The continuous emphasis on testing shifted the motivational system used by teachers to engage student learning from intrinsic motivation to extrinsic motivation (Deci et al., 1999; Ryan & Deci, 2000). The cumulative impact of threats, directives, distant deadlines, and competition within classrooms and between schools supplanted all other motivational techniques, even when a school attained Adequate Yearly Progress—because pressure to keep off the "in need of improvement" list only increased.

The responsibility of students in directing and evaluating their own learning did not change. The key component of CFL/ALEM—that students would self-select and self-direct their learning—was unacceptable to almost all teachers. What little student responsibility did exist actually diminished as pressure to improve test performance increased.

Finally, the climate of relationships within the class, with parents, and with the school remained the same or changed in a negative way. Social relationships in classrooms remained similar over the course of the change because most teachers retained all authority. However, there was increased conflict between teachers and administrators over the reforms and, in a few cases, conflict among teachers. The few attempts to include parents more in school met with little success.

Educational Outcomes

Standardized test scores did not improve because of *Abbott V*. For example, the College Avenue School, which had the highest percent increase and sustained improvement in standardized test scores, did not implement the court mandates or any element of CFL/ALEM. The other schools experienced uneven test scores and no sustained improvement, even in the few cases where components of CFL/ALEM affected teaching.

Because of NCLB, standardized test scores did improve but, with the exception of College Avenue, the improvements were not sustained. Consistent with this finding among the schools profiled here, the fourth-grade standardized test scores for schools throughout New Jersey indicate that from 1999 to 2005 a significant achievement gap remained, when test scores were analyzed by economic status and ethnicity.

Figure 8.1 compares the performance of economically disadvantaged (which includes the Abbott districts) and non-economically disadvantaged students on the fourth-grade language arts test.[3] Figure 8.2 shows the percent proficient and above on the fourth-grade language arts test by ethnicity.

In mathematics, as displayed in Figure 8.3, a narrowing of the proficiency gap was demonstrated on the fourth-grade test over 7 years when measured by economic status. Figure 8.4 indicates that the gap in mathematics also narrowed when results are disaggregated by ethnicity. It is noteworthy that the four groups—White, Black, Asian, and Hispanic—never intersect and, as in the preceding graphs, the test score increases are roughly parallel.

It is likely that pressure to perform well on standardized tests led other schools in Abbott districts to focus on test preparation using techniques similar to those used in the schools profiled here. However, Figures 8.2 and 8.4 indicate that throughout the state, the *Abbott V* reforms and the NCLB pressures did not improve test scores for minority students significantly.

Other studies support these conclusions. Research on a large sample of New Jersey fourth-grade standardized test results for 3 years (1998–1999, 1999–2000, and 2000–2001) found that the achievement gap for African American students increased (Camilli & Monfils, 2004). An analysis of test results correlated with the degree of pressure on standardized tests in 25 states demonstrated that NCLB "had almost no important influence on student academic performance" (Nichols, Glass, & Berliner, 2005, p. 1; 2006; also Lee, 2006).[4]

Because of the emphasis on learning how to prepare for and take tests, for most students school was not an enjoyable or interesting experience. The emphasis on discipline, combined with test preparation, reduced opportunities for school to be a "learning community" that would prepare students to value education.

In summary, the most important educational outcome was that NCLB, and particularly its corrective actions, created organizational isomorphism that changed the deep structure of education in urban schools (DiMaggio & Powell, 1983). As it became apparent that NCLB sanctions would be enacted, increased pressure to focus exclusively on the standardized test to avoid sanctions narrowed the curriculum, replaced classroom teaching and the Core Content Curriculum Standards with test preparation strategies, and, although CFL/ALEM was already in decline, supplanted it and the other *Abbott V* mandates (Diamond & Spillane, 2004).

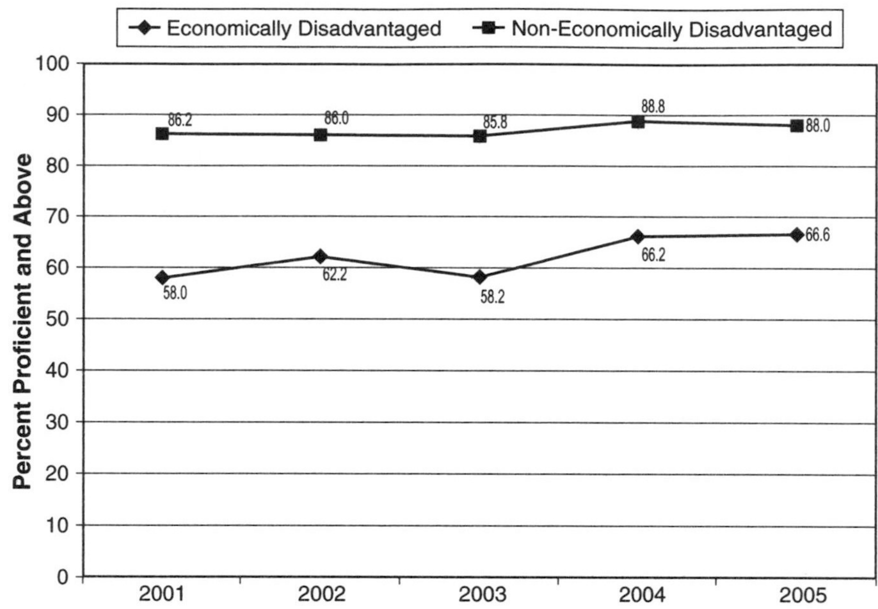

FIGURE 8.1. New Jersey Assessment of Fourth-Grade Students, Language Arts Literacy: Percent Proficient and Above by Economic Status (2001–2005). *Source:* New Jersey State Department of Education.

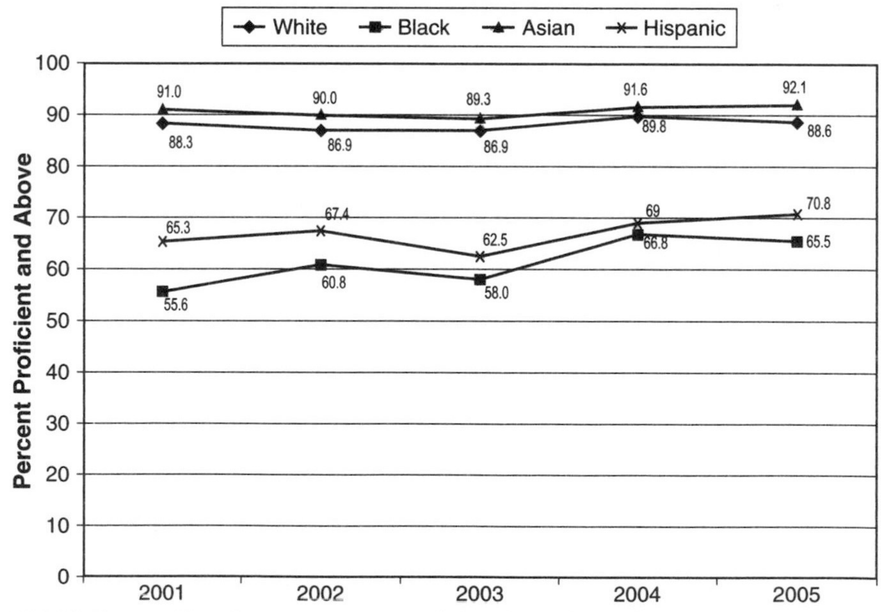

FIGURE 8.2. New Jersey Assessment of Fourth-Grade Students, Language Arts Literacy: Percent Proficient and Above by Ethnicity (2001–2005). *Source:* New Jersey State Department of Education.

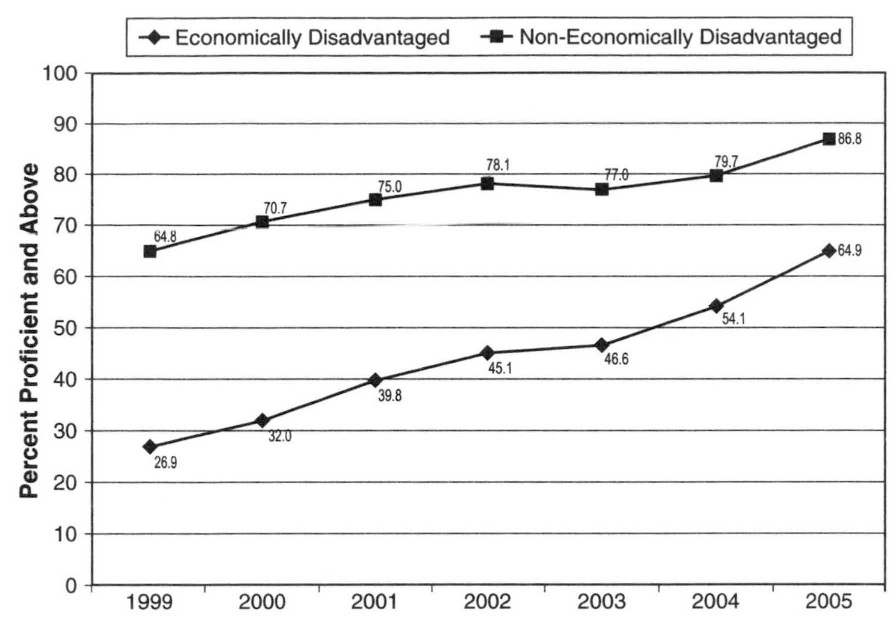

FIGURE 8.3. New Jersey Assessment of Fourth-Grade Students, Mathematics: Percent Proficient and Above by Economic Status (1999–2005). *Source:* New Jersey State Department of Education.

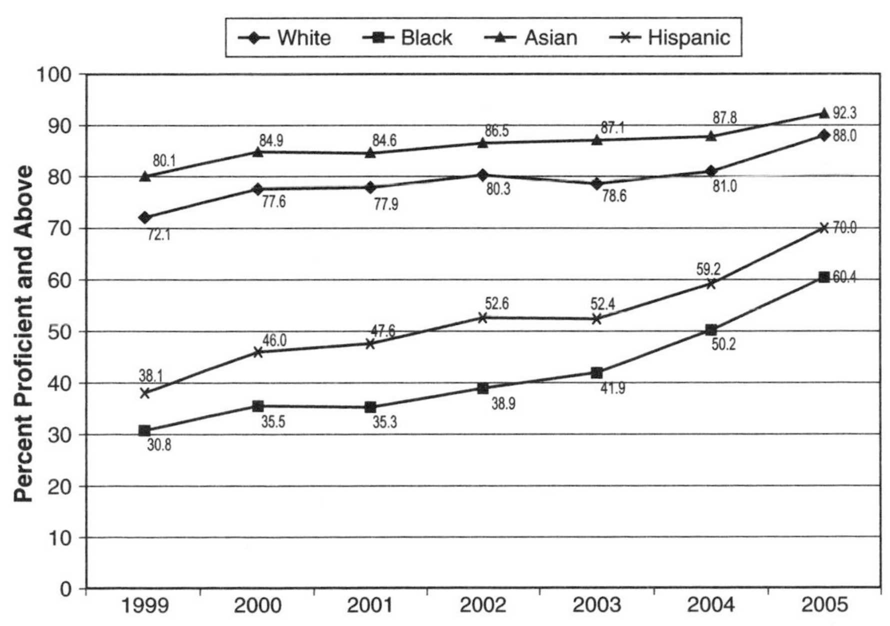

FIGURE 8.4. New Jersey Assessment of Fourth-Grade Students, Mathematics: Percent Proficient and Above by Ethnicity (1999–2005). *Source:* New Jersey State Department of Education.

Explaining the Changes

In all schools, administrators' and teachers' understanding of social class and race influenced the legitimacy of *Abbott V* and particularly the Whole School Reform model. Because of the eco-cognitive framework, most teachers rejected the court mandates as inappropriate for inner-city students. The eco-cognitive framework was a collective property of the schools as organizations, not an attribute of individuals.

The relationship among teachers' values, behavior, and change was complex, difficult to untangle, and not managed effectively by administrators. With the exception of Mrs. Smith, whose values changed before her behavior, the teachers who implemented the court mandates did so reluctantly (Mrs. Argent and Ms. Fadora, for example), and after they experienced success, changed their values retrospectively (Barnes, 2002; Weick, 1987) but retained reservations about the appropriateness of the reforms.

Basing reforms on scientific research, including CFL/ALEM, did not increase the legitimacy of the change process. In fact, most teachers rejected scientific studies of teaching methods and curriculum as either flawed or, more often, not appropriate or relevant for the social and cultural needs of the community, school, and classroom in which they taught.

Legitimacy influenced implementation, and the dynamics of legitimacy affected the change process. Delegitimation—as well as attempted construction, maintenance, and reconstruction of legitimacy—were the major catalysts of change in the schools (Gold, 1999). Specifically, teachers never viewed *Abbott V* as legitimate, and the state contributed to its delegitimation through lack of support and through implementation of Abbott Phase II, which substantially revised the initial mandates. By terminating the WSR models, the districts created a punctuation that eroded the legitimacy of the change process and contributed to a need to relegitimate change.

Finally, the result of the legitimacy dynamics over 7 years was that both school districts and the four schools experienced a complete change cycle. Because the change attempts were continuously delegitimated, the logical next step was to relegitimate reform with a return to local solutions. However, a key difference was that the legitimate coercion of NCLB reconfigured the deep structure of urban education and became the framework into which local reforms had to fit.

Abbott V, NCLB, and the Structure of Urban Education

The *Abbott V* funding parity and elementary reforms attempted to change the deep structure of urban education but did not succeed. For example, the court mandates tried to decentralize decision making to the level of the school and the classroom teacher. However, within a few years, the state recentralized the budget, and school management teams had no effect on classroom practice. In addition, instead of teachers making decisions regarding curriculum and instructional materials, the board of education, in an attempt to align instruction with standardized tests, made all curriculum decisions.

Under NCLB, the federal role in local education increased through application of pressure to improve accountability. The threat of sanctions contributed to the recentralization of decision making in the districts and in the state.

However, despite increased centralization and the coercion of NCLB, teachers retained significant power through their ability to modify the reforms. To a great extent this was because the local community—the context of education that neither *Abbott V* nor NCLB attempted to change—remained the same and influenced how teachers responded to the reforms. Neither reform was powerful enough or was enforced sufficiently to eliminate, modify, or override administrators' and teachers' understandings of how social class and race influence education.

Why Separate Cannot Be Equal

The Eco-Cognitive Framework

The primary reason for failure to implement the reforms was the effect of the eco-cognitive framework on all aspects of urban education. *Abbott V* and NCLB failed to close the achievement gap because even if the programs mandated could have closed it, during implementation administrators and teachers ignored, rejected, or modified them and reproduced existing education practices.

The segregated social structure legitimated segregated schools and the rejection of techniques intended to improve those schools. The evolutionary processes of variation, selection, and retention occurred within the context of a system differentiated by race and social class. In addition—facilitating an evolutionary process based on the values of the eco-cognitive framework—the management of change was inadequate and resulted in negative consequences that delegitimated potentially effective reforms. The inability to establish a new school culture contributed to the cycle of educational change, reducing the possibility of sustaining even minor changes (Fullan, 2005).

Teaching and Learning Did Not Improve

The achievement gap did not close because the conditions of teaching and learning did not change in a constructive way (Sarason, 2004). This was not because instruction was not the focus of change or because instruction could not improve. Instead, teachers disagreed with the need to change instruction and justified retaining the existing pedagogy. NCLB and the pressure it created to improve test scores reinforced the type of teaching that teachers were familiar with and approved.

Large-Scale Change as Experiment

Abbott V and NCLB were experimental strategies for changing urban schools. First, it is not clear that external coercive change is effective, whether mandated by a state court order or federal legislation (Rosenberg, 1991). However, the observations presented in Chapters 4–7 suggest that the more coercive and punitive a reform is, the more potential it has to create change. Second, the importation of externally developed instructional models is a new approach to reform. More important, research has found that implementing a model for comprehensive school reform does not improve achievement above levels found in schools that did not use a model (Good, Burross, & McCaslin, 2005). Finally, the models, which were developed by university researchers, address the needs of urban students, but scientific studies have not demonstrated that urban children need a distinctive type of education (King, 2005; Lee, 2005).

What has endured is the revolution that NCLB has created in urban education through narrowing the purpose and goals of schools to preparing students for tests. Evidence of this revolution is that, after the failure of *Abbott V* and NCLB to improve test scores, the local reforms selected by Newark and Elizabeth were aimed at fulfilling the new mission of urban schools to improve test scores.

THE NEXT CHAPTER discusses the limitations of *Abbott V*, NCLB, and other educational reforms, explores ways to improve the management of change in schools, and presents solutions beyond changing the financing and organization of separate schools.

CHAPTER 9

Segregation and the Future of Urban School Reform

Planning for a Post-Abbott and Post-NCLB Era

The Legacy of *Abbott V* and NCLB

The 1998 *Abbott V* New Jersey state court order on improving education in segregated urban schools and the No Child Left Behind federal legislation on accountability in elementary education (which took effect in 2002) instituted substantial reforms. However, after 7 years of operation under *Abbott V* and 3 years under NCLB, the four urban elementary schools documented in this book experienced only modest positive results, and these were overshadowed by significant negative outcomes. Driven by their own interpretations of social class and race, the administrations and faculty of these schools managed to reshape or resist the most powerful interventions to improve student learning that American society has developed.

Underscoring the lack of improvement, in August 2005 NCLB identified as at some phase of "in need of improvement" 544 schools, or 22.7% of the public and charter schools in New Jersey. The schools described in this book had varied, yet similar, experiences and, with one exception, did not perform well on tests. After achieving Adequate Yearly Progress (AYP) in 2004, Bridge Street was on the "early warning" list in 2005. College Avenue, which had achieved AYP the two previous years, failed to achieve it in language arts and entered "early warning" status, which an appeal reversed. Church Street achieved AYP in 2004, but in 2005 needed "corrective action." Park Avenue, among the first schools in New Jersey labeled in need of "restructuring," after an appeal received an additional year to improve.

In October 2005 NCLB identified Newark and Elizabeth, along with 13 other Abbott districts and 39 additional districts in New Jersey, as being in the second consecutive year of "in need of improvement." *Abbott V* and NCLB did not sufficiently improve these districts and, as a consequence of this failure and a part of the reform process, they faced loss of federal funds, replacement of administrators and teachers, removal of individual schools from the district, and future operation under receivers or trustees.

In an April 2006 lawsuit filed with the Supreme Court of New Jersey by Governor Jon Corzine to request a funding freeze for the Abbott districts, the brief stated,

> While gains in achievement in Abbott districts are evident, and the achievement gap is decreasing, collectively Abbott districts are still lagging behind the State average passing rates on these assessments. None of the Abbott districts is passing the language arts portion of the NJASK4 at the state average passing rate of 81.6%. Only three Abbott districts . . . are exceeding the State average passing rate of 80.2% on the math portion of the NJASK4. *(Abbott v. Burke,* 2006, p. 16)

The brief also noted that "success—or lack thereof—on the State assessments appears to have no correlation to the amount of money the district spends on a per pupil basis" *(Abbott v. Burke,* 2006, p. 17).

Explaining the Test Scores

The 2006 Corzine brief also stated that increases in test scores in some Abbott districts were attributable to a focus on standards-based education instead of implementation of the *Abbott V* mandates. Explaining this, Assistant Education Commissioner Gordon MacInnes (2005b), who led the shift away from the *Abbott V* mandates, wrote,

> Students in districts that have most faithfully implemented the specific remedies prescribed by the Supreme Court as interpreted by the Department of Education before 2002, have consistently performed less well than would be predicted when compared to other Abbott students. Districts that have relied on school-based curricular decisions [instead of the CCCS] have seen a decline in student performance relative to other Abbott districts. (p. 6)

In testimony before the New Jersey Senate Education Committee, MacInnes (2005b) elaborated on his explanation. He said,

> The most likely explanation for why Abbott students do not perform as well as their suburban peers is that *they are not taught what they are expected to learn and what they are tested on in the state assessments.* Most Abbott districts have not yet caught up with the changes introduced by the Core [Content Curriculum] standards. (p. 10)

When asked why, he responded, "I don't know, I can't explain it."

An Alternative Explanation

The experiences of the schools profiled in this book demonstrate that adherence to the original *Abbott V* mandates did not create low performance. Instead, a factor contributing to the inability to score higher on the tests was that the schools *did not* implement the mandated changes. In addition, the limited effectiveness of the Core Content Curriculum Standards was because administrators and teachers selected specific standards to focus on. More important, the change that *was* implemented—extensive continuous test preparation, forced by fear of NCLB sanctions—provided a limited and narrow education that was to a large extent based on speculation concerning the content of the test.

The pervasive influence of the eco-cognitive framework on the change process and classroom practice, explains the consistent, but often seemingly mysterious, finding that something occurs in schools to reduce minority student learning. What happened in the schools described here is that urban African American and Latino students received a different education delivered in a different way than did majority suburban students.

What Next?

In response to a Superior Court ruling that the state had to develop a management plan for the Abbott districts, an October 2005 report, "Closing the Achievement Gap: Two-Year Plan Instructional Priorities" (MacInnes, 2005c), presented the state plan. It continued the 2002 Abbott II revisions that reduced the emphasis on the Whole School Reform model, reemphasized the Core Content Curriculum Standards as the curriculum for every student in the state, and shifted from a uniform "Abbott Program" to customized approaches for each district.

After 7 years of reform that produced few positive results, instead of continuing the same policies, the state should have asked, What, beyond the reforms already attempted, is required to close the achievement gap? Based on the findings of this book, a more productive question would be, What policies, if any, can reconfigure the cognitive framework of administrators and teachers to change the dynamics of legitimacy that affect urban education reform?

To answer these questions, it is useful to view the research findings reported in Chapters 4 through 7 from the perspective of the literature on education change. Following that discussion, the argument is presented that schools contribute more to achievement than has previously been recognized. The chapter concludes with an examination of the future of *Abbott V*, NCLB, and other reforms in a segregated society.

The Findings in Perspective

Abbott V and NCLB were founded on two major premises: (a) that it was possible to implement large-scale education reform, and (b) that the framework of the New Accountability—which relied on externally developed, top-down reform that required accountability in exchange for local control and flexibility—could succeed. Based on these assumptions, the New Jersey state judicial system and the federal legislative process formulated landmark policies intended to equalize educational opportunity for low-income minority students.

However, despite periodic social and intellectual movements intended to improve education through radical reform, uneven incremental change characterized education reform in the 20th century (Tyack & Cuban, 1995). In fact, whether radical or conservative in its intent, most education reform failed (Ravitch, 2000; Sarason, 2004). For example, since the mid-1960s, the beginning of the use of social science theories to improve schools, most research has indicated that it is difficult to change schools because innovations often experience rapid failure, seldom reach full implementation, and if they survive, deteriorate over time (Fink, 2000; Gold, 1999).

Education change usually derails because of ineffective leadership, inadequate resources, a resistant organizational culture, and the tendency of reforms to focus on variables that have little effect on improving learning (Burke, 2002; Fink, 2000; Gold & Miles, 1981; Louis & Miles, 1990; Sarason, 1996, 2004). Attesting further to the difficulties of bringing about change, no research indicates that an original innovative vision for education reform has been replicated on a small scale with fidelity or has diffused to create large-scale change (Elmore, 2004). Contrary to the history of failure of small-scale reforms, and despite the fact that educational research did not underpin pedagogic practice (Lagemann, 2000), however, the reforms initiated by states and cities in response to the 1983 report "A Nation at Risk" (National Commission on Excellence in Education) did increase the complexity and scale of education change significantly (Bryk et al., 1998; Cuban & Usdan, 2003).

The experiences of the four schools profiled in this book—which were subject to attempts to increase the scale of reform—are consistent with research on school reform that has found that changing schools is difficult. Adding to the typical problems of instituting change, the large scale increased complexity, reduced resources, and adversely affected monitoring, assistance, appropriate measurement, and timely corrective action. Indeed, lack of experience with large-scale education reform and the problems encountered during *Abbott V* and NCLB indicate that large-scale reform is still an experimental and uncertain solution for reforming schools and, specifically, for closing achievement gaps.

A Revised Model of Urban Education and Change

The Contribution of Communities to Achievement

The failure of large-scale reform is consistent with another stream of research. Since 1966, family characteristics and community variables have eclipsed classroom behaviors as explanations for academic achievement (Arum, 2000; Coleman et al., 1966; Rothstein, 2004). For example, the negative effects of low economic status are more severe for minority students, particularly when they live in neighborhoods that are predominantly minority and poor (Sirin, 2005). Research on student composition in high schools concluded that "segregation still matters, but it is the socioeconomic composition, not the racial composition, of high schools that impacts student achievement" (Rumberger & Palardy, 2005, p. 2003).

New Jersey Assistant Education Commissioner Gordon MacInnes (2005a) recognized the importance of economic status on achievement and the difficulty in overcoming it. He wrote,

> For almost 40 years since the publication of the Coleman Report, the most certain relationship in educational research and policy is that parental economic and educational background and status are the best predictors of student performance. Until recently, no state or city has broken this connection; only small scale or heroic unreplicable exceptions are to be found. Consider that in the last two years, the state administered eight separate tests to about 700,000 4th, 8th, and 11th graders in 590 districts categorized by eight economic/educational District Factor Groupings "A" to "J." Thus, with 128 opportunities to upset the "demography-as-destiny" table, not once did a lower letter group outperform on average a higher letter group. Yet it is precisely this iron relationship that is to be broken in Abbott districts on a scale never achieved anyplace. (p. 3)

To some extent, the findings reported this book support other research conclusions that family and community socioeconomic status affects learning more than improvements in classrooms (Rothstein, 2004). Indeed, low socioeconomic status and race significantly influenced *Abbott V* and NCLB in multiple ways.

The strong evidence of the influence of social factors external to schools on educational achievement prompted David Berliner (2006) to ask,

> Why do we put so much of our attention and resources into trying to fix what goes on inside low performing schools when the causes of low performance may reside outside the school? Is it possible that we might be better off devoting more of our attention and resources than we now do toward helping the families in the communities that are served by those schools? (p. 963)

Although Berliner's focus on improving conditions external to schools is an important redirection, schools *do* contribute to achievement, and appropriate changes in schools *can* improve student performance.

The Contribution of Schools to Achievement

Abbott V and NCLB assumed that certain types of changes in schools could improve student achievement. In fact, recent research indicates that schools do make a difference and can challenge the influence of family and the local community on achievement (Fryer & Levitt, 2002). There is also increasing evidence that classroom behavior of teachers, specifically instructional techniques, has a significant impact on student learning (Coburn, 2004; Lampert, 2001; Roth et al., 2003; Weinstein, 2002; Wenglinsky, 2002, 2004). Particularly important is whether reform improves the conditions for learning (Sarason, 2004), employs effective instructional methods (Wenglinsky, 2002), and produces a high degree of implementation (Gold & Miles, 1981; Supovitz & May, 2003).

Supporting the position that schools contribute to learning, a recent study concluded that, instead of reproducing inequality, schools equalize cognitive skills for most groups of students (Downey, von Hippel, & Broh, 2004). An important exception is that "The gaps in cognitive skills between Blacks and Whites grow faster than expected when school is in session, directing our attention to schooling as a source of Black/White inequality" (Downey et al., 2004, p. 632). Another study documented unequal treatment with the finding that teachers of African American students spend more time on academic subjects and less time on enrichment and recess activities, compared with teachers of White students (Roth et al., 2003). Other studies document the creation of stereotype threat (Steele, 1997) and oppositional culture (Ogbu, 2003), which adversely affect the academic performance of African American students. In addition to the liabilities of high levels of family and community poverty, school and classroom instruction can affect achievement negatively (Lee, 2005; Weinstein, 2002). In summary, accumulating research indicates that what happens in school *is* important for minority students.

The Community, the School, and Large-Scale Reform

The externally initiated changes under *Abbott V* and NCLB brought to the foreground the eco-cognitive framework that permeated decision making by the teachers and administrators and made explicit their understanding of the contributions of the community and the school to learning (Sarason & Klaber, 1985, p. 128). Without the forced change, these extremely important views would have retained their power to affect behavior in classrooms but would have remained implicit. Although the processes that mediated implementation of reform through the eco-cognitive framework varied among the teachers and the schools (Olsen & Kirtman, 2002), the negative comparison of poor inner-city neighborhoods with wealthy White suburbs among most administrators and teachers was attributable to the collectively perceived—and objective—social conditions of the metropolitan area.

The pervasiveness of the eco-cognitive framework suggests that the schools described in this book did not passively reflect the social class and racial characteristics of a specific community (Coleman et al., 1966; Rothstein, 2004). Instead, teachers and administrators made conscious decisions and engaged in behavior that produced a specific type of education. Even under extreme external pressure to change, the schools intentionally reproduced the type of education that reflected social class occupational roles (Anyon, 1980) and established complex, often indirect, socialization processes that "influence which cultural models children are exposed to," along with a "structure of rewards and sanctions" (Bowles & Gintis, 2002, p. 18).

Abbott V and NCLB viewed administrators and teachers as passive agents who would simply implement external reforms. However, their interpretation of the reforms from the perspective of the eco-cognitive framework demonstrates that teachers and administrators were active participants in the change process.

Segregation and the Future of Urban School Reform

The Eco-Cognitive Myth

The eco-cognitive framework is misguided and harmful. Social science research does not support the widespread view that poor urban areas are disorganized (e.g., the idea that urban students need structure to compensate for dysfunctional families) or the notion of personal inferiority often attributed to the poor. Alejandro Portes (2000) wrote,

> The core finding of [the] empirical literature is that the poor are no different from anyone else. They simply lack the resources and information to climb out of this self-reproducing condition. Ultimately, poverty causes social pathology—not vice versa. Outside observers from the government, the elite press, and academia have consistently attributed to the poor—currently labeled the "underclass"—features that distinguish them from the rest of society and that "cause" their permanent disadvantage. (p. 5)

A theory of human nature and, by implication, variability in intelligence in different groups, underlies the eco-cognitive framework based on environmental variation (Pinker, 2002). Robert Sternberg and Elena Grigorenko

(1999) dispelled the importance for education of current the gene–environment debate. They wrote,

> Whether abilities or disabilities, personality attributes, or motivational inclinations are inherited fully or in part has virtually no bearing on what educators should do in their classrooms. In particular, what we know about heritability has no bearing on how modifiable attributes are (e.g., learning skills, thinking skills, motivation to learn, and so on). Evidence suggests that environment can make a powerful difference on academic skills and performance, whatever the heritabilities or various abilities may be. From the standpoint of education and psychology practitioners, the heredity versus environment debate is *an unnecessary detour.* (p. 536)

An important implication of these two correctives to the eco-cognitive framework is that instead of arranging classrooms to teach poor minority students "resilience," or using scripted lessons tailored to the needs of urban students, meaningful equalization of urban education for poor minority students requires teaching the same cognitive and social skills in the same way as they are taught to the majority population. At the Bridge Street School, Mrs. Smith did this with widely acknowledged success—in one of the most "socially disorganized," high-poverty, racially segregated communities in the United States.

This raises a fundamental question: Do reforms exist that can alter or overcome the effects of the eco-cognitive framework itself? Before proposing an alternative strategy for reform, it is critical to discuss whether *Abbott V* and NCLB can be changed to reduce the negative effects of the eco-cognitive framework.

The Future of *Abbott V*

Abbott V equalized resources in urban schools and introduced some innovative programs but had little effect on the selection of specific reforms and their continued implementation. One possible solution for encouraging long-term implementation would be to allow each school to perform a self-diagnosis and develop its own reform strategy rather than subject it to a court or federally imposed top-down reform.

A bottom-up change strategy may sound reasonable, but it is not likely to be effective unless the eco-cognitive framework changes first. The taken-for-granted understanding of social class and race would influence the diagnosis, the change strategy, and consequently whatever reforms were implemented. A self-diagnosis would probably simply reproduce urban education instead of changing it.

More monitoring of top-down change by the state is a possible solution. In fact, however, recognizing the limitations of monitoring and enforcement, the New Jersey Department of Education began to shift its focus in September 2005 such that it would "operate as partners to districts to untangle instructional challenges and improve financial and business efficiency" (MacInnes, 2005a, p. 4). The key shortcoming of the new emphasis was that, unless state employees received training that would allow them to understand accurately the social processes affecting the dynamics of change in schools, and developed techniques to change them, the eco-cognitive framework would continue to influence all aspects of reform.

This study found that the eco-cognitive framework prevalent in the culture of the elementary schools also operated in the Abbott preschools located within the schools. It is likely that the eco-cognitive framework affects Abbott preschool programs located in separate buildings as well.

The eco-cognitive framework will probably affect the Abbott secondary education reforms initiated in 2005. According to the New Jersey Department of Education, the goals of the Secondary Education Initiative are to create smaller "learning communities," increase instructional rigor, and have every student receive regular personalized attention from at least one adult.

Research supports the creation of small high schools for urban minority students because small size creates an organizational culture that encourages and supports academic achievement (Fine et al., 2005; National Academy of Sciences, 2003). A key benefit for minority urban students is that small schools decouple the culture of the school from the cultures of the low income urban family and the neighborhood that can exert a negative influence on achievement (Fine et al., 2005).

However, the national committee that evaluated research on urban high schools noted that "A system of schools that has fully implemented the core principles needed to provide engaging, rigorous education for all students is yet to be seen" (National Academy of Sciences, 2003, p. 2). Like the other elements of *Abbott V*, the creation of small high schools is experimental and a surrogate for integration that attempts to create separate but equal schools. Small schools may separate the culture of the community from the culture of education, but as Chapters 4 through 7 have demonstrated, the eco-cognitive framework brings a version of the culture of the community into classrooms through the values and behavior of the educators.

The Future of NCLB

NCLB was less comprehensive than *Abbott V* and simply pressured schools to improve standardized test scores through progressive corrective actions. The basic defect was that, even when resources were adequate, pressure alone was ineffective because it did not provide specific ways in which low-performing schools could change. Coupled with the minimal skills of most administrators in managing change, the result was the simple and direct solution of test preparation.

NCLB also contributed to the evolutionary processes of selection by narrowing the options for change, for example, by reducing the options generated by *Abbott V.* It influenced retention of change because it reinforced preexisting tendencies within the deep structure of urban education to simplify the curriculum, restrict the type of pedagogy, and, ultimately, reduce the meaning and type of education.

Redesigning NCLB to overcome its unintended negative consequences would be difficult because of the flexibility it granted states and school districts in implementing their own reforms in exchange for accountability. It is unlikely that the federal government will choose to micromanage classrooms. Instead, it will probably continue to focus on accountability, with a shift toward multidimensional measures of achievement. Even this minor change in emphasis would leave intact the multiple problems encountered by the schools profiled in this book.

In summary, modifications of *Abbott V* and NCLB are not easy to accomplish or likely to make much difference unless they address the underlying causes of the achievement gap. Although they had the potential to change the deep structure of urban education, only NCLB did—but negatively. Before presenting techniques for improving the change process, it is important to examine reforms based on some significant alternative approaches: business management principles, market forces, and legal strategies.

Schools as Businesses and Market Solutions

The application of business management techniques to education typically creates minor adjustments in existing practices (Ouchi, 2003). For example, the business management elements of *Abbott V,* particularly the use of zero-based budgeting, which was intended to give control over financial resources to schools, not only failed for technical and political reasons but did not result in significant improvements in learning. In the few years that it was used, the school-based allocation of resources was no more creative or effective than budgets formulated and administered by the Board of Education.

A problem with market solutions—vouchers and charter schools—for isolated, poor, monoracial schools is that although they may create choices, the demographic characteristics of districts like Newark and Elizabeth restrict the options. A charter school might provide a curriculum organized around a theme, and the teaching style might be distinctive, but the social, economic, and racial characteristics of the student population would be no different from those in neighborhood public schools. Also, it is not clear that school choice promotes competition that will induce public schools to improve (Tractenberg, Sadovnik, & Liss, 2004). Most important, business practices and markets are not likely to alter education significantly because they have only a limited effect on the eco-cognitive framework, which reinforces adherence to the existing deep structure of urban education.

A Legal Strategy for Change

According to James Liebman and Charles Sabel's (2003a, 2003b) analysis of recent state education reforms and NCLB, the reforms provide a legal framework for improving education. Essentially, *Abbott V* and NCLB created the ability to compare performance among schools and to identify the methods used to achieve it.

This framework creates the potential for individual or class-action litigation for improvements based on the demographic characteristics of schools. If a school with specific demographic characteristics performs better on standardized tests than a school with a similar population, the low-performing school could sue to obtain the successful methods.

Abbott V used a similar framework to compare student achievement across District Factor Groups (DFGs) designated A through J—the poorest to the wealthiest of New Jersey's over 600 school districts. Coupled with information on per pupil expenditures, these achievement comparisons supported, and eventually led to a mandate for, equal per pupil funding and sweeping school reform remedies.

However, as Chapters 4 through 7 document, after funding equalization and attempted implementation of the New Jersey Supreme Court mandates, significant achievement differences persisted even among schools in the same DFG. For example, Bridge Street consistently scored higher than Park Avenue, even though both had similar student and community characteristics.

The evidence suggests that identifying and transferring effective practices is difficult. For example, it was not entirely clear to the schools in this study why test scores fluctuated from year to year. In addition, the cultures of Bridge Street and Park Avenue were distinctive, and the culture of Bridge Street may have created a more effective learning atmosphere. Organizational cultures are not only difficult to change, they are usually rooted in a specific historical context that reduces the prospect of transfer.

Nevertheless, using the legal framework outlined above and the test results of *Abbott V* and NCLB, *Crawford v. Davy* (2006), a class-action lawsuit intended to serve as a national test case, was filed in the Superior Court of New Jersey in Newark in July 2006. The class was more than 60,000 students in 96 failing schools in 25 New Jersey districts. The suit argues that the denial of educational opportunities violates children's civil right to a thorough and efficient education under the New Jersey constitution, and to equal protection of the laws under the state and federal constitutions.

The two remedies the lawsuit seeks are an end to "compulsory attendance zones that prevent children from attending better performing public schools outside of their districts" and a share of public funds allocated to a student to permit enrollment in a public or private school. In other words, the litigants want interdistrict school choice with public funding or vouchers. The suit does not want to end *Abbott V* funding but instead to use it in a different way than to continue to support failing schools.

In addition to the difficulties of replicating effective teaching techniques and school cultures, potential limitations of the legal strategy are the same conditions that have historically affected education reform in the United States and the persistence of the eco-cognitive framework in schools students might attend with vouchers.

Alternative Strategies

Some Basic Elements of School Reform

Whether changes occur in *Abbott V* or NCLB, or the movement to turn schools into businesses becomes more successful, or a legal strategy for education equity propels a new civil rights movement, it is necessary to develop a model of what urban school reform should try to accomplish.

First, reform should create conditions that change the eco-cognitive framework. Without altering teachers' and administrators' understanding of the role of social class and race in education, any type of reform will fail.

Second, all students should be in an educational environment that provides equal resources. This includes equal per pupil funding but should also address the condition of school buildings, health care, safety, and nutrition.

Third, the educational programs introduced into high-poverty schools should not be experimental. Most Whole School Reform models and other programs for changing urban education have not produced significant improvement in student achievement over time. Often, these "new" programs use teaching methods that reflect or reinforce the eco-cognitive framework, for example, reliance on drills and rote learning (American Institutes for Research, 2005). Instead, programs that produce high achievement in affluent suburbs should serve as models for urban reform and, if necessary, should undergo only minor adaptations. Another approach is what research has identified as "active" teaching practices that correlate with improved student performance, including individualization, collaboration, and authentic assessment (Wenglinsky, 2002).

Fourth, program implementation requires an appropriate authority structure that includes leaders who understand and proactively manage the change process, coupled with predetermined monitoring systems to establish and maintain a high level of implementation fidelity. Although the emphasis in schools is usually collegiality and creativity rather than obedience to authority (Cuban, 2004), the use of a command and control authority structure in schools has the potential to improve the implementation of reforms. When the urgency for change is high, developing a more rigid, yet adaptive, hierarchy that can initiate and enforce change is necessary. Ironically, the creation of a more bureaucratic structure may be an important innovation because collegial or organic organizational structures, which are often advocated as a change that can improve learning compared with bureaucratic structures, are not a powerful determinant of student achievement (Miller & Rowan, 2006).

Finally, evaluating the results of the changes should include administrator and teacher self-evaluation, in addition to review by a panel of outside experts who also act as mentors and consultants. Student evaluation should measure individual academic growth based on more humanistic and flexible criteria than the current standardized tests, for example, a portfolio of accomplishments and performance-based assessment.

Managing Change More Effectively

Whatever the next education reform, improving management of the change process is essential.[1] Two issues that emerged as critical for the schools described in this book were the problems the reforms encountered and the management of legitimacy.

Each change influenced succeeding changes (Tushman & Romanelli, 1985, p. 180). The history of a particular organizational pattern of change framed the next phase, whether it was an equilibrium or a revolutionary period. For example, communication distortion shaped the information available for corrective action in the next phase. When policy makers and administrators were provided with incorrect information, change was delegitimated, perpetuating the very conditions that the initial and subsequent reforms were intended to solve.

No principal in the profiled schools employed a particular theory of individual or organizational change. A key element in any reform should be a mechanism for increasing the legitimacy of the need and the urgency for change (Kotter, 1996, pp. 35–50), especially with respect to the need for improving classroom instruction. This requires changing the school culture (Schein, 1992), with the objective of transforming external change into a common understanding of the needs of the school. Permitting each teacher to reject or modify the changes based on his or her own experience and preferences is a recipe for failure. Changing school culture requires critical examination of the assumptions and rationalizations underlying the eco-cognitive framework (Argyris, 2004).

Another approach to changing school culture is to use the typologies of schools and teachers in presented in Chapters 4 through 7 as a tool for administrators to use in analyzing the interaction of values and behaviors. The extent to which values or behaviors should be a focus of reform depends on the complexity of the needed change and the extent to which the new methods differ from pre-change conditions. Relatively minor changes that rationalize existing practice do not require values change. Complex, demanding changes such as *Abbott V* require values change before behavior change.

Finally, employing multiple change techniques—reason, research, resonance, redescription, resources and rewards, and real world events—which improves the probability of change (Gardner, 2004), can be an approach to altering the eco-cognitive framework. One application of this method that could specifically address the eco-cognitive framework would be to implement culturally relevant ways of teaching inner-city students (Delpit, 1995; Ladson-Billings, 1994; Weinstein, 2002).[2]

But changing the eco-cognitive framework is difficult. The training in the Community for Learning/Adaptive Learning Environments Model (CFL/ALEM) did not succeed, and the negative experiences of the administrators and faculty with the reforms only served to reinforce their concepts of social, racial, and economic bifurcation and provided a convenient explanation of why the court- and state-sponsored solutions would not work. Although changing the cognitive frameworks of individuals may have some effectiveness (Kegan & Lahey, 2001; Seligman, 1991), because the social structure produced the eco-cognitive framework, social change is required. This leads to consideration of changes outside of schools that can improve learning.

Expanding Education Policy

Economic Policies

As noted above, because of the failure of school reforms, recent arguments expand what counts as education policy to include economic policies that create and perpetuate poverty (Anyon, 2005; Berliner, 2006; Rothstein, 2004). For example, proponents of economic policy change champion a higher minimum wage, because research indicates that increased family income improves achievement (Anyon, 2005).

However, communities and families that will benefit from an increased minimum wage will remain significantly lower in the social class structure than families with middle-class incomes and wealth. Although increasing wages should help, it is unlikely to significantly reduce social class distinctions and mitigate the negative impact on education of race discrimination and class bias. This is particularly true for the racially and economically isolated communities described in this book.

Integration

The fundamental finding of this study is that a segregated social and economic structure legitimated segregated schools and influenced the selection of specific educational practices to fit the needs of students in those schools. The argument for social policy from this finding is that integration is not only a moral responsibility in a democratic society (Gutmann, 1987, pp. 160–171) or a necessity for improving economically and racially segregated urban schools (Orfield & Lee, 2005; Powell & Spencer, 2003), but it is the only way to reconfigure the deep structure of urban education by delegitimating the eco-cognitive framework.

It is possible that over time integration can change the deep structure of the environment of education, which eventually will reconfigure the cognitive framework of policy makers, administrators, and teachers through the evolutionary processes of variation, selection, and retention that now contribute to reproducing unequal education. In other words, the power of the environment over the type of education that can be provided in urban schools is currently regarded as legitimate and has been relegitimated by the shortcomings and failures of reforms such as *Abbott V* and NCLB; thus, by citing environment, teachers can successfully resist planned organizational change. The external environment of urban schools requires a fundamental change to increase racial and economic diversity, which in turn will affect organizational change processes. This is becoming increasingly important, because there is evidence that urban schools are becoming more segregated (Frankenberg & Lee, 2002; Kozol, 2005).

However, since *Brown* the politics of integration have been extremely contentious. Further, since the 1974 U.S. Supreme Court *Milliken v. Bradley* decision, involuntary interdistrict integration has not been available as a solution for improving urban schools (Eaton, Feldman, & Kirby, 1996).

In the face of the legal constraints on integration, alternative schemes have included the creation of magnet communities that, because of the enriched quality of life they offer, will attract a mixture of races and social classes (Wachtel, 1999, pp. 233–236). Another strategy is to use public school choice to create middle-class schools for all children (Kahlenberg, 2001, 2004). However, in Newark and Elizabeth, as well as in similar cities throughout the country, population characteristics do not permit economic integration through intradistrict choice. It is also possible that the eco-cognitive framework could affect middle-class schools through assignment of middle-class minority students to low-ability tracks.

Interdistrict voucher plans such as that proposed in *Crawford v. Davy* (2006) face significant political and social obstacles and provide limited, selective integration. Similarly, countywide integration could provide a solution, but it is problematic because of White flight.

Voluntary Integration

In June 2006, the U.S. Supreme Court agreed to hear *Parents Involved in Community Schools v. Seattle School District No. 1* and *Meredith v. Jefferson County*

Board of Education, which involve the use of race for school assignments (see Welner, 2006). The Court's ruling could have considerable impact on the extent to which race can influence school assignment.

In the meantime, an approach that can succeed, even if the Supreme Court upholds limits on the role of race or eliminates it completely, is small-scale voluntary integration of schools in working- and middle-class suburbs near cities. The voluntary aspect of the plan would reduce barriers to integration instead of forcing it on unwilling communities. One objective would be to create a higher level of integration than can be produced with vouchers, without leaving uninformed or less motivated families in the inner city. Also, as opposed to a voucher program, a critical mass of students is necessary because the ultimate goal is to change the external environment of schooling to reduce the effects of the eco-cognitive framework. This would require the selection a school that a student would contribute to by increasing its racial diversity.

To facilitate voluntary integration, the state could initially provide suburbs with financial support for integrated schools that would decrease over time. For example, participating suburban districts could receive an Abbott level of per pupil expenditure, which is higher than suburban funding, plus an administrative fee and transportation costs. Another incentive could be reduced property taxes for these districts, offset with a contribution to school funding from state revenues, for example, from the state lottery or (in the case of New Jersey specifically) a tax on Atlantic City casinos.

State and county funds could upgrade urban school facilities—a process started under *Abbott V*—and provide them with programs not available in the suburbs, ranging from preschools and elementary schools with extremely small class sizes to successful experiments such as the Bard High School Early College in New York City, which teaches college-level courses beginning in the 11th grade. Finally, the state should require research by an independent agency to monitor the effect on cognitive achievement and social development for all students involved in the integration program.

Enforcement of the Mount Laurel housing decision would also improve integration in New Jersey. High real estate values make residential integration of communities extremely difficult without the enforcement of fair housing laws.

Equal Opportunity

An alternative to the integration strategy discussed above is to create genuinely separate and equal schools. But how can it be done? What change process or instructional programs can create separate and equal education? How would it be determined that education that is separate is indeed equal? If it is, will it be consistent with American democratic ideals?

There are many reasons why integration is the solution to the problems that plague urban communities and schools. One might list them, but this most compelling statement from *Brown* really says it all:

> Does segregation of children in public schools solely on the basis of race, even though the physical facilities and other 'tangible' factors may be equal, deprive the children of the minority group of equal education opportunities? We believe that it does. . . . In the field of public education, the doctrine of 'separate but equal' has no place. (*Brown v. Board of Education*, 1954)

Ultimately, the type of educational opportunity provided for poor minority group children is a critical test of the legitimacy of American society.

APPENDIX A

Education Equity in New Jersey

A Summary of Cases and Continuing Litigation

Key decisions are in **bold**.

1875	The New Jersey constitution is amended to require the Legislature to establish a system of "thorough and efficient education."[1]
Feb. 1970	A lawsuit, ***Robinson v. Cahill***, brought on behalf or urban schoolchildren, charges that the state's system for funding schools discriminates against poorer districts and creates disparities in education.
April 1973	The New Jersey Supreme Court rules that heavy reliance on property taxes for education discriminates against poor districts.
July 1975	The **Public School Education Act**, Chapter 212, creates a new state funding formula for public schools, but lawmakers do not raise taxes to pay for it.
July 1976	The New Jersey Supreme Court shuts public schools for 8 days because the Legislature failed to fund the new formula. The first New Jersey state income tax is enacted.
Feb. 1981	The Education Law Center of Rutgers University, Newark, files ***Abbott v. Burke*** on behalf of urban schoolchildren, challenging the 1975 Act as inadequate to assure a thorough and efficient education. The Education Law Center charges that disparities between wealthy and poor districts increased under the Chapter 212 funding formula, which was supposed to reduce them.
1985	The New Jersey Supreme Court issues ***Abbott I***, remanding the case to the Office of Administrative Law, and rules that

to satisfy the Constitution, the State must assure urban children an education enabling them to compete with their suburban peers.

1986–1987 The trial in *Abbott* takes place over 9 months before Judge Steven LeFelt.

Aug. 1988 Administrative Law Judge LeFelt rules that funding for the system is unconstitutional and discriminates against poor districts; issues a 600-page initial decision recommending a complete overhaul of the State's system of providing urban education.

Feb. 1989 Education Commissioner Saul Cooperman rejects Judge LeFelt's decision, claiming that the existing funding system provides equal education opportunities.

May 1990 Governor James J. Florio introduces the **Quality Education Act** (QEA), including a new funding formula, in anticipation of a Supreme Court decision in favor of the Abbott children and introduces a $2.8 billion state tax increase to pay for the new law and the budget deficit he inherited.

June 1990 The New Jersey Supreme Court rules in ***Abbott v. Burke II*** that inadequate and unequal funding denies students in urban districts a thorough and efficient education and that the state must provide "parity-plus"—equal funding between suburban and urban districts for regular education plus extra or "supplemental" programs to "wipe out disadvantages as much as a school district can."

March 1991 Governor Florio signs an amendment to the QEA diverting $360 million to property tax relief.

July 1992 The Education Law Center files suit charging that the QEA fails to comply with the 1990 *Abbott II* ruling.

July 1994 The New Jersey Supreme Court, in ***Abbott III***, declares the QEA unconstitutional because it neither assures parity nor guarantees needed supplemental programs. The Court gives the State until 1997 to comply.

Nov. 1995 Governor Christine Todd Whitman unveils a plan to change the school funding formula by capping spending in suburban districts, shifting the State's role to guaranteeing minimum spending and achievement of the New Jersey Core Curriculum Content Standards for all students.

Dec. 1996 Governor Whitman signs the **Comprehensive Education Improvement and Financing Act** (CEIFA), which allows a difference of more than $1,200 in spending per pupil between Abbott and suburban district averages.

Jan. 1997 The Education Law Center files suit, charging CEIFA failure to comply with the 1990 and 1994 Abbott rulings.

May 1997 The New Jersey Supreme Court, in ***Abbott IV***, declares CEIFA unconstitutional and orders State officials to increase immediately funding for Abbott schools to parity with suburban schools. The Court also orders a special hearing before a Superior Court judge to determine the supplemental programs needed by disadvantaged children and to determine facility needs in urban districts.

Sept. 1997 The State allocates $246 million to the Abbott districts to comply with the *Abbott IV* ruling. The 1997–1998 school year is the first in which funding for education is equalized between urban and suburban school districts.

Jan. 1998 After 2 months of hearings, Remand Judge Michael Patrick King recommends to the Supreme Court implementation of a package of supplemental programs, including preschool, at an additional cost of $312 million per year, plus at least $2.7 billion for building deficiencies.

May 1998 The New Jersey Supreme Court issues ***Abbott V*** and orders unprecedented entitlements for Abbott children, including Whole School Reform, full-day kindergarten and preschool for all 3- and 4-year-olds, and a comprehensive state-managed and funded facilities program to correct code violations, to eliminate overcrowding, and to provide adequate space for all educational programs in the Abbott schools. Other required supplemental programs are health and social services, increased security, technology, alternative education, school-to-work, after-school, and summer school programs.

July 1999 The Education Law Center returns to the New Jersey Supreme Court to challenge the State's failure to implement well-planned, high-quality preschool education for all children in the Abbott districts.

March 2000 The New Jersey Supreme Court rules in ***Abbott VI*** that the State had failed to implement preschool education as directed, and orders the New Jersey Department of Education to ensure that day care centers meet the same standards as district schools, that classes be restricted to 15 students, and that all teachers be certified within 4 years.

May 2000 The New Jersey Supreme Court reaffirms in ***Abbott VII*** its prior ruling that the State fully fund the Abbott school construction program.

July 2000 The Legislature enacts the Educational Facilities Construction and Financing Act to finance and implement $6 billion in facilities improvements in Abbott schools and school districts statewide.

April 2001 Administrative Law Judge Jeff Masin rules that the State had failed again to properly implement the Abbott preschool program, as required in *Abbott V* and *Abbott VI*.

Sep. 2001 The New Jersey Supreme Court hears arguments on the State's continuing failure to implement preschool.

Oct. 2001 The Appellate Division of Superior Court hears arguments on the failure of the State to establish clear, effective, and comprehensive guidelines for local school and district implementation of Abbott programs and reforms.

Oct. 2001 The New Jersey Supreme Court issues the first half of ***Abbott VIII***, directing timely state decisions for preschool plans and budgets and the expected administrative appeal process to resolve disputes between districts and the State Department of Education over plans and budgets.

Feb. 2002 The New Jersey Supreme Court issues the second half of ***Abbott VIII***, further clarifying requirements for State implementation of the *Abbott V* preschool mandate, as augmented by *Abbott VI*.

Feb. 2002 Governor James E. McGreevey creates a commission to oversee implementation of Abbott remedies and pledges that the state will not be an obstacle to change.

March 2002 The Education Law Center agrees to support the McGreevey Administration's application before the Supreme Court for a 1-year freeze on further implementation of Abbott remedies at 2002–2003 levels. In exchange, McGreevey agrees to boost preschool spending by $150 million and maintain parity with an additional $83 million in a year when budget deficits require flat State funding to all other school districts.

June 2002 The New Jersey Supreme Court issues ***Abbott IX***, directing the 1-year freeze on further implementation of Abbott remedies.

July 2002 Governor McGreevey establishes the Schools Construction Corporation and calls for building "high performance" schools.

Dec. 2002 The Abbott Implementation and Compliance Coordinating Council stops meeting amid strong rumors the McGreevey Administration will seek a 2nd-year freeze on funding Abbott and will further seek to roll back the Court-ordered mandates.

March 2003 The McGreevey Administration applies to the Supreme Court to remove the mandates for Whole School Reform and supplemental programs.

April 2003 The New Jersey Supreme Court directs the parties to mediate the disputed matters before Judge Philip Carchman.

June 2003 The New Jersey Supreme Court accepts the mediation agreement, settling all matters except the Department of Education's request for a 2nd-year freeze on state funding of Abbott districts, and issues the first half of ***Abbott X***.

July 2003 The New Jersey Supreme Court directs the Department of Education to fund the districts at amounts sufficient to maintain expenditures authorized in the 2002–2003 budgets.

Aug. 2003 The Cooperative Rulemaking Group ordered in *Abbott X* concludes its work on new Abbott regulations.

Jan. 2004 The Appellate Division hears appeals by 21 districts challenging the State's failure to provide $150 million in disputed state aid.

Jan. 2004 The Secondary Education Workgroup ordered in *Abbott X* begins meeting to develop research-based reform initiatives for Abbott middle and high schools.

March 2004 The New Jersey Supreme Court directs the New Jersey Department of Education to restore immediately an estimated $78–100 million in programs and positions to the 2003–2004 budgets of the Abbott districts.

March 2004 Abbott districts ask the New Jersey Supreme Court to overturn an Appellate Court ruling that sanctioned the failure of the New Jersey Department of Education to fully fund the Abbott preschool program.

Aug. 2004 The New Jersey Supreme Court reaffirms New Jersey's prohibition of school segregation, ruling that "racial imbalance resulting from de facto segregation . . . is inimical" to the New Jersey constitutional guarantee of a thorough and efficient education.

Sept. 2004 The property tax task force meets to consider amending the New Jersey constitution. Among the proposals are amendments to the "thorough and efficient" clause of the constitution and other schemes to reduce property tax, including revision of *Abbott V* to provide Abbott districts with funds at the state average instead of matching or surpassing the wealthiest school districts, as the New Jersey Supreme Court mandated.

June 2005 The Education Law Center files a lawsuit against the New Jersey Department of Education for failure to have a plan to manage the Abbott programs and reforms.

July 2005 The Schools Construction Corporation runs out of the $6 billion allocated for school construction under Abbott and stops work on 200 urban school projects.

Aug. 2005 Superior Court Judge Neil Schuster orders the New Jersey Department of Education to prepare a plan for the Department's Abbott Division to manage implementation of the Abbott reforms for 2006–2007.

Nov. 2005 The Supreme Court hears arguments for more construction funds for Abbott districts.

Jan. 2006 In ***Bacon v. New Jersey State Department of Education***, the New Jersey State Board of Education rules that students in 16 rural districts are not receiving a "thorough and efficient" education under the state funding law.

April 2006 Governor Jon Corzine files suit in the New Jersey Supreme Court to preclude requests from Abbott districts for additional Education Opportunity Aid for 2007. The freeze on Abbott spending is requested because of a fiscal crisis in the State and because the State had not adequately monitored the spending of Abbott districts.

May 2006 The New Jersey Supreme Court rules that Abbott funding be frozen for the 2007 fiscal year and approves fiscal audits for several Abbott districts.

APPENDIX B

Research Methods

IT IS IMPORTANT to understand the research methods used in this book to evaluate the data, theory, and conclusions. Knowledge of the methods also assists in determining whether generalization to other types of reforms and different geographic locations is appropriate. Recently, the selection of a research method has become more important because federal education research policy requires scientifically rigorous research—often equated with randomized controlled trials—to inform education policy and practice (Anfara, Brown, & Mangione, 2002; Eisenhart & Towne, 2003).

The following discussion presents the research design, site selection process, the role of theory, data collection methods, and analysis strategies.

The Research Design: Comparative and Longitudinal

The research design was comparative and longitudinal. Comparisons between the two school districts, among the four schools, and among the teachers occurred continuously throughout data collection. Another key comparison was the responses to *Abbott V* versus reactions to No Child Left Behind. These comparisons identified common elements and significant variations as the change process developed.

The research was longitudinal because 7 years of data in Elizabeth—September 1998 to June 2005—and almost 6 years in Newark—March 2000 to June 2005—contributed to understanding change as a process that develops over time (Hargreaves & Goodson, 2006). To document changes that occurred because of the reforms, the research sampled schools at roughly regular intervals, varied by different days of the week and different times of day.

In addition to classroom observations—which averaged 2 hours per observation and approximately 60 observations for each school—school visits included attendance at training programs, observation of faculty meetings, and informal interviews with teachers and administrators.

Attendance at key events provided a way to measure the influence of time on the change process as participants experienced it. This strategy increased the ability to understand how specific information and actions affected participants' interpretation of events and their subsequent behavior.

The Research Sites

The Sample Size

Qualitative research on educational change usually produces a thick description (Geertz, 1973) of a single example of planned change (Barnes, 2002; Bensman, 2000; Duke, 1995; Fink, 2000). Recent exceptions are Bryk and Schneider's (2002) sample of four schools in Chicago and Harry, Sturges, and Klingner's (2005) study of 12 schools, which concluded that the abundance of data made interpretation difficult and that "we could have achieved a more refined analysis with a sample half [the] size" (p. 12).

This book presents four in-depth case studies of a complex, long-term change process. Because of the richness of the data, a small sample is appropriate; it avoids the issue of an overwhelming amount of data but reduces the limitations of a single case study. In addition, this book relies on data from other research on Abbott districts that used qualitative and quantitative data (Erlichson et al., 1999; Erlichson & Goertz, 2001; Muirhead, Tyler, & Hamilton, 2001; Supovitz & May, 2003; Walker, 2000; Walker & Gutmore, 2000).

Selecting School Districts

The method for selecting districts and schools was a purposive sample. The objective was to vary the size and population of the cities, the type of school district, and the features of the schools and their communities.

This strategy encountered immediate problems because the first three districts contacted refused to participate in the study. Eventually, Newark and Elizabeth agreed to participate. The districts differed primarily because of the larger population of Newark, key differences in their histories, and because the state operated Newark's school system before and during implementation of the *Abbott V* and NCLB reforms. The two districts are representative of many cities in the United States because they face the same social and economic issues—high crime rates, inadequate health care, extensive poverty, and education systems that need improvement—and most metropolitan areas have similar patterns of residential segregation (Glaeser & Vigdor, 2001; Jargowsky, 2003; Massey & Denton, 1993).

Selecting Schools

In Elizabeth, an assistant superintendent selected schools that varied by size, student population characteristics, and community type. Because the Bridge Street School was in one of the most economically depressed neighborhoods in Newark, it was a critical case for studying reform. It also provided an opportunity to study change in a district operated by the state. As documented in Chapters 4 through 7, the selected schools had most of the characteristics common to urban schools in poor minority communities throughout the United States.

Selecting Teachers

The research focused on first- and fourth-grade teachers. First grade is important because that is when most students learn to read. Since the inception of the New Jersey standardized test, fourth grade has been the first elementary class tested. Data from two grade levels provided an opportunity to observe the effects of change in different classroom settings.

Identifying teachers to participate in the study was an important issue. Teachers who were to be studied extensively were selected by the school principals. In Elizabeth, with the exception of one Latina, all teachers who were selected and agreed to participate were White, and only one was male. This accurately reflected the composition of the faculty in Elizabeth. Observations and interviews of the few African American and Latina teachers occurred during faculty meetings.

At Bridge Street, the teachers selected by the principal were White females. Observations of several African American teachers' classrooms provided additional data, and only female African American teachers participated in training for the Bank Street Literacy program.[1]

Ten teachers agreed to participate, and most volunteered their opinions and information on a wide variety of issues. However, several were less articulate and required more direct questioning. Even these teachers permitted extensive observation of their classrooms and did not disguise their values and behaviors. For example, after a few observations, an initially reticent teacher demonstrated how she satisfied administrators' unannounced classroom observations with false lesson plans for the Community for Learning/Adaptive Learning Environments Model (CFL/ALEM). In addition, she vigorously reprimanded students during every observation without embarrassment over her difficulty in managing fourth-grade students.

Sample Benefits and Limitations

All of the schools in the study selected the CFL/ALEM Whole School Reform (WSR) model. One advantage of studying the same model in four schools was the opportunity to examine variations in implementation of the same program. Another advantage was that, compared with the other models, the complexity of CFL/ALEM enabled exploration of wide-ranging restructuring of administrator, teacher, and student behaviors.

The limitation of studying one WSR model was the possibility that other models could have created different classroom and schoolwide change processes, been modified differently, and affected student achievement and behavior more or less than CFL/ALEM. Reducing the impact of this limitation, research indicates that many of the New Jersey Supreme Court approved models did not improve achievement, and insufficient research exists to evaluate the effectiveness of most models (American Institutes for Research, 2005; Berends, Chun, Schuyler, Stockly, & Briggs, 2002; Borman et al., 2000; Borman, Hewes, Overman, & Brown, 2002; Cook et al., 1999; Desimone, 2002).

The principals selected teachers whom they considered to be successful implementers of CFL/ALEM. In addition to a bias toward accepting the *Abbott V* mandates, these teachers were probably more receptive than their colleagues to implementing NCLB. Countering this bias, it became apparent early in fieldwork that the participating teachers varied widely in their values, teaching styles, willingness, and ability to change.

Overall, the limitations of a purposive sample appear to be minimal because of variation in the sample despite the demographic and economic similarities of Abbott schools and districts. Finally, the sample avoided problems associated with sampling on the dependent variable (see Firestone, Schorr, & Mackey, 2004).

The Role of Theory: Explaining Change

The punctuated legitimacy theory of educational change influenced all aspects of the research. It served to guide the data collection, the continuous analysis, and the final interpretation of the events initiated by *Abbott V* and NCLB. To reduce any tendency to force the data to fit the theory, during fieldwork and analysis, the research process included periodic written critical assessments of the data to explore alternative explanations. The simultaneous use of a theory and the collection of grounded data created a research process that alternated between deductive and inductive logics of inquiry (Peirce, 1931–1958).

As the research developed, it became clear that the theory explained much of the change. The central idea that legitimacy is the major causal variable in the organization change process expanded to include the authority and power of the state. However, the most significant contribution of the data to the theory—specification of the elements contained in the eco-cognitive framework—did not change it. Instead, the eco-cognitive framework demonstrated the extensive influence of the specific elements of a cognitive framework on the change process.

Data Collection Methods: Ethnography

Ethnography seeks to understand how people create meaning and act on it within a naturalistic setting. This requires documentation and interpretation of values and behaviors and their interaction. In this book, ethnographic methods also documented less complex objectively measurable behavior, particularly the level of implementation of *Abbott V* and NCLB.

Most important, instead of structuring responses through questionnaires, ethnographic methods allowed administrators and teachers to volunteer their understandings of *Abbott V* and NCLB, to supplement observations of their behavior.[2] Participants' cognitive frameworks emerged during training sessions, conversations in the faculty lounge, and in their management of the changes and their classroom behavior.

Fieldwork usually provided the information needed to answer the research questions. However, letting participants define the issues raised new questions that informed the next observation, facilitating extended rolling revisits (Burawoy, 2003, p. 668). In addition, most administrators and teachers experienced the changes as participants and as observers of the behavior of others. In the latter role they frequently provided insights that served as hypotheses to be informally tested during the ongoing data collection.

Newspaper articles in the *Star-Ledger*—the largest circulation paper in New Jersey—and the *New York Times* provided additional data. Another source of information was the plethora of documents generated by the New Jersey Department of Education and the Education Law Center.

Data Analysis: Continuous and Interactive

Data analysis was continuous and influenced fieldwork. After each observation, in addition to writing field notes, theoretical notes identified variables, organizational processes, and major themes (Miles & Huberman, 1994; Strauss & Corbin, 1998). This process also identified unclear and puzzling behavior, explored connections among emerging themes, and identified data that challenged the punctuated legitimacy theory. In addition, new research questions emerged from this process, as well as from major events such as the introduction of NCLB.

When data collection ended, the major task was to reconstruct the sequence of events for each school and classroom. The focus was the major decisions and behaviors related to *Abbott V* and NCLB. The description of the change process, the theoretical notes, and the punctuated legitimacy theory identified potential causal variables and variations (Maxwell, 2004). Finally, cross-site analysis (presented in Chapter 8) relied on systematic comparison of the narratives and the analysis for each school.

Notes

Introduction

1. Court-ordered financial equalization between the wealthiest and the poorest school districts in the state, in addition to the other *Abbott V* remedies, makes New Jersey a critical case for examining the effectiveness of the policy of separate but equal urban education. New Jersey also serves as a significant laboratory for studying the effects of No Child Left Behind. Critics of NCLB have argued that its implementation was ineffective because the federal government did not fund it adequately, and that its central reform—accountability—failed to change schools in meaningful ways. In New Jersey, as an unanticipated benefit of the funding of the *Abbott V* reforms, NCLB was implemented in an atmosphere of significantly increased expenditures in poor minority schools.

   Finally, the four urban elementary schools described and analyzed in this book are critical cases for studying *Abbott V* and NCLB because for several decades they have experienced the challenges confronted daily by urban schools in America.
2. In a press release accompanying the 2004–2005 NCLB Adequate Yearly Progress (AYP) Report, the New Jersey Commissioner of Education, William Librera, noted that

   > While New Jersey has supported the NCLB's focus on student achievement and adult accountability as consistent with our own priorities, we continue to have serious problems with the federal law's convoluted and confusing system of labeling schools and of calculating who is making progress and who is not.

   He then observed that

   > The biggest reason that we have more schools on the New Jersey Schools in Need of Improvement list is that this year, under NCLB, the state was required to increase the percentages of students within each of the ten subgroups at each school who must pass each test.

   Researchers have questioned the appropriateness of the AYP measure, observing that it unfairly labels schools with low-income minority populations as failing because AYP does not measure academic growth adequately and does not take into account the initial disadvantages that students bring to school (Kim & Sunderman, 2005).

3. This book uses pseudonyms for the schools and teachers that participated in the study. Alteration of facts in a few instances protects the anonymity of individuals but does not distort the research findings. Nonresearch locations and individuals retain their actual identities.

Chapter One

1. For information on the Abbott cases see http://www.nj.gov/njded/abbotts.
2. In 1975, every school district in New Jersey was categorized in a District Factor Group (DFG) ranging from A for the least affluent districts to J for the most affluent districts. The original purpose of this grouping was to compare students' performance on statewide assessments across demographically similar districts. The DFGs use six variables from census data that closely approximate socioeconomic status:

    1. Percentage of adults with no high school diploma
    2. Percentage of adults with some college education
    3. Occupational status
    4. Unemployment rate
    5. Percentage of individuals in poverty
    6. Median family income

3. The 1999 data (2000 Census) are more relevant to this research than the 1989 data (1990 Census), because the Abbott reforms began in 1998. The New Jersey Supreme Court, however, made its decision concerning which cities to designate as Abbott districts based on the 1989 data, when Irvington had a median family income of $35,787 and Plainfield's was $42,238. Millburn's 1989 median family income was $102,529, and Westfield's was $77,022.

    Median family income growth from 1989 to 1999 was significantly greater for Millburn (35.4%) and Westfield (31.9%) than for Irvington (12.9%) and Plainfield (16.8%). These statistics demonstrate the extreme differences in wealth and race in close proximity and indicate that the 1990s were significantly more prosperous for high-income families than for low-income families.
4. Teacher salaries in New Jersey are among the highest in the nation and, to some extent, reflect the income levels of communities. For several years the New Jersey Education Association, the statewide teacher union, advocated a statewide starting salary of $40,000. Because of the additional funds provided under *Abbott V,* Plainfield, Irvington, and other Abbott districts increased their starting teacher salaries to approximately $42,600 in 2005, which is competitive with many middle- and upper-income suburbs. Westfield negotiated the highest starting salary in the state: $51,453 beginning in 2006–2007.
5. For detailed studies of the financial equalization process in New Jersey, see Firestone, Goertz, and Natriello (1997) and Reed (2001).
6. The number of Abbott districts grew to 31 with the addition of Salem City in July 2004.

Chapter Two

1. The No Child Left Behind Act can be located at http://www.ed.gov/policy/elsec/leg/esea02/107-110.pdf and at http://www.ed.gov/nclb/landing.jhtml?src=pb

   For an overview of the history of NCLB and an analysis of the problems encountered between the federal government and states that affected its implementation, see Sunderman and Kim (2005) and Sunderman, Kim, and Orfield (2005).

Chapter Three

1. Appendix B describes in detail how the punctuated legitimacy theory informed the book.

Chapter Four

1. The population totals exceed 100% because of people who identify themselves in the census as White or African American and also of Latino ethnicity.
2. The Abbott decisions did not equalize education funding for all school districts in New Jersey, only for the poorest. Many districts just above the threshold for Abbott designation constitute the "poor but non-Abbott districts" (Ritter & Lauver, 2003). In November 2005, the legal committee of the State Board of Education issued a preliminary report warning that the state's school funding formula could be unconstitutional and that a new funding scheme should consider the financial needs of the non-Abbott poor districts (Mooney, 2005d). In January 2006, in *Bacon v. New Jersey State Department of Education,* the State Board of Education ruled that students in 16 rural districts were not receiving a "thorough and efficient" education. This could lead to these districts being included in the Abbott decision.
3. "Census tracts are small, relatively permanent statistical subdivisions of a county. . . . Designed to be relatively homogeneous units with respect to population characteristics, economic status, and living conditions, census tracts average about 4,000 inhabitants" (U.S. Census Bureau, http://ask.census.gov/).
4. This narrative, and those for the other three schools, describes chronologically the changes initiated by *Abbott V* and NCLB. All events in the schools occurred within the contexts presented in Chapters 1 and 2.
5. Although it seems incredible that an important court decision would be a surprise, that was in fact the case for some of the educators studied. The author discussed *Abbott V* with the superintendent of another Abbott district whose appointment began 1 week before announcement of the decision. He and the school board were unaware of the impending court action.
6. Most of the teachers observed for this book disliked Success for All. It is important to note that SFA was the model that had been the subject of the most research, and it had produced significant improvement in literacy in high-poverty schools (Borman et al., 2005). The developers of the Community for Learning/Adaptive Learning Environments Model (CFL/ALEM) claimed that it reflected scientific principles of learning. Although few studies had evaluated it, an American Institutes for Research (2005) assessment concluded that it was significantly less effective than other comprehensive reform models. The study rated CFL/ALEM as hav-

ing no overall positive effects on student achievement, whereas Success for All received a moderately strong rating, one of the highest.

7. By coincidence, all of the schools profiled in this book selected CFL/ALEM. Appendix B, Research Methods, discusses the implications of this program bias for the research.

   Six schools in Newark voted for CFL/ALEM, 17 for Success for All, 15 for Accelerated Schools, 11 for the Comer School Development Program, 3 for the Coalition of Essential Schools, 2 for Co-Nect Schools, 2 for America's Choice, and 1 for Micro Society.
8. In selecting teachers for the study, the principal immediately nominated Mrs. Smith because she was an outstanding teacher. The researcher was already familiar with Mrs. Smith from articles in the *Star-Ledger* that had praised her teaching. It was awkward not to include the Bridge Street School's "star" teacher and insist instead on an "average" teacher. It was also of interest to understand how *Abbott V* would influence an outstanding teacher.
9. After Mrs. Lake's departure, research resumed in Mrs. Ondine's fourth-grade class. Several observations of her class had occurred in previous years.

Chapter Five

1. Nine elementary schools and five middle schools implemented CFL/ALEM, making it the most widely used Whole School Reform (WSR) model in Elizabeth. Four elementary schools selected Success for All, and another four opted for the Comer model. One middle school selected The Coalition for Essential Schools, and an elementary school choose Accelerated Schools.
2. Many first-grade teachers criticized High/Scope as too socialization oriented and without sufficient attention to academics. In addition, teachers thought that when High/Scope did teach reading it was not effective. In fact, High/Scope emphasized a constructivist approach to reading, which was rejected by most teachers in Elizabeth, particularly by the teachers in the Park Avenue School described in Chapter 7.

   The blaming behavior of many teachers was because they were at the intersection of many professional relationships over which they had little, if any, control, particularly their students' previous teachers. Increasing accountability intensified criticism of others when students' performance was not satisfactory.
3. Implementation of Everyday Math and Open Court occurred over 3 years in Elizabeth, staggered by grade and school. Many suburban schools had used Everyday Math for more than 10 years before Newark and Elizabeth adopted it. Few, if any, suburbs used Open Court, which was considered a specifically urban reading series.
4. Research demonstrates that phonics instruction is effective (Ehri, Nunes, Stahl, & Willows, 2001). The issue for this study, however, is beliefs that either prevent or encourage teacher change.
5. Gutmore and Walker's (2002) research included College Avenue in a group of seven schools in Abbott districts with reading and math test scores equal to or better than suburban schools "to identify how and why these schools were more successful than their Abbott counterparts" (p. 3).

   The findings of the study, which applied to College Avenue, were that the schools shared six features. The first three, grouped under "Leadership," were

(1) "All of the schools have principals who focus on creating management structures and a climate where teachers and staff maximize their abilities through collegial leadership";
(2) "All of the schools manifested a high level of academic focus"; and
(3) "All of the building principals demonstrated a remarkable resistance to bureaucratic malaise and a resolute persistence in the face of difficulties." (p. 4)

Under the heading "Culture of Caring," the researchers listed the following findings:

(4) "All of the schools focused a high level of energy on services to children"; and
(5) "All of the schools embraced a collective responsibility for the 'well being' of the school." (p. 5)

The final finding, classified as "Teacher Professionalism," was

(6) "All of the schools demonstrated a high level of teacher professionalism as determined by direct observation of teaching behavior." (p. 5)

The conclusion was that the schools "stand as exemplars of high performance, not only in terms of their Abbott counterparts but of all school districts in New Jersey" (Gutmore & Walker, 2002, p. 3). In a personal communication, Gutmore and Walker reported that they did not observe implementation of any elements of the *Abbott V* mandates at College Avenue.

Although Gutmore and Walker's findings accurately describe important features of College Avenue, their research design did not generate enough data over a sufficient time to discover the real key to its success. They accepted uncritically what the teachers and administrators told them. In addition, a limitation of this research is that it sampled on the dependent variable.

Chapter Six

1. The principal wanted the two first-grade teachers and two fourth-grade teachers to be included in the study. However, one fourth-grade teacher declined to participate.
2. There was extraordinary sensitivity to outsiders during the standardized tests. On the day of the test, the principal could only see part of me through the window in the door. She was relieved to discover it was not a monitor from the central office. Her pacing in the class during the test made even *me* anxious and had to affect students negatively.

Chapter Seven

1. After termination of the research relationship, observation of Mrs. Monrose at meetings and information from other teachers indicated that she continued to oppose any changes and never used CFL/ALEM.

Chapter Eight

1. The *New York Times*, in a March 26, 2006, front page article by Sam Dillon titled, "Schools Cut Back Subjects to Push Reading and Math: Responding to No Child Left Behind Law, Thousands Narrow the Curriculum," cited the narrowing of the curriculum as documented in the March 2006 Center on Education Policy report "From the Capital to the Classroom" (available at http://www.cep-dc.org/nclb/Year4/Press/). The *Times* called this a "sea change in American instructional practice . . ." (p. 1).
2. Observations and interviews of an elementary school in an upper middle-class non-Abbott suburb indicated that after initial concern, the administration and teachers discovered that fourth-grade students scored in the low to mid-90% range on the standardized test every year in all subjects. The school focused on the test only a week before its administration to familiarize students with test-taking skills and conditions. More important, the school and district did not narrow the curriculum in order to perform better on the test.
3. For language arts literacy, the tests reported in Figures 8.1 and 8.2 are the Elementary School Proficiency Assessment (ESPA; 2001–2002) and the New Jersey Assessment of Skills and Knowledge (NJASK; 2003–2005). For language arts, 2001 was the standard-setting year for the ESPA and the NJASK. For mathematics, the tests reported in Figures 8.3 and 8.4 are the ESPA (1999–2002) and the NJASK (2003–2005). For mathematics, 1999 was the standard-setting year for the ESPA and the NJASK. In Figures 8.2 and 8.4, ethnic groups reported for 2005 do not include students who identified themselves as being of multiple ethnicities.
4. NCLB required biennial administration of the National Assessment of Educational Progress (NAEP) beginning in 2002–2003 to serve as a measure of how challenging state-constructed tests were. There has been a significant gap between the New Jersey test and NAEP scores, which is typical of most states (Carey, 2006).

   In addition, an analysis of NAEP reading scores indicates that they have remained unchanged since 1992, and an analysis of test items found that the math knowledge actually tested in the fourth grade was content learned in first and second grade (Loveless, 2004, pp. 6–17). For NAEP results, see http://nces.ed.gov/nationsreportcard/.

Chapter Nine

1. Although schools differ in important ways from other organizations, the organization and business literature contains models of organizations that are useful for managing school change—with appropriate modification. Examples are Edward Lawler and Christopher Worley's *Built to Change* (2006) and the organization-based approach to school improvement described in William Ouchi's *Making Schools Work* (2003). Also useful are studies of the role of leadership in organization change. Examples are John Kotter's *A Force for Change* (1990), which distinguishes between leadership and management, and his *Leading Change* (1996).
2. A problem with culturally appropriate and other classificatory schemes is that they can be misunderstood and misused. Several times during the research, trainers applied Howard Gardner's multiple intelligences (1999) to entire groups. For example, a Newark Board of Education trainer announced that "All learning disabled kids are high on bodily-kinesthetic intelligence."

Appendix A

1. The sources for this appendix were the Education Law Center (http://www.edlawcenter.org/); *New Jersey's Public Schools: A Biennial Report for the People of New Jersey,* 2002–2003 and 2004–2005 editions, by Philip E. Mackey (Rutgers University, Public Education Institute, Center for Government Services, Edward J. Blaustein School of Planning and Public Policy); and the *Star-Ledger,* 1998–2006.

Appendix B

1. The 2000 U.S. Census documented 8.4% of teachers as non-Hispanic Black and 5.5% as Hispanic.
2. Because observations were often of groups and meetings, which made tape recording impossible, notes were handwritten and later transcribed. On several occasions, teachers requested that the researcher stop taking notes (which was complied with) because they considered the information too critical of an administrator, a fellow teacher, students, parents, the New Jersey Department of Education, or President Bush's education policies.

References

The Abbott districts: Pare with care. (2005, May 29). *Star-Ledger,* Section 10, p. 2.

Abbott v. Burke, No. 42,170 (N.J. Sup. Ct., 2006). [Brief] Retrieved November 7, 2006, from http://www.edlawcenter.org/ELCPublic/elcnews_060410_StateSupremeCourt Brief.pdf

Abrahamson, E. (1991). Managerial fads and fashions: The diffusion and rejection of innovations. *Academy of Management Review, 16*(3), 586–612.

Addison, K., & Mooney, J. (2005, July 17). Schools takeover leaves shaky legacy. *Star-Ledger,* p. 13.

Aldrich, H. (1999). *Organizations evolving.* Thousand Oaks, CA: Sage Publications.

American Institutes for Research. (2005). *Comprehensive School Reform Quality Center report on elementary school comprehensive school reform models.* Washington, DC: Author.

Anfara, V. A., Brown, K. M., & Mangione, T. (2002). Qualitative analysis on stage: Making the research process more public. *Educational Researcher, 31*(7), 28–36.

Anyon, J. (1980). Social class and the hidden curriculum of work. *Journal of Education, 162*(1), 67–92.

Anyon, J. (1997). *Ghetto schooling: A political economy of urban educational reform.* New York: Teachers College Press.

Anyon, J. (2005). *Radical possibilities: Public policy, urban education, and a new social movement.* New York: Routledge.

Argyris, C. (2004). *Reasons and rationalizations: The limits to organizational knowledge.* New York: Oxford University Press.

Arum, R. (2000). Schools and communities: Ecological and institutional dimensions. *Annual Review of Sociology,* 26, 395–418.

Barnes, C. (2002). *Standards reform in high-poverty schools: Managing conflict and building capacity.* New York: Teachers College Press.

Bell, D. (2004). *Silent covenants: Brown v. Board of Education and the unfulfilled hopes for racial reform.* New York: Oxford University Press.

Bensman, D. (2000). *Central Park East and its graduates: "Learning by heart."* New York: Teachers College Press.

Berends, M., Chun, J., Schuyler, G., Stockly, S., & Briggs, R. J. (2002). Challenges of conflicting school reform: Effect of new American schools in a high-poverty district. Santa Monica, CA: Rand.

Berliner, D. C. (2006). Our impoverished view of educational reform. *Teachers College Record, 108*(6), 949–995.

Bolden, M. A. (2001, September 10). Whole school reform [in parts]. *Star-Ledger,* p. 15.

Booher-Jennings, J. (2005). Below the bubble: "Educational triage" and the Texas accountability system. *American Educational Research Journal,* 42(2), 231–268.

Borman, G. D., Hewes, G. M., Overman, L. T., & Brown, S. (2002). *Comprehensive school reform and student achievement: A meta-analysis.* Baltimore: Center for Research on the Education of Students Placed at Risk.

Borman, G. D., Rachuba, L., Datnow, A., Alberg, M., MacIver, M., Stringfield, S., & Ross, S. (2000). *Four models of school improvement: Successes and challenges in reforming low-performing, high-poverty Title I schools* (CRESPAR Report No. 48). Baltimore: Johns Hopkins University, Center for Research on the Education of Students Placed at Risk.

Borman, G. D., Slavin, R. E., Cheung, A. C. K., Chamberlain, A. M., Madden, N. M., & Chambers, B. (2005). The national randomized field trial of success for all: Second-year outcomes. *American Educational Research Journal, 42,* 673–696.

Boudon, R. (2003). Beyond rational choice theory. *Annual Review of Sociology, 29,* 1–21.

Bowles, S., & Gintis, H. (2002). Schooling in capitalist America revisited. *Sociology of Education, 75*(2), 1–18.

Braun, B. (2005, June 2). In state's schools, segregation isn't history but a current event. *Star-Ledger,* p. 15.

Brown v. Board of Education, 347 U.S. 483 (1954). Retrieved November 7, 2006, from http://www.nationalcenter.org/brown.html

Bryk, A. S., & Schneider, B. (2002). *Trust in schools: A core resource for improvement.* New York: Russell Sage Foundation.

Bryk, A. S., Sebring, P. B., Kerbow, D., Rollow, S., & Easton, J. Q. (1998). *Charting Chicago school reform: Democractic localism as a lever for change.* Boulder, CO: Westview Press.

Burawoy, M. (2003). Revisits: An outline of a theory of reflexive ethnography. *American Sociological Review, 68,* 645–679.

Burke, W. (2002). *Organization change: Theory and practice.* Thousand Oaks, CA: Sage.

Camilli, G., & Monfils, L. F. (2004). Test scores and equity. In Firestone, W. A., Schorr, R. Y., & Monfils L. F. (Eds.), *The ambiguity of teaching to the test: Standards, assessment, and educational reform* (pp. 143–158). Mahwah, NJ: Erlbaum.

Capuzzo, J. P. (2001, November 25). Mount Laurel: A battle that won't go away. *New York Times,* Section 14, p. 1.

Carey, K. (2006). *Hot air: How states inflate their education progress under NCLB.* Washington, DC: The Education Sector.

Chambers, S. (2004, September 8). Six new schools lead overhaul. *Star-Ledger,* pp. 1, 16.

Chambers, S. (2005, June 26). Thirty years after Mr. Laurel: What went wrong? *Star-Ledger,* Section 10, p. 1.

Chen, D. (2005, September 9). Corzine vows to seek bonds to finish school construction. *New York Times*, p. B7.

Clotfelter, C. T. (2004). *After Brown: The rise and retreat of school desegregation*. Princeton, NJ: Princeton University Press.

Coburn, C. E. (2004). Beyond decoupling: Rethinking the relationship between the institutional environment and the classroom. *Sociology of Education, 77*, 211–244.

Coleman, J. S., Campbell, E. Q., Hobson, C. J., McPartland, J., Mood, A. M., Weinfeld, F. D., & York, R. L. (1966). *Equality of educational opportunity.* Washington, DC: U.S. Government Printing Office.

Cook, T., Habib, F., Phillips, M., Settersten, R., Shagle, S., & Degirmencioglu, S. (1999). Comer's school development program in Prince George's County, Maryland: A theory-based evaluation. *American Educational Research Journal, 36*(3), 543–598.

Crawford v. Davy (N.J. Super. Ct., Ch. Div., Gen. Eq., July 13, 2006). [Complaint] Retrieved November 7, 2006, from http://www.nje3.org/complaint.pdf

Cuban, L. (2001). *Oversold and underused: Computers in the classroom*. Cambridge, MA: Harvard University Press.

Cuban, L. (2004). *The blackboard and the bottom line: Why schools can't be businesses*. Cambridge, MA: Harvard University Press.

Cuban, L., & Usdan, M. (Eds.). (2003). *Powerful reforms with shallow roots: Improving America's urban schools*. New York: Teachers College Press.

Datnow, A. (1999). *How schools choose externally developed reform designs*. Baltimore: Center for Research on the Education of Students Placed at Risk, Johns Hopkins University.

Deci, E., Koestner, R., & Ryan, R. (1999). A meta-analytic review of experiments examining the effects of extrinsic rewards on intrinsic motivation. *Psychological Bulletin, 125*(6), 617–668.

Delpit, L. (1995). *Other people's children: Cultural conflict in the classroom*. New York: The New Press.

Desimone, L. (2002). How can comprehensive school reform models be successfully implemented? *Review of Educational Research, 72*(3), 433–479.

Diamond, J. B., & Spillane, J. P. (2004). High-stakes accountability in urban elementary schools: Challenging or reproducing inequality? *Teachers College Record, 106*(6), 1145–1176.

Dillon, S. (2006, March 26). Schools cut back subjects to push reading and math: Responding to No Child Left Behind Law, thousands narrow the curriculum. *New York Times*, Section 1, p. 1.

DiMaggio, P., & Powell, W. (1983). The iron cage revisited: Institutional isomorphism and collective rationality in organizational fields. *American Sociological Review, 48*, 147–160.

Downey, D. B., von Hippel, P. T., & Broh, B. A. (2004). Are schools the great equalizer? Cognitive inequality during the summer months and the school year. *American Sociological Review, 69*, 613–635.

Duke, D. (1995). *The school that refused to die*. Albany: State University of New York Press.

Eaton, S. E., Feldman, J., & Kirby, E. (1996). Still separate, still unequal: The limits of *Milliken II*'s monetary compensation to segregated schools. In G. Orfield & S. E.

Eaton, *Dismantling desegregation: The quiet reversal of* Brown v. Board of Education (pp. 143–178). New York: The New Press.
Ehri, L. C., Nunes, S. R., Stahl, S. A., & Willows, D. M. (2001). Systematic phonics instruction helps students learn to read: Evidence from the national reading panel's meta-analysis. *Review of Educational Research, 71*(3), 393–447.
Eisenhart, M., & Towne, L. (2003). Contestation and change in national policy on "scientifically based" education research. *Educational Researcher, 32*(7), 31–38.
Elmore, R. (2004). *School reform from the inside out: Policy, practice, and performance.* Cambridge, MA: Harvard Education Press.
Epstein, J. (2005). Attainable goals? The spirit and letter of the No Child Left Behind Act on parental involvement. *Sociology of Education, 78*(2), 179–182.
Erlichson, B., & Goertz, M. (2001). *Implementing whole school reform in New Jersey: Year two.* New Brunswick, NJ: Rutgers, The State University of New Jersey, Public Education Institute.
Erlichson, B., Goertz, M., & Turnbull, B. (1999). *Implementing whole school reform in New Jersey: Year one in the first cohort schools.* New Brunswick, NJ: Rutgers, The State University of New Jersey, Public Education Institute.
Expect more of Bolden. (2005, July 2). *Star-Ledger,* p. 8.
Fine, M., Bloom, J., Burns, A., Chajet, L., Buishard, M., Payne, Y., Perkins-Munn, T., & Torre, M. E. (2005). Dear Zora: A letter to Zora Neale Hurston 50 years after *Brown. Teachers College Record, 107*(3), 496–528.
Firestone, W., Goertz, M., & Natriello, G. (1997). *From cashbox to classroom: The struggle for fiscal reform and educational change in New Jersey.* New York: Teachers College Press.
Firestone, W., Schorr, R., & Mackey, P. (2004). Curriculum and culture: Findings from New Jersey's illustrative best practices study. Retrieved November 7, 2006, from http://www.cepa.gse.rutgers.edu/Best%20Practices%20JFTK%20Final%20Report%20pem%2005-10-04.pdf
Fink, D. (2000). *Good schools/real schools: Why school reform doesn't last.* New York: Teachers College Press.
Fishman, T. C. (2005). *China Inc.: How the rise of the next superpower challenges America and the world.* New York: Scribner.
Frankenberg, E., & Lee, C. (2002). *Race in American public schools: Rapidly resegregating school districts.* Cambridge, MA: Harvard University, The Civil Rights Project.
Frankenberg, E., Lee, C., & Orfield, G. (2003). *A multiracial society with segregated schools: Are we losing the dream?* Cambridge, MA: Harvard University, The Civil Rights Project.
Fryer, R., & Levitt, S. (2002). *Understanding the Black-White test score gap in the first two years of school.* Cambridge, MA: National Bureau of Economic Research.
Fullan, M. (with Stiegelbauer, S.). (1991). *The new meaning of educational change.* New York: Teachers College Press.
Fullan, M. (2005). *Leadership & sustainability: System thinkers in action.* Thousand Oaks, CA: Corwin Press.
Gans, H. J. (1962). *The urban villagers: Group and class in the life of Italian-Americans.* New York: The Free Press.
Gans, H. J. (1995). *The war against the poor: The underclass and antipoverty policy.* New York: Basic Books.

Gardner, H. (1999). *Intelligence reframed: Multiple intelligences for the 21st century.* New York: Basic Books.

Gardner, H. (2004). *Changing minds: The art and science of changing our own and other people's minds.* Cambridge, MA: Harvard Business School Press.

Gebeloff, R. (2005, May 30). In North Jersey, race affects where we choose to live. *Star-Ledger,* p. 1.

Geertz, C. (1973). *The interpretation of cultures: Selected essays.* New York: Basic Books.

Gersick, C. (1991). Revolutionary change theories: A multilevel exploration of the punctuated equilibrium paradigm. *Academy of Management Review, 16,* 10–36.

Gersick, C. (1994). Pacing strategic change: The case of a new venture. *Academy of Management Journal, 37,* 9–45.

Glaeser, E., & Vigdor, J. (2001). *Racial segregation in the 2000 census: Promising news.* Washington, DC: The Brookings Institution.

Gold, B. (1999). Punctuated legitimacy: A theory of educational change. *Teachers College Record, 101*(2), 192–219.

Gold, B., & Miles, M. (1981). *Whose school is it anyway? Parent-teacher conflict over an innovative school.* New York: Praeger.

Golson, J. (2005, May 25). Ousted school chief says board gave him no warning. *Star-Ledger,* p. 27.

Good, T. L., Burross, H. L., & McCaslin, M. M. (2005). Comprehensive school reform: A longitudinal study of school improvement in one state. *Teachers College Record, 107*(10), 2205–2226.

Gould, S. J. (2002). *The structure of evolutionary theory.* Cambridge, MA: Harvard University Press.

Gutmann, A. (1987). *Democratic education.* Princeton, NJ: Princeton University Press.

Gutmore, D., & Walker, E. (2002). *Urban schools that work: A report by citizens for better schools.* South Orange, NJ: Seton Hall University.

Hannan, M. T., & Freeman, J. (1989). *Organizational ecology.* Cambridge, MA: Harvard University Press.

Hargreaves, A., & Goodson, I. (2006). Educational change over time? The sustainability and nonsustainability of three decades of secondary school change and continuity. *Educational Administration Quarterly, 32*(1), 3–41.

Harry, B., Sturges, K. M., & Klingner, J. K. (2005). Mapping the process: An exemplar of process and challenge in grounded theory analysis. *Educational Researcher, 34*(2), 3–13.

Helmreich, W. B. (1999). *The enduring community: The Jews of Newark and Metrowest.* New Brunswick, NJ: Transaction Publishers.

Ingram, P., & Clay, K. (2000). The choice-within-constraints new institutionalism and implications for sociology. *Annual Review of Sociology, 26,* 525–546.

Jargowsky, P. (2003). *Stunning progress, hidden problems: The dramatic decline of concentrated poverty in the 1990s.* Washington, DC: The Brookings Institution.

Johnson, D. E., & Johnson, B. (2002). *High stakes: Children, testing, and failure in American Schools.* New York: Rowman & Littlefield.

Kahlenberg, R. D. (2001). *All together now: Creating middle-class schools through public school choice.* Washington, DC: Brookings Institution Press.

Kahlenberg, R. D. (2004). *Can separate be equal? The overlooked flaw at the center of No Child Left Behind.* New York: The Century Foundation.

Kegan, R., & Lahey, L. L. (2001). *How the way we talk can change the way we work: Seven Languages for Transformation.* San Francisco: Jossey-Bass.

Kelman, H. C. (2001). Reflections on social and psychological processes of legitimization and delegitimization. In J. T. Jost & B. Major (Eds.), *The psychology of legitimacy: Emerging perspectives on ideology, justice, and intergroup relations* (pp. 54–73). New York: Cambridge University Press.

Kim, J. S., & Sunderman, G. L. (2005). Measuring academic proficiency under the No Child Left Behind Act: Implications for educational equity. *Educational Researcher, 34*(8), 3–13.

King, J. E. (Ed.). (2005). *Black education: A transformative research and action agenda for the new century.* Mahwah, NJ: Lawrence Erlbaum Associates.

Kotter, J. P. (1990). *A force for change: How leadership differs from management.* New York: The Free Press.

Kotter, J. P. (1996). *Leading change.* Boston: Harvard Business School Press.

Kogut, B. (Ed.). (2003). *The global internet economy.* Cambridge, MA: MIT Press.

Kozol, J. (1991). *Savage inequalities: Children in America's schools.* New York: Harper Perennial.

Kozol, J. (2005). *The shame of the nation: The restoration of apartheid schooling in America.* New York: Crown.

Ladson-Billings, G. (1994). *The dreamkeepers: Successful teachers of African American children.* San Francisco, CA: Jossey-Bass.

Lagemann, E. C. (2000). *An elusive science: The troubling history of education research.* Chicago: University of Chicago Press.

Lampert, M. (2001). *Teaching problems and the problems of teaching.* New Haven, CT: Yale University Press.

Lawler, E. E., & Worley, C. G. (2006). *Built to change: How to achieve sustained organizational effectiveness.* San Francisco: Jossey-Bass.

Lee, C. D. (2005). The state of knowledge about the education of African Americans. In J. E. King (Ed.), *Black education: A transformative research and action agenda for the new century* (pp. 45–71). Mahwah, NJ: Erlbaum.

Lee, J. (2006). *Tracking achievement gaps and assessing the impact of NCLB on the gaps: An in-depth look into national and state reading and math outcome trends.* Cambridge, MA: Harvard University, The Civil Rights Project.

Levine, E. (2002). *One kid at a time: Big lessons from a small school.* New York: Teachers College Press.

Liebman, J. S., & Sabel, C. F. (2003a). What are the likely impacts of the accountability movement on minority children?: The federal No Child Left Behind Act and the post-desegregation civil rights agenda. *North Carolina Law Review, 81,* 1703–1750.

Liebman, J. S., & Sabel, C. F. (2003b). A public laboratory Dewey barely imagined: The emerging model of school governance and legal reform. *New York University Review of Law and Social Change, 28,* 183–304.

Logan, J. R., Oakley, D., Stowell, J., & Stults, B. (2001). *Living separately: Segregation rises for children.* Albany: State University of New York, Lewis Mumford Center.

Louis, K. S., & Miles, M. B. (1990). *Improving the urban high school: What works and why.* New York: Teachers College Press.

Loveless, T. (2004). *How well are American students learning?* Washington, DC: The Brookings Institution.

MacInnes, G. (2005a). *Proposal for assessment of achievement in Abbott districts.* Request for Quotation for Evaluation of "Abbott" Programs, Appendix B, State of New Jersey, Department of Education Division of Finance Office of State Budget and Accounting.

MacInnes, G. (2005b, February 3). *Student achievement in the Abbott districts.* Statement of Gordon MacInnes, Assistant Commissioner for Abbott Implementation, New Jersey Senate Education Committee.

MacInnes, G. (2005c, October 6). *Closing the achievement gap: Two-year plan instructional priorities.* Trenton: New Jersey State Department of Education.

Mackey, P. E. (2002). *New Jersey's public schools: A biennial report for the people of New Jersey, 2002–2003 edition.* New Brunswick, NJ: Public Education Institute, Rutgers University.

Marsico, R. (2005, March 17). Chinese imports boost port activity to record levels: Nearly 4.5 million containers came through area. *Star-Ledger,* 51.

Martin, J., & Ryan, J. (2005, June 16). Big raid targets gang in Elizabeth. *Star-Ledger,* p. 17.

Massey, D. S., & Denton, N. A. (1993). *American apartheid: Segregation and the making of the underclass.* Cambridge, MA: Harvard University Press.

Maxwell, J. A. (2004). Causal explanation, qualitative research, and scientific inquiry in education. *Educational Researcher, 33*(2), 3–11.

McNamara, D. (2005, May 19). Superintendent: Removal was out of the blue. *Elizabeth/Hillside Gazette Leader,* p. 1.

McNeil, L. (2000). *Contradictions of school reform: Educational costs of standardized testing.* New York: Routledge.

McNichol, D. (2005, March 11). Jersey halts new pacts for school construction: Inspector general to review contracts. *Star-Ledger,* p. 1.

McNichol, D., & Chambers, S. (2005, November 27). Projected costs soar for fixing needy schools. *Star-Ledger,* p. 1.

Measuring school reforms. (2002, June 6). *Star-Ledger,* p. 20.

Meier, D., & Wood, G. (Eds.). (2004). *Many children left behind: How the No Child Left Behind Act is damaging our children and our schools.* Boston: Beacon Press.

Merton, R. K. (1936). The unanticipated consequences of purposive social action. *American Sociological Review, 1,* 894–904.

Merton, R. K. (1948). The self-fulfilling prophecy. *Antioch Review, 8,* 193–210.

Meyer, J. W., & Rowan, B. (1977). Institutionalized organizations: Formal structures as myth and ceremony. *American Journal of Sociology, 83,* 340–363.

Miles, M. B., & Huberman, A. M. (1994). *Qualitative data analysis: An expanded sourcebook* (2nd ed.). Thousand Oaks, CA: Sage.

Miller, R. J., & Rowan, B. (2006). Effects of organic management on student achievement. *American Educational Research Journal, 43*(2), 219–253.

Mooney, J. (2004a, August 29). . . . formerly known as the education president. *Star-Ledger,* Section 10, p. 1.

Mooney, J. (2004b, October 29). Reading and writing scores rise in needy school districts. *Star-Ledger,* p. 23.

Mooney, J. (2005a, March 15). School aid pits haves against the have-nots: New limits on spending add to funding concerns. *Star-Ledger,* p. 11.

Mooney, J. (2005b, May 18). State looks to shrink needy school list: Abbott districts gear up to fight proposal revising criteria for who gets aid. *Star-Ledger,* pp. 1, 10.

Mooney, J. (2005c, August 11). More schools fail to reach U.S. standard: Number in Jersey jumps to 851 as 'Left Behind Act' gets tougher. *Star-Ledger,* p. 13.

Mooney, J. (2005d, November 4). A call to revamp school funding. *Star-Ledger,* p. 19.

More than just test scores. (2005, May 19). *Elizabeth/Hillside Gazette Leader,* p. 4.

Mr. Bush's ABC's: He stresses accountability. Will Republicans stick with him on choice? (2001, January 25). *Wall Street Journal,* p. A18.

Muirhead, M., Tyler, R., & Hamilton, M. (2001). *Study of whole school reform implementation in New Jersey Abbott districts: Perceptions of key stakeholders.* Washington, DC: George Washington University.

National Academy of Sciences. (2003). *Engaging schools: Fostering high school students' motivation to learn.* Washington, DC: National Academies Press.

National Commission on Excellence in Education. (1983). *A nation at risk: The imperatives for educational reform.* Washington, DC: U.S. Department of Education.

New Jersey Department of Education. (1998, 2002). New Jersey Core Curriculum Content Standards. Current standards available at http://www.nj.gov/njded/aps/cccs/

New Jersey Supreme Court. (2004). *In the matter of the petition for authorization to conduct a referendum on the withdrawal of North Haledon School District from the Passaic County Manchester Regional High School District.* 181 N.J. 161, 854 A.2d327.

Newman, K. (1988). *Falling from grace: The experience of downward mobility in the American middle class.* New York: The Free Press.

Nichols, S. L., Glass, G. V., & Berliner, D. C. (2005). High-stakes testing and student achievement: Problems for the no child left behind act. Tempe: Arizona State University, Educational Policy Studies Laboratory.

Nichols, S. L., Glass, G. V., & Berliner, D. C. (2006). High-stakes testing and student achievement: Does accountability pressure increase student learning? *Education Policy Analysis Archives, 14,* 1.

No Child Left Behind Act of 2001 [NCLB Act]. Public Law 107-110. Available at http://www.ed.gov/policy/elsec/leg/esea02/107-110.pdf

Noddings, N. (2005). Rethinking a bad law. *Education Week, 24*(24), 38.

Ogbu, J. U. (2003). *Black American students in an affluent suburb: A study of academic disengagement.* Mahwah, NJ: Erlbaum.

Olsen, B., & Kirtman, L. (2002). Teacher as mediator of school reform: An examination of teacher practice in 36 California restructuring schools. *Teachers College Record, 104*(2), 301–324.

Orfield, G., & Eaton, S. (1996). *Dismantling desegregation: The quiet reversal of* Brown v. Board of Education. New York: The New Press.

Orfield, G., & Lee, C. (2005). *Why segregation matters: Poverty and educational inequality.* Cambridge, MA: The Civil Rights Project, Harvard University.

Orr, J. S. (2004, August 23). Corzine sees 'crisis of confidence' in N.J. *Star-Ledger,* pp. 1, 7.

Ouchi, W. G. (2003). *Making schools work: A revolutionary plan to get your children the education they need.* New York: Simon & Schuster.

Parsons, C., & Fidler, B. (2005). A new theory of educational change—Punctuated equilibrium: The case of the internationalization of higher education institutions. *British Journal of Educational Studies, 53*(4), 447.

Peirce, C. S. (1931–1958). *Collected papers of Charles Sanders Peirce* (C. Hartshorne, P. Weiss, & A. Burks, Eds.). Cambridge, MA: Harvard University Press.

Pinker, S. (2002). *The blank slate: The modern denial of human nature.* New York: Viking.

Popham, W. J. (2004). *America's "failing" schools: How parents and teachers can cope with No Child Left Behind.* New York: RoutledgeFalmer Press.

Portes, A. (2000). The hidden abode: Sociology and analysis of the unexpected. *American Sociological Review, 65,* 1–18.

Powell, J. A., & Spencer, M. L. (2003). *Brown* is not *Brown* and educational reform is not reform if integration is not a goal. *New York University Review of Law and Social Change, 28,* 343–352.

Rae, D. (2001). Viacratic America: *Plessy* on foot v. *Brown* on wheels. *Annual Review of Political Science, 4,* 417–438.

Ravitch, D. (2000). *Left back: A century of failed school reforms.* New York: Simon & Schuster.

Reed, D. (2001). *On equal terms: The constitutional politics of education opportunity.* Princeton, NJ: Princeton University Press.

Reock, E. C., Jr. (2004, April 30). *Trends in New Jersey school finance.* Paper presented at the Public Education Institute Roundtable at Rutgers University, Piscataway, NJ.

Ritter, G. W., & Lauver, S. C. (2003). School finance reform in New Jersey: A piecemeal response to a systemic problem. *Journal of Education Finance, 28,* 575–598.

Romanelli, E., & Tushman, M. L. (1994). Organizational transformation as punctuated equilibrium: An empirical test. *Academy of Management Journal,* 37, 1141–1166.

Rosenberg, G. N. (1991). *The hollow hope: Can courts bring about social change?* Chicago: University of Chicago Press.

Roth, J., Brooks-Gunn, J., Linver, M., & Hofferth, S. (2003). What happens during the school day? Time diaries from a national sample of elementary school teachers. *Teachers College Record, 150*(3), 317–343.

Rothstein, R. (2004). *Class and schools: Using social, economic, and educational reform to close the Black-White achievement gap.* Washington, DC: Economic Policy Institute.

Rumberger, R. W., & Palardy, G. J. (2005). Does segregation still matter? The impact of student composition on academic achievement in high school. *Teachers College Record, 101*(9), 1999–2045.

Runge, M. (2001, May 31). Elizabeth Whole School Reform effort to be enhanced with $120,000 grant. *Elizabeth/Hillside Gazette Leader,* p. 3.

Ryan, J. E. (2004). The perverse incentives of the No Child Left Behind Act. *New York University Law Review, 79*(3), 932–989.

Ryan, R., & Deci, E. (2000). Intrinsic and extrinsic motivations: Classic definitions and new directions. *Contemporary Educational Psychology, 25,* 54–67.

Sarason, S. B. (1996). *Revisiting the culture of the school and the problem of change.* New York: Teachers College Press.

Sarason, S. B. (2004). *And what do you mean by learning?* Portsmouth, NH: Heinemann.

Sarason, S. B., & Klaber, M. (1985). The school as a social situation. *Annual Review of Psychology, 36,* 115–140.

Sassen, S. (1991). *The global city: New York, London, Tokyo.* Princeton, NJ: Princeton University Press.

Schein, E. H. (1992). *Organizational culture and leadership* (2nd ed.). San Francisco: Jossey-Bass.
Schemo, D. J. (2004, April 7). Kennedy demands full funding for school bill. *New York Times,* p. B9.
Schuppe, J. (2005, May 12). Double-barrel crackdown on shootings. *Star-Ledger,* p. 15.
Schutz, A. (1967). *Collected papers: The problem of social reality.* The Hague: Martinus Nijhoff.
Schwaneberg, R. (2004, April 18). A work in progress, 50 years after *Brown vs. Board of Ed*: New Jersey is among states still confronting segregation in schools. *Star-Ledger,* p. 1.
Sciarra, D. (2004, September 29). A Trojan horse threatens urban schools. *Star Ledger,* p. 17.
Scott, W. R. (1995). *Institutions and organizations.* Thousand Oaks, CA: Sage.
Seligman, M. E. P. (1991). *Learned optimism.* New York: Knopf.
Shafir, E., & LeBoeuf, R. A. (2002). Rationality. *Annual Review of Psychology, 53,* 491–517.
Sieber, S. (1981). *Fatal remedies: The ironies of social intervention.* New York: Plenum Press.
Silin, J. G., & Lippman, C. (Eds.). (2003). *Putting the children first: The changing face of Newark's public schools.* New York: Teachers College Press.
Sirin, S. R. (2005). Socioeconomic status and academic achievement: A meta-analytic review of research. *Review of Educational Research, 75*(3), 417–453.
Steele, C. M. (1997). A threat in the air: How stereotypes shape intellectual identity and performance. *American Psychologist, 52*(6), 613–629.
Sternberg, R., & Grigorenko, E. (1999). Myths in psychology and education regarding the gene–environment debate. *Teachers College Record, 100*(3), 536–553.
Strauss, A., & Corbin, J. (1998). *Basics of qualitative research: Techniques and procedures for developing grounded theory.* Thousand Oaks, CA: Sage.
Strunsky, S. (2002, May 12). Prosperity beckons: For Elizabeth, once down on its luck, now a dynamic time. *New York Times,* Section 14, p. 1.
Sunderman, G. L., & Kim, J. S. (2005, November 3). The expansion of federal power and the politics of implementing the No Child Left Behind Act. *Teachers College Record.* Retrieved November 7, 2006, from http://www.tcrecord.org/content.asp?contentid=12227
Sunderman, G. L., Kim, J. S., & Orfield, G. (2005). *NCLB meets school realities: Lessons from the field.* Thousand Oaks, CA: Corwin.
Supovitz, J. A., & May, H. (2003). *The relationship between teacher implementation of America's choice and student learning in Plainfield, New Jersey.* Philadelphia: University of Pennsylvania, Consortium for Policy Research in Education.
Teacher builds up kids' ability to learn. (2000, February). *Star-Ledger.*
Tractenberg, P., Holzer, M., Miller, J., Sadvonik, A., & Liss, B. (2002). *Developing a plan for reestablishing local control in the state-operated school districts.* Newark, NJ: Rutgers University, Institute of Education Law & Policy, Joseph C. Cornwall Center for Metropolitan Studies.
Tractenberg, P., Sadovnik, A., & Liss, B. (2004). *Tough choices: Setting the stage for informed, objective deliberation on school choice.* Newark, NJ: Rutgers University, Institute of Education Law and Policy.
A truce in New Jersey's school war. (2002, February 9). *New York Times,* Section A, p. 18.

Tushman, M., & Romanelli, E. (1985). Organizational evolution: A metamorphosis model of convergence and reorientation. In L. L. Cummings & B. M. Straw (Eds.), *Research in organizational behavior* (pp. 171–222). Greenwich, CT: JAI Press.

Tyack, D. (1974). *The one best system: A history of American urban education*. Cambridge, MA: Harvard University Press.

Tyack, D., & Cuban, L. (1995). *Tinkering toward utopia: A century of public school reform*. Cambridge MA: Harvard University Press.

Tye, B. (2000). *Hard truths: uncovering the deep structure of schooling*. New York: Teachers College Press.

Wachtel, P. (1999). *Race in the mind of America: Breaking the vicious circle between Blacks and Whites*. New York: Routledge.

Walker, E. (2000). *Decentralization and participatory decision-making: Implementing school-based management in the Abbott districts*. South Orange, NJ: Seton Hall University.

Walker, E., & Gutmore, D. (2000). *The quest for equity and excellence in education: A study on whole school reform in New Jersey special needs districts*. South Orange, NJ: Center for Urban Leadership, Renewal and Research, Department of Educational Administration and Supervision, Seton Hall University.

Wang, M. C. (1992). *Adaptive education strategies: Building on diversity*. Baltimore: Paul H. Brookes Publishing.

Weber, M. (1947). *The theory of social and economic organization*. New York: The Free Press.

Weick, K. (1987). Perspectives on action in organizations. In J. Lorsch (Ed.), *Handbook of organizational behavior* (pp. 10–28). Englewood Cliffs, NJ: Prentice Hall.

Weick, K., & Quinn, R. (1999). Organizational change and development. *Annual Review of Psychology, 50*, 361–386.

Weinstein, R. S. (2002). *Reaching higher: The power of expectations in schooling*. Cambridge, MA: Harvard University Press.

Welner, K. G. (2006). K–12 race-conscious student assignment policies: Law, social science, and diversity. *Review of Educational Research, 76*(3), 349–382.

Wenglinsky, H. (2002). How schools matter: The link between teacher classroom practices and student academic performance. *Education Policy Analysis Archives*, 10(12). Retrieved November 7, 2006, from http://epaa.asu.edu/epaa/v10n12/

Wenglinsky, H. (2004). Closing the racial achievement gap: The role of reforming instructional practices. *Education Policy Analysis Archives, 12*(64). Retrieved November 7, 2006, from http://epaa.asu.edu/epaa/v12n64/

Williams, R. F. (1990). *The New Jersey State Constitution: A reference guide*. Westport, CT: Greenwood Press.

Wilson, W. J. (1996). *When work disappears: The world of the new urban poor.* New York: Alfred A. Knopf.

Zelditch, M. (2001). Theories of legitimacy. In J. T. Jost & B. Major (Eds.), *The psychology of legitimacy: Emerging perspectives on ideology, justice, and intergroup relations* (pp. 33–53). New York: Cambridge University Press.

Index

Page numbers followed by italic letter *f* refer to figures; those followed by *t* refer to tables.

Abbott V, 1
  budgetary constraints on, 18
  eco-cognitive framework in, 164–165
  evaluation of, 19
  as experimental strategy, 156
  failure of, in perspective, 160
  funding inequalities preceding, 7–8
  governors' approach to, 15–17
  governor's lawsuit against, 20
  legitimacy of. *See* legitimacy of change
  mandates of, 8–9
  origin of, 14–15
  socioeconomic context of, 11–14
  student demographics in, 9
  theoretical perspective on, 37–38
  underfunding of, 64
  vs. NCLB, 29
Abbott Phase II, 70
Abbott Secondary Initiative, 20, 165
Abbott v. Burke, 158
Abrahamson, E., 149
academic achievement
  African Americans and, 151
  community role in, 161–162
  district factor groups in, 167
  by economic status, 152*f*, 153*f*
  by ethnicity, 152*f*, 153*f*
  school role in, 162
  school size in, 165
Addison, K., 46
Adequate Yearly Progress (AYP)
  at Bridge Street School, 72, 74, 157
  case study failure in, 157
  at Church Street School, 118, 119, 157
  at College Avenue School, 98, 100, 101, 157
  corrective action on, 24–26
  in Elizabeth, 157
Adequate Yearly Progress (*continued*)
  in Newark, 157
  at Park Avenue School, 139, 157
  state determination of, 24
adoption stage, 30
African Americans. *See also* ethnicity; race
  achievement gap and, 151, 162
  in Newark, 41–42
  residential patterns of high-income, 12–13
Alberg, M., 184
Aldrich, H., 34, 35
American Institutes for Research, 168, 184, 188
Anfara, V. A., 181
Anyon, J., 11, 13, 36, 41, 163, 170
Argyris, C., 169
Arum, R., 41, 160
attention deficit/hyperactivity disorder (ADHD), 131
automobile's impact, 42
AYP. *See* Adequate Yearly Progress

Bank Street College of Education, 72, 73
Bard High School Early College, 172
Barnes, C., 30, 154, 182
Bell, D., 26
benchmarking tests, 68
Bensman, D., 30, 182
Berends, M., 184
Berliner, D. C., 151, 161, 170
Bloom, J., 165
Bolden, M. A., 64
Booher-Jennings, J., 150
Borman, G. D., 184, 188
Boudon, R., 35
Bowles, S., 163
Braun, B., 11

Bridge Street Elementary School
AYP failure at, 72, 157
CFL/ALEM terminated at, 70–71
demographics of, 47–48
faculty training at, 56–57
faculty typology at, 78–79
leadership at, 79
legitimacy of *Abbott V* at, 77–78
model selection at, 49
NCLB impact at, 72–73
standardized test scores at, 63, 69, 72, 74, 76
Briggs, R. J., 184
Broh, B. A., 162
Brooks-Gunn, J., 162
Brown, K. M., 181
Brown, S., 184
Brown v. Board of Education, 1, 29, 173
Bryk, A. S., 160, 182
budget, zero-based, 9, 62, 86, 92, 132, 166
Buishard, M., 165
Burawoy, M., 185
Burke, W., 160
Burns, A., 165
Burross, H. L., 156
business management models, 166

California Achievement Test, 90
Camilli, G., 151
Campbell, E. Q., 38, 41, 161, 163
Capuzzo, J. P., 13
Carey, K., 191
CFL/ALEM
in adult workshop, 126
Degree of Implementation instrument, 58
description of, 49–50, 51*f*
evaluation criteria for, 58
faculty autonomy and, 62
faculty objections to, 59, 93
faculty resistance to, 65, 79, 93, 102, 140, 149
faculty training in, 56–57, 65–66, 86, 108, 125–126
implementation failure in, 148–149
learning centers in. *See* learning centers
model classroom in, 50–51
selection as model, 49, 85–86, 107, 125
Chajet, L., 165
Chamberlain, A. M., 188
Chambers, B., 188
Chambers, S., 14, 17, 18
change. *See also* educational change theory; legitimacy of change
in classroom reform, 149–150
covert active resistance to, 79
covert passive resistance to, 102
effective management of, 169–170
experimental strategies in, 156
externally coercive, 120
externally triggered, 103
normal appearance of, 102–103
change (*continued*)
overt active resistance to, 102, 140
planned, 34
selective incremental, 79
self-motivated value driven, 78–79
structural coercive, 121
structural coercive reverse, 121
teacher resistance to, 149
unanticipated incremental, 79
voluntary reverse, 140
change triggers, 32
charter schools, 166
Cheung, A. C. K., 188
Chun, J., 184
Church Street School
AYP at, 157
demographics, 106–107
Everyday Math at, 116
faculty training at, 108
faculty typology at, 121
legitimacy of *Abbott V* at, 119–120
model selection at, 107
NCLB at, 118
socialization at, 119–120
standardized test scores at, 111, 113, 114, 117, 119
Church Street School community, 105
class-action lawsuits, 167
class size, 86, 95, 128, 135
classroom change, 149–150
Clay, K., 35
Clotfelter, C. T., 1, 9
Coburn, C. E., 34, 162
Codey, Richard, 18, 19
cognitive frameworks, legitimacy in, 35
Coleman, J. S., 38, 41, 161, 163
College Avenue Elementary School
AYP at, 98, 157
CFL/ALEM in, 89–90
decision-making process at, 100
demographics of, 84–85
faculty training at, 86
faculty typology at, 102
implementation timeline at, 90
individualization at, 94–95
invidious distinctions in, 101
legitimacy of *Abbott V* at, 101–102
model selection at, 85–86
standardized test scores at, 90, 93, 95, 97, 98, 100, 101
WSR model selection at, 85–86
College Avenue School community, 83–84
Comer School Development Program. *See* SDP
Community for Learning/Adaptive Learning Environments Model. *See* CFL/ALEM
community variables, 161–162
compulsory attendance zones, 167
computer labs, 62, 114, 128
constructivist techniques, 70, 109, 117, 120, 150

Cook, T., 184
Corbin, J., 185
Core Curriculum Content Standards (CCCS), 9
  for language arts, 55
  state vs. district objectives, 113
  test preparation displacement of, 133
  "thorough and efficient" education in, 14, 54
corrective action, 24–26
Corzine, Jon, 17, 18, 19, 158
covert active resistance to change, 79
covert passive resistance to change, 102
Crawford v. Davy, 167, 171
Cuban, L., 160, 168
cultural biases, in ESPA, 61

Datnow, A., 49, 184
Deci, E., 78, 150
decision-making
  centralized, at College Avenue, 100
  in CFL/ALEM program, 79–80
  cognitive frameworks in, 35
  eco-cognitive frameworks in, 36, 163
  in implementation failure, 154–155
deep structure of organizations
  components of, 31
  in learning changes, 37
  NCLB impact on, 151
Degirmencioglu, S., 184
Degree of Implementation (DOI), 58, 66
Delpit, L., 170
demographics
  of *Abbott V,* 9
  of Bridge Street School, 47–48
  of Church Street School, 106–107
  of College Avenue School, 84–85
  of Elizabeth, 82–83
  in market solution options, 166
  of Newark, 43–44
  of Park Avenue School, 124
"demography-as-destiny," 161
Denton, N. A., 11, 12, 13, 36, 182
Department of Education, 116
Desimone, L., 184
Diamond, J. B., 151
Dillon, S., 191
DiMaggio, P., 31, 151
District Factor Groups (DFG), 167
Downey, D. B., 162
Drop Everything and Read program, 131
Duke, D., 30, 182

Easton, J. Q., 160
Eaton, S. E., 1, 171
eco-cognitive framework
  in *Abbott V,* 164–165
  at Bridge Street School, 77–78
  at Church Street School, 119–120
  at College Avenue School, 101–102
  in decision-making process, 163
  description of, 36
eco-cognitive framework (*continued*)
  negative implications of, 163–164
  at Park Avenue School, 139
  in reform implementation failure, 155
economic policies, 17, 170, 172
economic status. *See also* socioeconomic context
  in academic achievement, 161–162
  language arts literacy by, 152*f*
  math proficiency by, 153*f*
  proficiency gap and, 151
  racial segregation and inequalities in, 12
Education Law Center, 8, 9, 16
educational change theory. *See also* change; legitimacy of change
  evolutionary processes in, 34–35
  incremental, 30–31
  punctuated equilibrium, 31–32
  punctuated legitimacy, 32–33, 184
  role of, 184
Ehri, L. C., 189
Eisenhart, M., 181
Elementary and Secondary Education Act (ESEA), 21
Elementary School Proficiency Assessment. *See* ESPA
Elizabeth, New Jersey
  AYP failure in, 157
  demographics of, 82–83
  ethnicity in, 81–82
  history of, 81
  per pupil expenditure in, 83, 84*t*
Elizabeth/Hillside Gazette Leader, 116, 132, 142
Elizabeth reform model (E3), 142–143
Elizabeth School District, 83
Elmore, R., 80, 160
Epstein, J., 23
equal opportunity, 172–173
equilibrium periods, 32
Erlichson, B., 49, 149, 182
ESPA, 56. *See also* NJASK
  Bridge Street School scores, 63, 69
  Church Street School scores, 111, 113, 114
  College Avenue School scores, 90, 93, 95, 97
  cultural biases in, 61
  Everyday Math and, 117
  focus on preparation for, 88–89, 110
  multiple intelligences theory in, 128
  objections to, 61
  Park Avenue School scores, 129, 130, 132, 134
ethnicity. *See also* race
  in Elizabeth, 81–82
  language arts literacy by, 152*f*
  math proficiency by, 153*f*
  in New Jersey, 10*t*
  in Newark, 43–44
  in proficiency gap, 151
ethnography, 185

evaluation. *See also* standardized test scores
  Degree of Implementation, 58
  of student learning, 150
Everyday Math, 69, 72, 94, 95, 99, 101, 116, 135
evolutionary processes, 34–35
externally coercive change, 120

faculty. *See* teaching and teachers
Feldman, J., 171
Fidler, B., 30
Fine, M., 165
Fink, D., 30, 31, 160, 182
Firestone, W., 184, 187
Fishman, T., 105
Frankenberg, E., 11, 171
Freeman, J., 31
Fryer, R., 162
Fullan, M., 31, 155
funding
  inequalities in, pre-*Abbott,* 7–8
  in NCLB enforcement, 26
  in Newark school district, 44–46
  zero-based budget, 9, 62, 86, 92, 132, 166
funding freeze request, 158

Gans, H. J., 13, 41
Gardner, H., 170, 191
Gardner, Howard, 65
Gebeloff, R., 12, 13
Geertz, C., 182
Gersick, C., 30, 31, 32
Gintis, H., 163
Glaeser, E., 182
Glass, G. V., 151
Goertz, M., 49, 149, 182, 187
Gold, B., 15, 30, 32, 34, 154, 160, 162
Golson, J., 142
Good, T. L., 156
Goodson, I., 181
Gould, S. J., 30
Grigorenko, E., 163
guided reading, 59, 76
Gutmann, A., 171
Gutmore, D., 182, 189, 190

Habib, F., 184
Hamilton, M., 182
Hannan, M. T., 31
Harcourt Brace, 76
Hargreaves, A., 181
Harry, B., 182
Harvard Civil Rights Project, 11
Helmrich, W. B., 41
Hewes, G. M., 184
high implementers, 132
High/Scope kindergarten program, 92, 108, 113, 127, 133, 134
high-stakes tests. *See* standardized tests
Hobson, C. J., 38, 41, 161, 163
Hofferth, S., 162
Holzer, M., 46
Huberman, A. M., 185

implementation of initial use stage, 31
incremental change theory, 30–31
indentation, 88
individualization of instruction, 59, 62, 87, 94–95, 150
Ingram, P., 35
institutionalization stage, 31
integration, 1, 170–172. *See also* segregation
intentional variation, 35
Internet, 62
invidious distinctions, 101

Jargowsky, P., 182
Johnson, B., 27
Johnson, D. E., 27

Kahlenberg, R. D., 171
Kegan, R., 170
Kelman, H. C., 33
Kennedy, Edward M., 21
Kerbow, D., 160
Kim, J. S., 187, 188
kindergarten program. *See* High/Scope
Kirby, E., 171
Kirtman, L., 163
Klaber, M., 162
Klingner, J. K., 182
Koestner, R., 78, 150
Kogut, B., 105
Kotter, J. P., 169, 191
Kozol, J., 7, 12, 171

Ladson-Billings, G., 170
Lagemann, E. C., 160
Lahey, L. L., 170
Lampert, M., 162
language arts proficiency
  Bridge Street School scores, 63, 69, 74, 76
  CCCS standards for, 55
  Church Street School scores, 111, 113, 114, 117, 119
  College Avenue School scores, 90, 93, 95, 97, 98, 100, 101
  in E3 reform model, 143
  funding freeze request and, 158
  gap in, 151, 152*f*
  Park Avenue School scores, 129, 130, 132, 134, 136, 138, 139
Lauver, S. C., 188
Lawler, E. E., 191
lawsuits
  Governor Corzine's, 20
  on segregation, 167
leadership
  external vs. local, 148
  passive, 121–122
  in urban school reform, 168

learning centers
  faculty training and concerns, 56, 57
  importance of, 65
  model, 50–51
  reading programs in, 109
  rotation difficulties in, 108, 109, 112
  self-scheduling in, 58
learning variables, 37
LeBoeuf, R. A., 35, 49
Lee, C., 11, 171
Lee, C. D., 162
Lee, J., 151
legitimacy of change. *See also* change; educational change theory
  at Bridge Street School, 77–78
  at Church Street School, 119–120
  cognitive frameworks in, 35
  at College Avenue School, 101–102
  in educational change theory, 32–33
  moral basis of, 33–34
  at Park Avenue School, 139
  passive leadership and, 121–122
  planned change and, 34
  in program implementation, 154
Levine, E., 30
Levitt, S., 162
Librera, William L., 19
Liebman, J. S., 21, 28, 33, 167
Linver, M., 162
Lippman, C., 30, 71
Liss, B., 46, 166
literacy training, 72, 73
Logan, J. R., 11, 43, 44
Louis, K. S., 31, 160
Loveless, T., 191

MacInnes, G., 15, 158, 159, 161, 165
MacIver, M., 184
Mackey, P. E., 184, 192
Madden, N. M., 188
Mangione, T., 181
manipulatives, 99, 135
market solutions, to education, 166
Marsico, R., 81
Martin, J., 82
Massey, D., 11, 12, 13, 36, 182
math proficiency scores
  Bridge Street School, 63, 69, 74, 76
  Church Street School, 111, 113, 114, 117, 119
  College Avenue School, 90, 93, 95, 97, 98, 100, 101
  by ethnicity and economic status, 151, 153*f*
  Everyday Math and, 117
  funding freeze request and, 158
  Park Avenue School, 129, 130, 132, 134, 136, 138, 139
math programs
  in E3 reform, 143
  Everyday Math, 69, 72, 94, 95, 99, 101, 116, 135
Maxwell, J. A., 185
May, H., 149, 162, 182
McCaslin, M. M., 156
McGreevey, James, 15–16, 55, 70
McNamara, D., 142
McNeil, L., 27
McNichol, D., 18
McPartland, J., 38, 41, 161, 163
Meier, D., 26, 34
Meredith v. Jefferson County Board of Education, 171–72
Merton, R. K., 27, 80
Meyer, J. W., 31, 34
Miles, M. B., 31, 160, 162, 185
Miller, J., 46
Miller, R. J., 169
Milliken v. Bradley, 171
minimum wage, 170
model program selection
  at Bridge Street School, 49
  at Church Street School, 107
  at College Avenue School, 85–86
  at Park Avenue School, 125
model programs
  business management models, 166
  CFL/ALEM. *See* CFL/ALEM
  Comer School Development, 52*f,* 124
  Elizabeth reform, 142–143
  in NCLB, 23
  Newark Reform, 72
  Success for All, 50*f,* 107
  for urban school reform, 168–169
  Whole School Reform. *See* Whole School Reform
Monfils, L. F., 151
Mood, A. M., 38, 41, 161, 163
Mooney, J., 18, 19, 21, 46, 77, 188
moral basis of legitimacy, 33–34
Mount Laurel ruling, 13–14, 172
Muirhead, M., 182
multiple intelligences, 65–66, 128

National Academy of Sciences, 165
National Assessment of Educational Progress (NAEP) test, 24
National Commission on Excellence in Education, 160
Natriello, G., 187
NCLB. *See* No Child Left Behind
New Jersey Assessment of Skills and Knowledge. *See* NJASK
New Jersey Department of Education, 54, 55, 66, 138–139, 165
New Jersey Supreme Court, 184, 187
New York Times, 13, 15, 191
Newark, New Jersey
  AYP failure in, 157
  demographics of, 43–44, 47
  per pupil expenditure in, 44–46

Newark, New Jersey (*continued*)
race riots in, 42
socioeconomic context of, 41–44
Newark Reform Model, 72
Newark school district
funding of, 44–46
state takeover of, 46
Newman, K., 81
Nichols, S. L., 151
NJASK, 56. *See also* ESPA
Bridge Street School scores, 72, 74, 76
Church Street School scores, 117, 119
College Avenue School scores, 98, 100, 101
Park Avenue School scores, 136, 138, 139
state average passing rate in, 158
No Child Left Behind Act, 22, 23, 24
No Child Left Behind (NCLB)
academic achievement goals of, 22–23
assessment tools in, 23–24
bipartisan support for, 21–22
at Bridge Street School, 72–73
at Church Street School, 118
coercive legitimacy of, 77
at College Avenue School, 97
corrective action requirements in, 24–25
enforcement of, 26
as experimental strategy, 156
failure of, in perspective, 160
impact of, 151
inadequacies of, 165–166
integration not included in, 1
model programs in, 23
at Park Avenue School, 135–136
purpose of, 22–23
reality vs. philosophy of, 118
scientific research as requirement of, 23, 26
states' rights in, 27
test score improvement in, unsustainable, 151
theoretical perspective on, 37–38
vs. *Abbott V*, 29
Noddings, N., 34
Nunes, S., 189

Oakley, D., 11, 43, 44
Ogbu, J. U., 162
Olsen, B., 163
Open Court reading series, 94, 95, 101, 118, 137
Orfield, G., 1, 11, 171, 188
organizational change. *See* change; educational change theory; legitimacy of change
Orr, J. S., 17
Ouchi, W. G., 166, 191
Overman, L. T., 184
overt active resistance to change, 102, 140

Paige, Rod, 21
Palardy, G. J., 161
parents and parental involvement
changes in, 150
lack of, in reading support, 99
parents and parental involvement (*continued*)
in NCLB, 23
non-English speaking, 112, 113
Parents Involved in Community Schools v. Seattle School District No. 1, 171
Park Avenue School
AYP at, 157
control issues at, 140–141
demographics of, 124
faculty training at, 125–126
faculty typology at, 140
high implementers at, 132
legitimacy of *Abbott V* at, 139
model selection at, 125
NCLB at, 135–136
standardized test scores at, 129, 130, 132, 134, 136, 138, 139
test preparation at, 140
Park Avenue School community, 123–124
Parsons, C., 30
Payne, Y., 165
Peirce, C. S., 184
per pupil expenditure
Elizabeth, 83, 84*t*
Newark, 44–46
Perkins-Munn, T., 165
Phillips, M., 184
phonics, 59, 60, 87, 101, 109, 137
Pinker, S., 163
planned change, 34
play, as learning, 113, 127, 134
Plessy v. Ferguson, 10
Popham, W. J., 27, 37
population. *See* demographics
Portes, A., 163
Powell, J. A., 171
Powell, W., 31, 151
prescription sheet, 53, 56, 89, 129
Price, Clement, 12
privatization, NCLB in facilitating, 27–28
property tax reform, 17, 172
pull-out program, 114
punctuated equilibrium theory, 31–32
punctuated legitimacy theory, 32–33, 184

Quinn, R., 32

race. *See also* demographics; ethnicity
in *Abbott V* demographics, 9
in New Jersey, 10*t*
in Newark, 42, 43–44
in school assignments, 171
Rachuba, L., 184
Rae, D., 42
Ravitch, D., 160
reading programs
Drop Everything and Read, 131
guided reading, 59, 76
Harcourt Brace, 76
in learning center, 109

reading programs (*continued*)
  Open Court, 94, 95, 101, 118, 137
  phonics in, 59, 60, 87, 109
  tutorials, 99
  whole language in, 87
Reed, D., 1, 187
Reock, E. C., Jr., 45
research. *See* scientific research
residential patterns
  of high-income African Americans, 12–13
  Mount Laurel ruling on, 13–14
  segregation by race, 11–12, 14
resilience, 54, 120, 164
revolutionary periods, 32
Ritter, G. W., 188
Rollow, S., 160
Romanelli, E., 31, 32, 169
Rosenberg, G. N., 33, 156
Ross, S., 184
rote learning, 101, 103, 110, 128
Roth, J., 162
Rothstein, R., 38, 41, 161, 163, 170
routines, 74
Rowan, B., 31, 34, 169
Rumberger, R. W., 161
Ryan, J. E., 27, 28
Ryan, J., 82
Ryan, R., 78, 150

Sabel, C. F., 21, 28, 33, 167
Sadvonik, A., 46, 166
San Antonio Independent School District v. Rodriguez, 14
Sarason, S. B., 149, 155, 160, 162
Sassen, S., 36, 41, 105
Savage Inequalities (Kozol), 7
Schein, E. H., 169
Schemo, D. J., 21
Schneider, B., 182
school construction
  by *Abbott V* mandate, 17
  in Elizabeth, 84
  in urban school reform, 172
school reform. *See* urban school reform
school size, and academic achievement, 165
Schorr, R., 184
Schuppe, J., 47
Schutz, A., 34
Schuyler, G., 184
Schwaneberg, R., 10
Sciarra, D., 17
scientific research
  in NCLB mandate, 23, 26
  on school reform failure, 160
  teacher rejection of, 154
Scientific Research Associates, 92
Scott, W. R., 31
SDP (Comer School Development Program)
  description of, 52*f*
  at Park Avenue School, 124
Sebring, P. B., 160
segregation. *See also* integration
  Brown on, 173
  class-action lawsuits on, 167
  residential, post-WWII, 11–12
selection, in evolutionary process, 35
selective incremental change, 79
self-motivated value-driven change, 78–79
self-scheduling
  difficulties with, 134
  importance of, 58
  objections to, 131
  purpose of, 131–132
  training on, 57
Seligman, M. E. P., 170
Settersten, R., 184
SFA (Success for All)
  description of, 50*f*
  negative response to, 107, 125
Shafir, E., 35, 49
Shagle, S., 184
Sibert, Joan, 67
Sieber, S., 27
Silin, J. G., 30, 71
Sirin, S. R., 38, 161
Slavin, R. E., 188
social emotional training, 143
social interaction, moral basis of, 33
socialization, 119–120
socioeconomic context. *See also* economic status
  of *Abbott V*, 11–14
  in Newark, 41–44
spelling test, 137
Spencer, M. L., 171
Spillane, J. P., 151
Stahl, S. A., 189
standardized test scores. *See also* ESPA; NJASK
  at Bridge Street School, 63, 69, 72, 74, 76
  at Church Street School, 111, 113, 114, 117, 119
  at College Avenue School, 90, 93, 95, 97, 98, 100, 101
  at Park Avenue School, 129, 130, 132, 134, 136, 138, 139
standardized tests
  Abbott V schools' failure in, 158–159
  impact of, on creative teaching, 27
  lack of improvement in, 150–151
  in NCLB, 24
  preparation for, 88–89, 103, 110, 133, 140
  selection of, in Elizabeth, 90
  teaching to, 91
Star-Ledger, 12, 13, 16, 17, 60, 76
states' rights, 27, 28
Steele, C. M., 162
Sternberg, R., 163
Stockly, S., 184
Stowell, J., 11, 43, 44
Strauss, A., 185

Stringfield, S., 184
structural coercive change, 121
structural coercive reverse change, 121
Strunsky, S., 82
student population. *See* demographics
Stults, B., 11, 43, 44
Sturges, K. M., 182
suburbs and suburban schools
  invidious distinctions in, 101
  reform as incidental to success at, 118
  voluntary integration in, 172
  vs. urban education, 147
  as White, vs. urban, 13
Success for All/Roots and Wings. *See* SFA
Sunderman, G. L., 187, 188
Supovitz, J. A., 149, 162, 182
Supreme Court, 171

tax reform, 17, 172
"teacher call," 53, 56, 112
teacher-centered learning, 127, 139, 140–141
teaching and teachers
  in academic achievement, 162
  CFL/ALEM high implementers, 132
  CFL/ALEM threat to, 62
  control issues in, 140–141
  standardized tests impact on, 27
  typology of, 78–79, 102, 121, 140, 169
teaching to test, 91
team teaching, 87, 95, 150
Temple University Center for Research in Human Development and Education, 49–50
Temple University facilitators. *See* training facilitators
TerraNova test, 90, 96, 137
test preparation, 88–89, 103, 110, 133, 140
test-taking skills, 75
theory of multiple intelligences, 65–66, 128
"thorough and efficient" education, 14, 54
Title I schools
  funding actions against, 26
  NCLB corrective actions for, 24–25
Torre, M. E., 165
Towne, L., 181
Tractenberg, P., 10, 46, 166
training
  at Bridge Street School, 56–57, 65–66
  at Church Street School, 108
  at College Avenue School, 86
  at Park Avenue School, 125–126
training facilitators
  CFL/ALEM techniques not used by, 126
  high implementer grants, 132
  turn-over rate of, 86
  on whole class instruction, 111
  workshop format of, 65–66
Turnbull, B., 49, 149, 182
Tushman, M. L., 31, 32, 169
tutorials, 99
Tyack, D., 31, 160
Tye, B., 31
Tyler, R., 182
typology of teachers, 78–79, 102, 121, 140, 169

unanticipated incremental change, 79
urban decay, post-WWII, 11
urban school reform
  alternative strategies for, 168–169
  change management in, 169–170
  economic policies in, 170
  integration in, 170–172
  legislation's impact on, 2
Usdan, M., 160

value-driven change, 78–79
Vigdor, J., 182
voluntary integration, 171–172
voluntary reverse change, 140
von Hippel, P. T., 162
vouchers, 166

Wachtel, P., 171
wait-time folder
  in CFL classroom, 53
  purpose of, 56–57
Walker, E., 182, 189, 190
Wall Street Journal, 22
Wang, M. C., 54, 131
Weber, M., 33
Weick, K., 32, 154
Weinfeld, F. D., 38, 41, 161, 163
Weinstein, R. S., 37, 80, 162, 170
Welner, K. G., 172
Wenglinsky, H., 162, 168
Whitman, Christine Todd, 15, 54
whole class instruction, 111, 127
whole language, 87, 101, 150
Whole School Reform, 8, 23. *See also* model programs
  at Bridge Street School, 49
  at Church Street School, 107
  at College Avenue School, 85–86
  cost of, 107
  at Park Avenue School, 142–143
Williams, R. F., 14
Willows, D. M., 189
Wilson, W. J., 11, 42
Wood, G., 26, 34
Worley, C. G., 191
writing samples, 75

York, R. L., 38, 41, 161, 163

Zelditch, M., 33
zero-based budget, 9, 62, 86, 92, 132, 166

About the Author

BARRY A. GOLD earned a Ph.D. in Sociology and Education from Columbia University. He taught elementary grades for several years in urban schools similar to those in this book. He currently teaches Organizational Behavior and Leadership Skills in the Lubin School of Business, Pace University, New York City.

Gold is the author of numerous papers and books, including *Whose School Is It Anyway? Parent–Teacher Conflict Over an Innovative School* (with Matt Miles; 1981), "Punctuated Legitimacy: A Theory of Educational Change" (*Teachers College Record*, 1999), and *International Organizational Behavior*, second edition (2005).